AN INTRODUCTION TO LITERARY STUDIES

Third edition

In this classic beginner's guide to English literature, Mario Klarer offers a concise and accessible discussion of central issues in the study of literary texts, looking at:

- definitions of key terms such as literature and text
- the genres of fiction, poetry, drama, and film
- periods and classifications of literature
- theoretical approaches to texts
- the use of secondary resources
- guidelines for writing research essays.

The new and expanded edition is fully updated to include:

- a wider range of textual examples from world literature
- additional references to contemporary cinema
- a section on comparative literature
- an extended survey of literary periods and genres
- recent changes in MLA guidelines
- information on state-of-the-art citation management software
- the use and abuse of online resources.

An Introduction to Literary Studies also features suggestions for further reading as well as an extensive glossary of key terms.

Mario Klarer is Professor of English and Chair of the American Studies Department at the University of Innsbruck, Austria.

AN INTRODUCTION TO LITERARY STUDIES

Third edition

Mario Klarer

Routledge
Taylor & Francis Group

LONDON AND NEW YORK

Published 2011
by Wissenschaftliche Buchgesellschaft, Darmstadt
as *Einführung in die Grundlagen der Literaturwissenschaft:
Theorien, Gattungen, Arbeitstechniken*

First published in English in 1999, second edition published 2004,
this edition published 2013 by Routledge
2 Park Square, Milton Park, Abingdon, Oxon OX14 4RN

Simultaneously published in the USA and Canada
by Routledge
711 Third Avenue, New York, NY 10017

Routledge is an imprint of the Taylor & Francis Group, an informa business

© 1999, 2004, 2013 Mario Klarer

British Library Cataloguing in Publication Data
A catalogue record for this book is available from the British Library

Library of Congress Cataloging in Publication Data
Klarer, Mario, 1962 – [Einführung in die Grundlagen der
    Literaturwissenschaft: Theorien, Gattungen, Arbeitstechniken. English]
    An Introduction to Literary Studies/Mario Klarer. – Third edition.
    pages cm
    Includes bibliographical references and indexes.
    1. English literature – History and criticism – Theory, etc.
    2. English literature – Research – Methodology – Handbooks, manuals,
    etc. 3. American literature – Research – Methodology –Handbooks,
    manuals, etc. 4. American literature – History and criticism – Theory,
    etc. 5. Criticism – Authorship – Handbooks, manuals, etc.
    6. Literature – Research – Handbooks, manuals, etc. I. Title.
    PR21.K5213 2013
    820.9 – dc23   2012046372

ISBN: 978-0-415-81191-0 (hbk)
ISBN: 978-0-415-81190-3 (pbk)
ISBN: 978-0-203-06891-5 (ebk)

Typeset in Perpetua
by Florence Production Ltd, Stoodleigh, Devon, UK

For Bernadette, Johanna and Moritz

CONTENTS

Preliminary remarks   ix
Preface to the third edition   xi
Acknowledgements   xiii

1   **What is literature? What is a text?**   1

    Genre, text type, and discourse   3
    Primary and secondary sources   4

2   **Major genres in literary studies**   9

    Fiction   9
    Poetry   36
    Drama   58
    Film   72

3   **Periods of literature**   85

4   **Theoretical approaches to literature**   99
    Text-oriented approaches   103
    Author-oriented approaches   114
    Reader-oriented approaches   116

Context-oriented approaches 119
Literary critique or evaluation 127
Film theory 129

5 Where and how to find secondary literature **133**

6 How to write a research paper **139**

7 Suggestions for further reading **153**

General literary terminology 153
Authors and works 154
Literary theory 155
Genres 157
Literary history 164
How to write a research paper 165

8 Glossary of literary and cinematographic terms **167**

References 197
Author and title index 201
Subject index 211

PRELIMINARY REMARKS

This concise introduction provides a general survey of various aspects of literary studies for college students who intend to specialize in English or American literature or want to acquire a basic familiarity with the entire field of literary studies in general. The book targets both the European and American college market: it is not only designed for beginners in the European system, where students have to specialize in one or two disciplines upon entering university, but it also meets the requirements for American undergraduates who have opted for a major in English or another language, and need an introduction to the more scholarly aspects of literary studies, one that goes beyond freshman "Introduction to Literature" courses. It therefore serves as a textbook for Introduction to Literature classes at all major European universities or advanced undergraduate English (honors) courses in the USA and as an independent study guide. Its simple language and accessible style make the book equally apt for English native speakers as well as students of literature whose native language is other than English.

Unlike most of the existing American textbooks geared toward freshman "Introduction to Literature" courses, which emphasize the firsthand reading of primary texts, this book targets a slightly more advanced audience interested in the scholarly aspects of literature. The book does not include entire literary texts, but rather draws on a number of very short excerpts to illustrate major issues of literary studies as an academic discipline.

An Introduction to Literary Studies deals with questions concerning the nature of "literature" and "text," discusses the three major literary genres, as well as film and its terminology, gives an overview of the most important literary periods, and raises issues of literary theory. A separate section explains basic research and composition techniques pertinent for the beginner. An extensive glossary of the major literary and cinematic terms gives easy and quick access to terminological information and also serves as a means to test one's knowledge when preparing for exams.

In order to meet the expectations of contemporary literary studies, the book places major emphasis on the accessibility of literary theory for beginners. It presents all major schools and approaches, including the latest developments, with reference to concrete textual examples. Film features as a fourth genre alongside fiction, poetry, and drama, to highlight the interdependence of literature and film in both artistic production and scholarly inquiry. The chapters on basic research and composition techniques explain standard research tools such as the *MLA International Bibliography* as well as the most important rules of the MLA style sheet and composition guidelines for writing research papers.

The book owes a great deal to my interaction with students in "Introduction to Literature" courses that I taught at the American Studies and Comparative Literature departments of the University of Innsbruck (Austria), and the English departments of the University of Pennsylvania (Philadelphia), Columbia University (New York), and the Université de Neuchâtel (Switzerland). Large parts of the original manuscript of the first edition were written during an Erwin Schrödinger Fellowship at the Getty Center for the History of Art and the Humanities in Santa Monica, California, from 1992 to 1994. The current edition was completed in 2012–2013 at the National Humanities Center in North Carolina. Geoffrey Galt Harpham, the director of the Center, as well as his excellent staff made this year possible. Brooke Andrade and Joel Elliott generously shared their expertise in citation management software for this project.

I am also indebted to a number of friends and colleagues for comments and suggestions. Sonja Bahn, Karen Carroll, Monika Datterl, Monika Fludernik, Roberta Hofer, J. Paul Hunter, Ulrich C. Knoepflmacher, Wolfgang Koch, Steven Marcus, Christian Quendler, Eliott Schreiber, Devin J. Stewart, and Hilde Wolfmeyer have been very helpful in their advice. I am particularly thankful to Cornelia Klecker and Johannes Mahlknecht for generously sharing their insights into narratology and recent developments in film for this new edition.

My biggest thanks go to my companion Bernadette Rangger for critically discussing every chapter of the book from its earliest conception to its final version, for having been with me during all these years, and for having made these years a wonderful time.

PREFACE TO THE THIRD EDITION

This third, revised, and expanded edition of *An Introduction to Literary Studies* builds on the basic structure of the 1999 and 2004 English editions but considerably widens its focus by also incorporating non-Anglophone literary traditions. In this respect, this third edition follows my German *Einführung in die Grundlagen der Literaturwissenschaft: Theorien, Gattungen, Arbeitstechniken* (Darmstadt: Wissenschaftliche Buchgesellschaft, 2011). However, all chapters have undergone major changes and expansion, so that, in total, this edition includes more than 40 pages of additional material. While only minor modifications have been made to the first chapter, Chapters 2–7 have been completely revised in order to meet current standards in research and composition techniques:

- Chapter 2, "Major genres in literary studies," underwent significant expansion in all of its sections, including additional examples from different historical periods and world literature. The section on fiction now includes a more detailed explanation of narratological models with further sample passages. The discussion on film substitutes recent releases for older examples, also integrating aspects of television and new media formats.
- Chapter 3, "Periods of literature," expands the discussion of English and American literary history, and now also offers glances at periods and movements outside these traditions, thus providing a more inclusive and global awareness of literary history in general.

- Chapter 4, "Theoretical approaches to literature," underwent updates and revision with respect to newer trends, such as cultural studies. An entirely new section on film theory provides a historical survey of the major developments in this particular field, as does the discussion of comparative literature as an independent methodological approach.
- Chapter 5, "Where and how to find secondary literature," now provides basic guidelines for evaluating Internet resources for student papers.
- Chapter 6, "How to write a research paper," benefits from new sample paragraphs of seminar papers in order to enhance the practical use for students. The section on the MLA style sheet has been completely redone, thus incorporating the new standards set by the seventh edition of the *MLA Handbook* in 2009, as well as discussing the use of citation management software.
- Chapter 7, "Suggestions for further reading," has been updated with recent publications on literary studies pertinent for the beginner.

In researching and writing this new material, I have tried to stay true to the principles of the first edition: to provide an up-to-date and accessible introduction to literary studies.

National Humanities Center (North Carolina)
May 2013

WHAT IS LITERATURE?
WHAT IS A TEXT?

Look up the term **literature** in any current encyclopedia and you will be struck by the vagueness of its usage as well as by an inevitable lack of substance in the attempts to define it. In most cases, literature is referred to as the entirety of written expression, with the restriction that not every written document can be categorized as literature in the more exact sense of the word. The definitions, therefore, usually include additional adjectives such as "aesthetic" or "artistic" in order to distinguish literary works from texts for everyday use such as telephone books, newspapers, legal documents, and scholarly writings.

Etymologically, the Latin word *litteratura* derives from *littera* (letter), which is the smallest element of alphabetical writing. The word **text** is related to *textile* and translates as "fabric": just as single threads form a fabric, so words and sentences form a meaningful and coherent text. The origins of the two central terms are, therefore, not of great help in defining literature or text. It is more enlightening to look at literature or text as cultural and historical phenomena and to investigate the conditions of their production and reception.

Underlying literary production is certainly the human desire to leave behind a trace of oneself through creative expression, which will exist detached from the individual and, therefore, outlast its creator. The earliest manifestations of this creative wish are prehistoric cave paintings, which pass on encrypted messages through visual signs. This visual component inevitably remains closely connected to literature throughout its various historical and social manifestations. In some periods, however, the pictorial dimension is pushed into the background and is hardly noticeable.

Not only the visual – writing is always pictorial – but also the acoustic element, the spoken word, is an integral part of literature, as the alphabet translates spoken words into signs. Before writing developed as a system of signs, whether pictographs or alphabets, texts were passed on orally. This predecessor of literary expression, called **oral poetry**, consisted of texts stored in a bard or minstrel's memory from which the singers could recite upon demand. Some scholars assume that most of the early classical and Old English epics originated in this tradition and were only later preserved in written form. But even classical literary genres such as ancient Greek poetry were – as its name "lyrical" poetry suggests – sung and accompanied by musical instruments, such as the lyre. Also, classical Greek drama contained large song-like parts, similar to the modern opera. Gradually, this acoustic dimension of texts lost momentum and gave way to non-hybrid formats that privilege pure text. This oral component, which runs counter to the modern way of thinking about texts, has been revived in the twentieth century through the medium of radio and other sound carriers. Audio-literature and the lyrics of songs still display the acoustic features of literary phenomena.

The visual aspect of literary texts, as well as the oral dimension, has been pushed into the background in the course of history. While the Middle Ages highly privileged the visual component of writing in such forms as richly decorated handwritten manuscripts, the arrival of the modern age – along with the invention of the printing press – made the visual element disappear or reduced it to a few illustrations in the text. "Pure" writing became more and more stylized as an abstract medium devoid of traces of material or physical elements. The medieval union of word and picture, in which both components of the text formed a single, harmonious entity, slowly disappeared. This modern *iconoclasm* (i.e., hostility toward pictures) not only restricts the visual dimensions of texts but also sees writing as a medium that can function with little connection to the acoustic element of language.

It is only in drama that the union between the spoken word and visual expression survives in a traditional literary genre, although this feature is not always immediately noticeable. Drama, which we traditionally

PREFACE TO THE THIRD EDITION

This third, revised, and expanded edition of *An Introduction to Literary Studies* builds on the basic structure of the 1999 and 2004 English editions but considerably widens its focus by also incorporating non-Anglophone literary traditions. In this respect, this third edition follows my German *Einführung in die Grundlagen der Literaturwissenschaft: Theorien, Gattungen, Arbeitstechniken* (Darmstadt: Wissenschaftliche Buchgesellschaft, 2011). However, all chapters have undergone major changes and expansion, so that, in total, this edition includes more than 40 pages of additional material. While only minor modifications have been made to the first chapter, Chapters 2–7 have been completely revised in order to meet current standards in research and composition techniques:

- Chapter 2, "Major genres in literary studies," underwent significant expansion in all of its sections, including additional examples from different historical periods and world literature. The section on fiction now includes a more detailed explanation of narratological models with further sample passages. The discussion on film substitutes recent releases for older examples, also integrating aspects of television and new media formats.
- Chapter 3, "Periods of literature," expands the discussion of English and American literary history, and now also offers glances at periods and movements outside these traditions, thus providing a more inclusive and global awareness of literary history in general.

- Chapter 4, "Theoretical approaches to literature," underwent updates and revision with respect to newer trends, such as cultural studies. An entirely new section on film theory provides a historical survey of the major developments in this particular field, as does the discussion of comparative literature as an independent methodological approach.
- Chapter 5, "Where and how to find secondary literature," now provides basic guidelines for evaluating Internet resources for student papers.
- Chapter 6, "How to write a research paper," benefits from new sample paragraphs of seminar papers in order to enhance the practical use for students. The section on the MLA style sheet has been completely redone, thus incorporating the new standards set by the seventh edition of the *MLA Handbook* in 2009, as well as discussing the use of citation management software.
- Chapter 7, "Suggestions for further reading," has been updated with recent publications on literary studies pertinent for the beginner.

In researching and writing this new material, I have tried to stay true to the principles of the first edition: to provide an up-to-date and accessible introduction to literary studies.

National Humanities Center (North Carolina)
May 2013

ACKNOWLEDGEMENTS

"Stop All the Clocks" on p. 42 by W. H. Auden from *Collected Poems* Ed. Edward Mendelson. © 1976 by Faber and Faber. Reprinted by permission of Faber and Faber. [USA and Rest of World]

"Stop All the Clocks" on p. 42 by W. H. Auden from *Collected Poems* Ed. Edward Mendelson. © 1976 by Faber and Faber. Reprinted by permission of Curtis Brown Ltd. [UK and Commonwealth]

"Anecdote of the Jar" on p. 45 by Wallace Stevens from *Selected Poems* © 1985 by Faber and Faber. Reprinted by permission of Faber and Faber.

"l(a" on p. 50 by e. e. cummings, from *Complete Poems 1904–1962* © 1991 by the Trustees for the e. e. cummings Trust and George James Firmage. Reprinted by permission of W.W. Norton.

"This Is Just to Say" on p. 57 by William Carlos Williams, from *The Collected Poems: Volume I, 1909–1939* © 1938 by New Directions Publishing Corp. Reprinted by permission of Carcanet Press. [UK and Commonwealth]

"This Is Just to Say" on p. 57 by William Carlos Williams, from *The Collected Poems: Volume I, 1909–1939* © 1938 by New Directions Publishing Corp. Reprinted by permission of New Directions Publishing Corp. [USA and Rest of World]

"In a Station of the Metro" on p. 46 by Ezra Pound, from *Personae* © 1926 by Ezra Pound. Reprinted by permission of New Directions Publishing Corp. [USA and Rest of World]

"In a Station of the Metro" on p. 46 by Ezra Pound, from *Personae* © 1926 by Ezra Pound. Reprinted by permission of Faber and Faber. [UK and Commonwealth] and without hesitation – read as one of the major representatives of literature, combines acoustic and visual elements more than any other literary genre. Even more obviously than in drama, the symbiosis of word and image culminates in film. This young medium is particularly interesting for textual studies, since film records spoken words and pictures in a manner that is reminiscent of books, allowing multiple viewings or readings. Methods of literary and textual criticism are, therefore, useful tools for the analysis of cinema and acoustic media. Computer hypertexts, such as web pages, are the most common contemporary hybrids of the textual and various other media; here, writing is linked to sounds, pictures, or video clips within an interdependent network. A relatively recent phenomenon, which also amalgamates the verbal and the visual, is the graphic novel. In the past few decades, these comic-book-like narratives have received the attention of traditional literary scholars. Although the written medium is obviously the main concern in the study of literature or texts, this field of inquiry has opened up to other areas of media, such as the stage, painting, film, music, or the Internet.

The permeation of modern textual studies with other media has recently resulted in controversies over the definition of "text." Many authors and critics have deliberately left the traditional paths of literature, abandoning old textual forms in order to find new ways of literary expression and analysis. On the one hand, visual and acoustic elements are being reintroduced into literature; on the other, literature mixes with other media, genres, text types, and discourses.

GENRE, TEXT TYPE, AND DISCOURSE

Literary criticism, like biology, resorts to the concept of evolution or development and to criteria of classification to distinguish various genres. The evolutionary approach is referred to as "literary history," whereas the generic approach is termed "poetics." Both fields are closely related to the issue at hand, as every attempt to define text or literature touches not only upon differences between genres but also upon the historical dimensions of these literary forms of expression.

The term **genre** usually refers to one of the three classical literary forms of epic, poetry, or drama. This categorization is slightly confusing since the epic, despite its verse form, does not qualify as poetry. It is, in fact, a precursor of the modern novel (i.e., prose fiction) because of its structural features, such as plot, character presentation, and narrative perspective. Although this old classification is still in use, the tendency today is to abandon the term "epic" and use "prose," "fiction," or "prose fiction" for the relatively young literary forms of the novel and the short story.

Besides the genres that define or demarcate the general areas of traditional literature, the term **text type** has gained wide currency under the influence of linguistics. Texts that do not fit into the canonical genre categories of fiction, drama, and poetry often become objects of inquiry for modern linguistics. But literary scholars have also been looking increasingly at texts that were previously deemed to be worthless or irrelevant for textual analysis. The term text type refers to highly conventional written documents, such as instruction manuals, sermons, obituaries, advertising texts, catalogues, and scientific or scholarly writing. It can, of course, also include the three main literary genres and their subgenres.

A further key term in theoretical treatises on literary phenomena is **discourse**. Like text type, it is used as a term for any kind of classifiable linguistic expression. It has become a useful denotation for various linguistic conventions that refer to areas of content and theme; for instance, we may speak of male or female, political, sexual, economic, philosophical, or historical discourse. The classifications for these forms of linguistic expression are based on levels of content, vocabulary, and syntax, as well as stylistic and rhetorical elements. Whereas the term text type refers to written documents, discourse includes written and oral expression.

In sum, the term genre applies primarily to the three classical forms of the literary tradition; text type is a broader term that is also applicable to "non-canonical" written texts (i.e., those that traditionally do not qualify as literature); and discourse is the broadest term, referring to a variety of written and oral manifestations that share common thematic or structural features. The boundaries of these terms are not fixed and vary depending on the context in which they appear.

PRIMARY AND SECONDARY SOURCES

Whether analyzing a traditional genre, or an unconventional text type or discourse, literary studies distinguishes between the artistic object, or primary source, and its scholarly treatment in a critical text, or the secondary source. **Primary sources** denote the traditional objects of analysis in literary criticism, including texts from all literary genres, such as fiction, poetry, or drama.

The term **secondary source** applies to texts such as **articles** (or essays), **book reviews**, and **notes** (brief comments on a very specific topic), all of which are published primarily in scholarly journals. In literary studies, as in any other academic discipline, articles of approximately 15 to 25 pages in regularly published **journals** inform the scientific community about the latest results of researchers (see Chapter 5, "Where and how to find secondary literature"). Articles also appear in **collections of essays** (or anthologies) compiled by one or several editors on a specific theme. Collections of essays published in honor of a famous researcher on one of his or her research topics go by the German name *Festschrift*. Results of scholarly research are not only published as articles but also as **monographs** (i.e., larger book-length treatises on a single theme). Most dissertations and books published by university presses or scholarly publishing houses belong to this group.

In terms of content, secondary literature tries to uphold those standards of scholarly practice that have, over time, been established for scientific discourse, including objectivity, documentation of sources, and general validity. It is vital for any reader to be able to check and follow the arguments, results, and statements of literary criticism. Since the interpretation of texts always contains subjective traits, secondary sources can only to a certain degree apply and maintain objective criteria or the general validity of the thesis. This idiosyncrasy can be seen as the main difference between literary criticism and the natural sciences. At the same time, it is the basis for the tremendous creative potential of this academic field. Slight changes of perspective and varying methodological approaches can produce new and original results in the interpretation of texts.

As far as documentation of sources is concerned, however, the requirements in literary criticism are as strict as those of the natural sciences. The reader of a secondary source should be able to retrace every quotation or paraphrase (summary) to the primary or secondary source from which it has been taken. Although varying and subjective opinions on texts will remain, the scholarly documentation of the sources should permit the reader to refer back to the original texts and thus make it possible to compare results and judge the quality of the interpretation.

As a consequence of these conventions in documentation, a number of formal criteria have evolved in literary criticism. Literary studies uses the term **critical apparatus** to refer to the list of sources of a scholarly paper or monograph, including: footnotes or endnotes, providing comments on the main text or references to further secondary or primary sources; a **bibliography** (or list of works cited); and, possibly, an index. Historically speaking, this documentation format has not always been followed in scholarly texts, but, rather, it has developed into a convention in the field only over the last several centuries (see also Chapter 6, "How to write a research paper").

Secondary literature

text types	publication media
monograph	book
essay (article)	journal
note	collection of essays
book review	Festschrift
review article	DVD, CD-ROM
	Internet

formal aspects	goals
footnotes	originality
bibliography	objectivity
quotations	lucidity of arguments
paraphrases	traceability of sources
index	general validity of thesis

In most cases, it is easy to distinguish between primary and secondary literature. However, every literary period produces works that, for various reasons, attempt to blur the boundaries between these two text types. In the late Middle Ages, Giovanni Boccaccio (1313–1375) added glosses (i.e., footnote-like explanations) to his Italian epic *Teseida* (c.1339), thus placing it on one level with the scientific works of his time, which also employed a critical apparatus.

The essay is another historical example, underlining the fact that earlier periods did not always follow today's literary classifications. Essays discuss a well-defined, abstract, or theoretical topic in a literary style. With the works of French writer Michel de Montaigne (1533–1592) and the English philosopher Francis Bacon (1561–1626), the genre reached its first heyday in the late sixteenth and early seventeenth centuries, and became especially popular in the eighteenth century. Essays exhibit the stylistic features of primary literature, while simultaneously approaching topics and questions in a very scientific manner. Consequently, following today's standards, essays are very much located in between these two different text types.

Many twentieth-century authors also deliberately neglected the traditional classification of primary and secondary sources. A famous example is T. S. Eliot's (1888–1965) modernist poem "The Waste Land" (1922), in which the American poet includes footnotes (a traditional element of secondary sources) in the primary text. The second half of the twentieth century develops and employs this feature even further: elements of secondary sources enter literary texts, and elements of primary sources – for example, the absence of a critical apparatus or an overtly literary style – are incorporated in secondary texts. Demarcating the boundaries of the two text types can therefore become quite challenging.

Vladimir Nabokov's (1899–1977) novel *Pale Fire* (1962) is an example of the deliberate confusion of text types in postmodernist American literature. *Pale Fire* consists of certain parts – for instance, the text of a poem – that can be labeled as primary sources; other parts would be characteristic of scholarly treatises or critical editions of texts, such as a foreword by the editor of the poem, a commentary with stylistic analysis as well as critical comments on the text, and an index of the characters in the poem. In the (fictitious) foreword signed by the (fictitious) literary critic Charles Kinbote, Nabokov introduces a poem by the (fictitious) author Francis Shade. Nabokov's novel borrows the form of a critical edition, in which the traditional distinction between literary text and scholarly commentary or interpretation remains clearly visible. In the case of *Pale Fire*, however, all text types are created by the author Vladimir Nabokov himself, who tries to point out the arbitrariness of this artificial categorization of primary and secondary sources. The fact that this text is called a novel, even though it has a poem at its center, calls attention to the relativity inherent in the traditional categorization of genres as well.

MAJOR GENRES IN LITERARY STUDIES

As early as Greco-Roman antiquity, the classification of literary works into different genres has been a major concern of literary theory, which has since then produced a number of divergent and sometimes even contradictory categories. Among the various attempts to classify literature into genres, the triad "epic," "poetry," and "drama" has proven to be the most common in modern literary criticism. Because the traditional epic gave way to the new prose form of the novel in the seventeenth and eighteenth centuries, recent classifications prefer the terms "fiction," "poetry," and "drama" as designators of the three major literary genres. The following sections will explain the basic characteristics of these literary genres, as well as those of film, a fourth textual manifestation in the wider sense of the term. We will examine these types of texts with reference to concrete examples and introduce crucial terminology and methods of analysis that are helpful for understanding the respective genres.

FICTION

Although the novel emerged as the most important form of prose fiction in the modern period, its precursors go back to the oldest texts of literary history. Homer's **epics**, the *Iliad* and the *Odyssey* (*c.* seventh century BC), and Virgil's (70–19 BC) *Aeneid* (*c.*31–19 BC) influenced the major medieval epics, such as Dante Alighieri's (1265–1321) Italian *Divine Comedy* (*c.*1307–1321), and the early modern epics, such as Edmund Spenser's (*c.*1552–1599) *Faerie Queene* (1590; 1596), Lodovico Ariosto's (1474–1533) *Orlando Furioso* (1532), and John Milton's (1608–1674) long baroque poem *Paradise Lost* (1667). The majority of traditional epics revolve around a hero who has to fulfill a number of tasks of national or cosmic significance in a multiplicity of episodes. In particular, classical epics, through their roots in myth, history, and religion, reflect an all-encompassing worldview of their respective periods and nations. The fragmentation of a unified worldview in the early modern period weakened the position of the epic and eventually paved the way for the modern novel. This new prose genre developed into the mouthpiece of relativism that was emerging in all aspects of cultural discourse.

Although traditional epics are written in verse, they clearly distinguish themselves from other forms of poetry by their length, narrative structure, depiction of characters, and plot patterns. Because of these features, the epic – together with the romance – functions as a precursor of the modern novel. As early as classical times, but more strongly in the late Middle Ages, the romance established itself as an independent genre. Ancient romances, such as Apuleius's *Golden Ass* (second century AD), were usually written in prose, while medieval works of this genre used verse forms, as in the anonymous Middle English Arthurian romance *Sir Gawain and the Green Knight* (fourteenth century). Despite its verse form and its eventful episodes, the romance is nevertheless considered to be a forerunner of the novel mainly because of its tendency toward a focused plot and innovative use of narrative situations (see also the sections on "Plot" and "Narrative situation" in this chapter).

While the scope of the traditional epic is usually broad, the romance condenses the action and directs the plot toward one particular goal. At the same time, the protagonist or main character is depicted in more detail and with greater care. The heroes of the classical epic, as, for example, Aeneas in Virgil's *Aeneid*, are usually flat characters who function mainly as embodiments of abstract heroic ideals. Romances, on the other hand, foreground individual traits, such as insecurity, weakness, or other facets of character, thereby anticipating distinct aspects of the novel. The hero of the anonymous *Sir Gawain and the*

Green Knight is a prime example of the way in which the courtly romance moves toward more realistic character depictions. The Arthurian knight Gawain still lives through a series of adventures that are structurally reminiscent of the traditional epic but he simultaneously develops into a multifaceted figure with highly idiosyncratic character traits. This psychological realism on the level of character presentation parallels detailed realistic descriptions of everyday life situations, such as a hunting scene that pays specific attention to all the steps of eviscerating the prey. On a narratological level, Gawain leaves behind the traditional omniscient, god-like point of view of the classical epic by using a figural narrative situation that adopts the perspective of the protagonist. A good example of this technique is the passage where Gawain pretends to be still asleep while the lady of the castle enters his bedroom and subsequently tries to seduce him:

> And the good man, Gawain, in gay bed sleeping
> Lies snug till any gleam glimmers on wall,
> Under coverlet clean, curtain'd about
> As on slumber he slid, a sly noise heard he,
> A little din at his door, which daintily open'd;
> He heav'd up his head out of the clothes,
> A corner of the curtain he caught up a little,
> And watched full warily what it might be.
> 'Twas the lady herself, lovely to look on,
> Who drew the door after, so stealthy and still,
> And boun'd toward the bed: and he blush'd and shamed him,
> Slipt him down slyly, and look'd as if sleeping.
>
> (xlviii, V. 2–13)

Everything is told in the third person (i.e., Gawain is referred to as "he") although we experience every detail of the action as if through Gawain's eyes (see the section on "Narrative situation" in this chapter). We gain deep insights into the mental reflections, insecurities, and ambivalent thoughts of the main character. The individualization of the protagonist, the perspectival narrative situation, and, above all, the linear plot structure, directed toward a specific climax that no longer centers on national or cosmic problems, are among the crucial features that distinguish the romance from epic poetry.

The **novel**, which emerged in Spain during the seventeenth century and in England during the eighteenth century, employs these elements in an even more obvious manner. Nevertheless, the early novel remains deeply rooted in the older genre of the epic. Miguel de Cervantes's (1547–1616) *Don Quixote* (1605; 1615), for instance, puts an end to the epic and to the *chivalric romance* by parodying and profaning their traditional elements: a not-so-noble knight who is involved in quite unheroic adventures courts a lady who is not so deserving of adoration. At the same time, however, Cervantes initiates a modified epic tradition in a new genre format. Similarly, the Englishman Henry Fielding (1707–1754) characterizes his novel *Joseph Andrews* (1742) as a "comic romance" and "comic epic poem in prose" (i.e., a parody and synthesis of existing genres). Also, in the plot structure of the early novel, which often tends to be episodic, elements of the epic survive in new attire, as, for example, Hans Jacob Christoph von Grimmelshausen's (*c.*1621–1676) *Simplicissimus* (1669) in Germany. In England, Daniel Defoe's (*c.*1660–1731) *Robinson Crusoe* (1719) marks the beginning of this new literary genre. Subsequently, Samuel Richardson's (1689–1761) *Pamela* (1740–1741) and *Clarissa* (1748–1749), Henry Fielding's *Tom Jones* (1749), and Laurence Sterne's (1713–1768) *Tristram Shandy* (1759–1767) establish the novel as one of the most productive genres of modern literature.

The terms "realism" and "individualism" characterize the newly established novel, thereby summarizing some of the basic innovations of this new medium. While the traditional epic exhibited a cosmic and allegorical dimension, the modern novel distinguishes itself by grounding the plot in a distinct historical and geographical reality. The allegorical and typified epic hero metamorphoses into the protagonist of the novel, with individual and realistic character traits.

These features of the novel, which, in their attention to individualism and realism, reflect basic socio-historical tendencies of the seventeenth and eighteenth centuries, soon made the novel a dominant literary genre. The novel thus mirrors the modern disregard for the collective spirit of the Middle Ages that heavily relied on allegory and symbolism. The rise of an educated middle class, the spread of the printing press, and changing economic circumstances, which allowed authors to pursue writing as an independent profession, underlie these major shifts in seventeenth- and eighteenth-century literary production. To this day, the novel maintains its leading position as the genre that has produced the most innovations in literature over the past three centuries.

The term "novel," however, subsumes a number of subgenres, such as the **picaresque novel** (from Spanish "*pícaro*" – "rogue"), which relates the experiences of a vagrant rogue in his conflict with the norms of society. Structured as an episodic narrative, the picaresque novel tries to lay bare social injustices in a satirical way. One of the earliest examples or precursors is the Spanish novel *Lazarillo de Tormes* (published anonymously in 1554), which initiates the genre. Grimmelshausen's *Simplicissimus*, and Fielding's *Tom Jones*, both display specific traits of this form of prose fiction. Picaresque novels share features with the **Bildungsroman** (novel of education), generally referred to by its German name. It describes the development of a protagonist from childhood to maturity, which is why it is also often called a coming-of-age story. Other examples include Johann Wolfgang von Goethe's (1749–1832) *Wilhelm Meisters Lehrjahre* (1795–1796) or Jean-Jacques Rosseau's (1712–1778) *Émile, or On Education* (1762). Italo Calvino's (1923–1985) Italian novel *The Baron in the Trees* (1957) also counts as a novel of education, as the reader learns about the life of a baron, starting with his childhood when he decides to live in trees, to his death as an old man in the treetops. In English literature, famous examples are Charles Dickens's (1812–1870) *David Copperfield* (1850) or J. D. Salinger's (1919–2010) American novel *The Catcher in the Rye* (1951).

Another early form of the novel is the **epistolary novel**, in which letters relate a first-person narration – a technique that was first employed in Samuel Richardson's (1689–1761) *Pamela* (1740–1741). In the German-speaking world, epistolary novels reached their peak with Goethe's *The Sorrows of Young Werther* (1774), and, in France, with Pierre Choderlos de Laclos's (1741–1803) *The Dangerous Liaisons* (1782). Interestingly, this subgenre developed in the eighteenth century, when the postal service also evolved in order to enable more efficient communication.

Another subgenre, still popular today, is the **historical novel**, which mostly draws from real occurrences and real historic people, or depicts historically accurate settings. Sir Walter Scott's (1771–1832) English novel *Waverly* (1814) influenced many other literatures, such as Alexander Dumas's (1802–1870) historical adventure story *The Count of Monte Christo* (1844–1846) in France. *The Name of the Rose* (1980) by

Italian literary critic Umberto Eco (1932–) revived the genre toward the end of the twentieth century. By depicting an entanglement around several mysterious murders in an Italian abbey of the fourteenth century, Eco proved that the genre can indeed work on many different levels, both literary and theoretical. The novel mirrors Eco's concerns in literary theory, especially semiotics, while also offering an exciting mystery story, as well as a survey of the zeitgeist in the late medieval period.

While satires unmask social plights through humorous caricatures, the **utopian novel**, as well as the **science fiction novel**, creates alternative worlds as a way of criticizing real socio-political issues. Thomas More (1477–1535) founded the genre in early modern England with his novel *Utopia* (1516), which led to other works that created similar societal visions. Some famous examples are Tommaso Campanella's (1568–1639) *City of the Sun* (1602) in Italy, *Christianopolis* (1619) by the German theologian Johann Valentin Andreae (1586–1654), and the novel *We* (1924) by the Russian author Yevgeny Zamyatin (1881–1937). In the past few decades, female authors have given literary utopias a new kind of dynamics, as evident in the dystopia (a negative utopia) of *The Handmaid's Tale* (1985) by Canadian author Margaret Atwood (1939–), which paints a gloomy picture of society from a female point of view.

Other popular forms of prose fiction are the **gothic novel**, enriching English literature of the eighteenth century with works such as Horace Walpole's (1717–1797) *The Castle of Otranto* (1764), and German literature with E. T. A. Hoffman's (1772–1822) *The Devil's Elixirs* (1816). Toward the end of the nineteenth century, the gothic novel had established itself as a serious literary genre, celebrating its heyday with Bram Stoker's (1847–1912) *Dracula* (1897). In later years, the genre mainly retired to the realms of trivial literature, film adaptations, and television, where it is currently experiencing a major revival.

The **detective novel** is a relatively young subgenre, originating in the nineteenth century. Similar traits, however, can already be observed in eighteenth-century works such as Friedrich Schiller's (1759–1805) *The Criminal of Lost Honour* (1792). In the English-speaking world, detective novels first gained popularity in the twentieth century with texts such as Agatha Christie's (1890–1976) *Murder on the Orient Express* (1934). In the past few decades, female detectives – such as in

Patricia Cornwell's (1956–) novels – have added new impulses to the genre, as have investigators with "ethnic" backgrounds – such as a Native American detective in Tony Hillerman's (1925–2008) novels. The thriller *The Da Vinci Code* (2003) by American author Dan Brown (1964–) showed the popularity of the genre in an impressive way, outselling many other publications with its mixture of religion, occultism, and the detective novel. Due to its broad appeal, television and cinema also display a strong affinity to this genre.

As we have seen with the detective novel, borders between subgenres are often blurred, meaning that novels such as Eco's *The Name of the Rose* can be seen both as a historical and a detective novel. Similarly, novels of education often bear features of picaresque novels. As with genre distinctions in general, one always assumes ideal criteria when trying to define longer narrative forms, which, however, hardly any work of literature can really completely fulfill. Even distinguishing a novel from shorter forms of prose fiction is not always an easy task.

Unlike the novel, concise forms of prose fiction, such as the **short story**, have received relatively little attention from literary scholars. As with the novel, the roots of the short story lie in antiquity and the Middle Ages. Story, myth, and the fairy tale relate to the oldest kinds of text types when "texts" were primarily transmitted orally. The term tale (from "to tell"), like the German *Sage* (from *sagen* – "to speak"), reflects this oral dimension that is inherent in short fiction. Even the Bible includes stories, such as "Job" (*c*. fifth to fourth century AD) or "The Prodigal Son" (*c*. first century BC), whose structures and narrative patterns resemble modern short stories. Other forerunners of this subgenre of fiction are the ancient satire and the medieval romance.

Indirect precursors of the short story are medieval and early modern narrative cycles. The Arabian *Thousand and One Nights*, compiled in the fourteenth and subsequent centuries, Giovanni Boccaccio's Italian *Decameron* (1349–1351), Geoffrey Chaucer's (*c*.1343–1400) *Canterbury Tales* (*c*.1387), and Marguerite de Navarre's (1494–1549) Spanish *Heptameron* (1558) anticipate important features of modern short fiction. These cycles of tales are characterized by a frame narrative that unites a number of otherwise heterogeneous stories. As a frame narrative for his *Decameron*, Boccaccio introduces a group of young Florentine men and women who flee from the plague to the countryside, and, as a way of killing time, tell each other stories over a period of ten days; hence *Decameron*, from the Greek terms *deka* ("ten") and *hemerai* ("days"). Similarly, the most important Middle English collection of stories, Chaucer's *Canterbury Tales*, uses a pilgrimage to the tomb of Saint Thomas Becket in Canterbury as a framing device. On their way to Canterbury, the pilgrims tell different, rather self-contained tales that are only connected through Chaucer's use of a "general prologue." This frame story not only describes the setting but also introduces the individual pilgrims who will later tell their respective tales. Chaucer renders these character portraits with a great deal of psychological realism, thereby establishing an indirect connection between the tellers and their respective stories. Both Chaucer and Boccaccio try to structure their works by introducing such narrative frames, thereby connecting relatively heterogeneous stories that, with regard to their individual content, have little or nothing in common.

The short story as we know it today emerged as a more or less independent text type at the end of the eighteenth century, parallel to the development of the novel and the newspaper. Regularly issued magazines of the nineteenth century exerted a major influence on the establishment of the short story by providing an ideal medium for the publication of this prose genre of limited length. Forerunners of these journals are the *Tatler* (1709–1711) and the *Spectator* (1711–1712 and 1714), published in England by Joseph Addison and Richard Steele, who tried to address the educated middle class in short literary texts and essay-like commentaries of general interest. Even today, magazines such as the *New Yorker* (since 1925) still function as privileged organs for first publications of short stories. Many of the early novels appeared as serial stories in these magazines before being published as independent books, as, for example, Charles Dickens's *The Pickwick Papers* (1836–1837). Apart from the famous American short stories by Washington Irving (1783–1859) and Edgar Allan Poe (1809–1849), the stories of Russian author Anton P. Chekhov (1860–1904) also proved to be very influential internationally. In the German-speaking part of the world, E. T. A. Hoffmann's romantic and gothic texts, which often gravitate around mechanical automata, are early examples of this genre. In the twentieth century, important authors, such as Heinrich Böll (1917–1985) in Germany or Ernest Hemingway (1899–1961) in the United States, continued this tradition. A major source of inspiration for modern writers and literary theorists are the philosophically oriented short stories of the Argentine author Jorge Luis Borges (1899–1986), such as, for example, his collection *The Library of Babel* (1941).

While the novel has always attracted the interest of literary theorists, the short story has never actually achieved the status held by book-length fiction. The short story, however, surfaces in comparative definitions of other prose genres, such as the novel or its shorter variants, namely the novella and the novelette. A crucial feature that Poe had already identified with the short story is its impression of unity, since it can be read – in contrast to the novel – in one sitting without interruption. Due to restrictions of length, the plot of the short story has to be highly selective, which necessitates an idiosyncratic temporal dimension that usually focuses on one central moment of the action. The slow and gradual build-up of suspense in the novel must be accelerated in the short story by means of certain techniques. The action of the short story therefore often begins close to the climax (*in medias res* – "the middle of the matter"), reconstructing the preceding context and plot development through flashbacks. Focusing on one main figure or location, the characters and the setting normally receive less detailed and careful depictions than in the novel. In contrast to the novel's generally descriptive style, the short story, for the simple reason of its limited length, has to be more suggestive. While the novelist can experiment with various narrative perspectives, the short story author usually chooses one particular narrative situation, relating the action through the eyes of a particular figure or narrator.

The **novella** or **novelette** holds an intermediary position between novel and short story since its length and narratological elements cannot be strictly identified with either of the two genres. Classical examples of this genre are *The Abbess of Castro* (1832) by French writer Stendhal (1783–1842) and Guy de Maupassant's (1850–1893) *Le Horla* (1887). In Germany, a notable novella is Theodor Storm's (1817–1888) *Aquis Submersus* (1876). In English, Joseph Conrad's (1857–1924) *Heart of Darkness* (1902) is one of the most famous examples, partly because of Francis Ford Coppola's (1939–) film adaptation *Apocalypse Now* (1979).

As this juxtaposition of the main elements of the novel and the short story shows, attempts to explain the nature of these genres rely on different methodological approaches, among them reception theory with respect to reading without interruption, formalist notions for the analysis of plot structures, and contextual approaches for delineating their boundaries with other comparable genres. The terms plot, time, character, setting, narrative situation, and style emerge not only in the definitions and discussions of the genre of the novel, but also function as the most important areas of inquiry in film and drama. Since we can isolate these aspects most easily in prose fiction, the following section will highlight them in greater detail by drawing on examples from novels and short stories. The most important dimensions are:

Plot	What happens?
Characters	Who acts?
Narrative situation	Who speaks and who sees?
Setting	Where and when do events take place?

Plot

The term **plot** refers to the way a story unfolds in a text. According to the philosopher and first literary theorist Aristotle (384–322 BC), a plot (or *mythos*, as he called it) needs to have a beginning, middle, and an end. In well-written plots, all of its elements must connect logically and produce something probable. A simple way to analyze a plotline is to divide it into four main stages:

exposition – complication – climax or turning point – resolution

The **exposition** or presentation of the initial situation is disturbed by a **complication** or **conflict** that produces suspense and eventually leads to a climax, crisis, or turning point. The **climax** is followed by a resolution of the complication (**denouement**), with which the text usually ends. Traditional fiction, drama, and film normally rely on this basic plot structure.

If we use this terminology for William Shakespeare's (1564–1616) play *Romeo and Juliet* (1595), we can trace the following plot structure: Initially, we encounter two families at war with each other (exposition). When Romeo falls in love with Juliet, this love challenges the relationship between their rivaling families (complication). This struggle consequently leads to the murder of Mercutio (climax), triggering a chain of events, including the deaths of Romeo and Juliet, which eventually compel the two families to put an end to the hostilities between them (resolution). As this example demonstrates, the narratological term "climax" denotes a "point of no return" that is the cause of all following actions. It should not be confused with the everyday use of the term climax as a "final showdown."

If, as in this example, all of these elements follow a chronological order, we speak of a linear plot. In many cases – even in linear plots – **flashbacks** and foreshadowing introduce information concerning the past or future into the narrative. Even the oldest surviving epic, the Mesopotamian *Epic of Gilgamesh*, the oldest parts of which go back to the third millennium BC, works with these techniques. For example, the first-person narration by Utnapishti, a figure who clearly resembles the biblical Noah, relates the story of the great flood as an elaborate flashback. Equally, in Homer's *Odyssey* (*c.* seventh century BC), flashbacks are an important narrative device. Even though the epic spans across the entire 10 years of Odysseus's voyages, the story begins shortly before the hero returns home. Several first-person narratives then tell of his adventures in episodic flashbacks.

The opening scene in Billy Wilder's (1906–2002) *Sunset Boulevard* (1950) is a famous example of **foreshadowing** in film: in a voice-over, the first-person narrator posthumously relates the events that led to his death while his dead body is drifting in a swimming pool. The only break with a linear plot or chronological narrative is the anticipation of the film's ending – the protagonist's death – thus eliminating suspense as an important narrative effect. This technique directs the audience's attention to aspects of the film other than the outcome of the action.

Many contemporary novels alter the linear narrative structure in rather unorthodox ways. The *Dictionary of the Khazars: A Lexicon Novel* (1984) by Serbian author Milorad Pavić (1929–2009), for instance, breaks the linearity by presenting parts of the novel as dictionary entries that the reader can follow in any order, from one cross-reference to another. The preface to the novel *Hopscotch* (1963) by Argentinian author Julio Cortázar (1914–1984) works with similar techniques, offering two ways of reading the book, each of which suggests a different combination of chapters, thus making the plot nonlinear and variable:

> In its own way, this book consists of many books, but two books above all. The reader is invited to choose between these two possibilities:

The first can be read in a normal fashion and it ends with chapter 56, at the close of which there are three garish little stars which stand for the words *The End*. Consequently, the reader may ignore what follows with a clean conscience.

The second can be read by beginning with chapter 73 and then following the sequence indicated at the end of each chapter. In case of confusion or forgetfulness, one need only consult the following list:

73 – 1 – 2 – 116 – 4 – 84 – 4 – 71 – 5 – 81 – 74 – 6 – 7 – 8 – 93 – 68 – 9 – 104 – 10 – 65 – 11 – 136 – 12 – 106 – 13 – 115 – 14 – 114 – 117 – 15 – 120 – 16 – 137 – 97 – 18 – 153 [. . .]
(xx)

The book thereby contains (at least) two distinct plotlines, depending on the order in which we choose to read the chapters of the novel.

Kurt Vonnegut's (1922–2007) postmodernist novel *Slaughterhouse-Five* (1969) is another striking example of an experimental plot structure that mixes various levels of action and time, such as the experiences of a young soldier in World War II, his life in America after the war, and a science-fiction-like dream world in which the protagonist is kidnapped by an extraterrestrial force. All three levels are juxtaposed as fragments by rendering the different settings as well as their internal sequences of action in an achronological way.

Kurt Vonnegut offers an explanation of this complex plot structure in his protagonist's report on the unconventional literary practice of the extraterrestrial people on the planet Tralfamadore:

[Our] books were laid out – in brief clumps of symbols separated by stars. [. . . E]ach clump of symbols is a brief, urgent message – describing a situation, a scene. We Tralfamadorians read them all at once, not one after the other. There isn't any particular relationship between all the messages, except that the author has chosen them carefully, so that, when seen all at once, they produce an image of life that is beautiful and surprising and deep. There is no beginning, no middle, no end [. . .]. What we love in our books are the depths of many marvelous moments seen at one time.
(70–71)

Kurt Vonnegut is actually talking about the structure of his own novel, which is composed of similarly fragmented parts. The different levels of action and time converge in the mind of the protagonist as seemingly simultaneous. Vonnegut's technique of nonlinear narrative, which interweaves several plotlines, conveys the schizophrenic mind of the shell-shocked protagonist through parallel presentations of different levels of experiences.

Such postmodernist narratives borrow techniques from the visual arts, whose representational structures are considered to be different from the literary practice. The eighteenth-century German author and literary theorist Gotthold Ephraim Lessing (1729–1781) regarded literature as a temporal art form since action develops in a temporal sequence of events. The visual arts, however, pertain to the spatial arts since they are able to capture one particular segment of the action, which the viewer can then perceive in one instant. Vonnegut and other experimental authors try to apply this pictorial structure of simultaneity to literary texts. Fragmented narratives of this sort, which abandon linear plots, surface in various genres and media, including film and drama. It is not surprising that these narrative experiments always indirectly determine other main elements, such as setting and character presentation.

Characters

While formalist approaches to the study of literature traditionally focus on plot and narrative structure, methods informed by psychoanalysis shift the center of attention to the characters of a text. A psychological approach is, however, merely one way of evaluating or interpreting characters; it is also possible to analyze character presentation in the context of narrative structures. Generally speaking, characters in a text can be rendered either as types or as individuals. A typified or **flat character** in literature is dominated by one specific trait. The term **round character** usually denotes a persona with more complex and differentiated features. This basic distinction between flat and round character goes back to the British author and literary theorist E. M. Forster (1879–1970).

Flat or typified characters often represent the general traits of a group of persons or abstract ideas. Classical Roman comedy excelled at presenting a whole cast of stock characters, such as the *miles gloriosus* ("the boastful soldier"), or the grumpy old man, as well as the cunning servant. Medieval allegorical depictions of characters preferred typification in order to personify vices, virtues, or philosophical and religious positions. In the extremely popular fourteenth-century English long poem *Piers Plowman* (c.1360–1386) by William Langland (c.1332–1387), most characters represent one specific feature, as, for example, the allegorical figures Do-well, Do-better and Do-best. The Everyman figure, a symbol of the sinful Christian, is another major example of this general pattern in the representation of man in medieval literature. In today's advertisements, typified character presentations re-emerge in magazines, posters, film, and television. The temporal and spatial limitations of advertising media revive allegorical and symbolic characterization for didactic and persuasive reasons that are comparable to those of the Middle Ages.

A good example of the purposeful use of typified character presentation occurs in the opening scene of Mark Twain's (1835–1910) "A True Story" (1874):

> It was summer-time, and twilight. We were sitting on the porch of the farmhouse, on the summit of the hill, and "Aunt Rachel" was sitting respectfully below our level, on the steps – for she was our servant, and colored. She was a mighty frame and stature; she was sixty years old, but her eye was undimmed and her strength unabated. She was a cheerful, hearty soul, and it was no more trouble for her to laugh than it is for a bird to sing. [. . .] I said: "Aunt Rachel, how is it that you've lived sixty years and never had any trouble?" She stopped quaking: She paused, and there was a moment of silence. She turned her face over her shoulder toward me, and said, without even a smile in her voice, "Misto C——, is you in 'arnest?"

(265)

The first paragraph of this short story provides a very formal configuration, where characters are reduced to mere types, yet still reflect a highly meaningful structure. The most significant constellation is rendered in one sentence: "'Aunt Rachel' was sitting respectfully below our level, on the steps – for she was our servant, and colored." The phrase "Misto C——, is you in 'arnest?" further specifies the inherent relationship. Twain manages not only to juxtapose African Americans and whites, slaves and slave owners, but also female and male. In this very short passage, Twain delineates a formal relationship between two character types that also represents a multileveled structure of dependence. He introduces typified characterization for several reasons: as a stylistic feature of the short story, which does not permit lengthy depictions, and as a meaningful frame within which the story evolves. The analyses of African American and feminist literary theory focus on mechanisms of race, class, and gender as analogously functioning dimensions. By juxtaposing a black, female slave with a white, male slave owner, Twain highlights these patterns of oppression in their most extreme forms. The setting – a farm in the US South – and, above all, the spatial positioning of the figures according to their social status ("'Aunt Rachel' was sitting respectfully *below* our level, on the steps") emphasize the mechanisms of dependence inherent in these mere character types.

The **individualization** of a character, however, has evolved into a main feature of the medieval romance, as we have seen in the example of *Sir Gawain and the Green Knight*, but even more so in the novel. Many modern fictional texts reflect a tension between these modes of representation by introducing both elements simultaneously. Herman Melville's (1819–1891) novel *Moby Dick* (1851), for instance, combines allegorical and individualistic elements in the depiction of its main character, the mysterious Captain Ahab. This lends a universal dimension to the action, which, despite being grounded in the particularities of a round figure, nevertheless points beyond the specific individual.

Both typified and individualized characters can be rendered in a text through showing and telling as two different **modes of presentation**. The explanatory characterization, or **telling**, describes a person or a setting through a narrator; for example, the depiction of Quasimodo in Victor Hugo's (1802–1885) French novel *The Hunchback of Notre Dame* (1831):

> The melancholy of the poor fellow became as incurable and complete as his deformity. His deafness rendered him in some measure dumb. For, the moment he lost his hearing, he resolved to avoid the ridicule of others by a silence that he never broke except when he was alone. He voluntarily tied up that tongue [. . .]; from then on, when necessity forced him to speak, his tongue was swollen and awkward, and like a door whose hinges have grown rusty.

(138–139)

In this example, the character is represented through the filter of a selective and sympathetic narrator. This technique deliberately places the narrator in the foreground, inserting him or her as a critical mediator between the action and the reader (see the section on "Narrative situation" in this chapter).

Dramatic characterization, or **showing**, does away with the position of an obvious narrator, thus avoiding any overt influence on the reader by a narrative mediator. This method of presentation creates the impression on the reader that he or she is able to perceive the acting figures without any intervening agency, as if witnessing a dramatic performance. The image of a person is "shown" solely through his or her actions and utterances without interfering commentary, thereby suggesting an "objective" narrative that leaves the interpretation and evaluation solely to the reader. Ernest Hemingway's (1899–1961) texts are among the most famous for this technique, which aims at an "objective" effect by means of a drama-like presentation:

> "The Express is an hour late, sir," she said. "Can I bring you some coffee?"
> "If you think it won't keep me awake."
> "Please?" asked the waitress.
> "Bring me some," said Mr. Wheeler.
> "Thank you."
> She brought the coffee from the kitchen and Mr. Wheeler looked out of the window at the snow falling in the light from the station platform.
> "Do you speak other languages besides English?" he asked the waitress.
> "Oh, yes, sir. I speak German and French and the dialects."
>
> (422)

This passage from "Homage to Switzerland" (1933) exemplifies this technique, typical of Hemingway, which offers only the facade of his characters by dwelling solely on the exterior aspects of dialogue and actions without further commentary or evaluation. Dramatic presentation, however, only pretends to represent objectively while it always necessarily remains biased and selective.

A more recent example of this style is *Kiss of the Spider Woman* (1976) by Argentinian author Manuel Puig (1932–1990). The entire novel is written in direct speech, almost like a movie script:

– Well, but as a farewell, I do want to ask you for something . . .

– What?

– Something you never did, even though we did a lot worse things.

– What?

– A kiss . . .

– You're right . . .

– But tomorrow, before I go. Don't get scared, I'm not asking for it now.

(260)

In addition to its script-like quality, the novel overtly discusses cinema. The main character, for example, indulges in re-narrating old films. As Puig himself worked in the film industry, and the novel was also adapted into a movie, these similarities are definitely intended. The drama-like dialogue creates an objective view of the action, presenting only a character's facade with its external aspects. Interpretation and evaluation are left to the reader. Naturally, however, this dramatic characterization is only superficially objective, and nevertheless takes a very specific perspective on the action.

As shown above, we can distinguish between two basic kinds of characters (flat or round), as well as between two general **modes of presentation** (telling or showing):

Kinds of characters	Modes of presentation
typified character (flat)	explanatory method = telling (narration)
individualized character (round)	dramatic method = showing (dialogue – monologue)

Similar to typification and individualization, explanatory and dramatic methods hardly ever appear in their pure forms, but rather as hybrids of various degrees, since most novels and short stories use description as well as dialogue. Questions concerning character presentation are always connected with problems of narrative situation and are therefore hard to isolate or deal with individually. The following section on "Narrative situation" thus inevitably touches upon aspects that have already been mentioned.

Narrative situation

The term **narrative situation** consists mainly of two aspects: the narrative voice (who speaks?) and the focalization (who sees?). The subtleties of narrative situations developed parallel to the emergence of the novel. The influential Austrian narratologist Franz Karl Stanzel (1923–) distinguishes between three typical narrative situations: the action of a text is either mediated through an exterior, unspecified narrator (authorial narrative situation), through a person involved in the action who refers to himself or herself as "I" (first-person narrative situation), or presented from the perspective of an involved figure in the third person (figural narrative situation). This tripartite structure can only summarize the most extreme manifestations, which, particularly in modernist and postmodernist fiction, hardly ever occur in their pure form; individual literary works are often hybrids combining elements of various types of narrative situations.

The most common manifestations of narrative situation in prose fiction can, therefore, be structured according to the following pattern:

authorial narrative situation
external narrator with an omniscient point of view
who refers to the protagonist in the third person

first-person narrative situation
by the protagonist or by a minor
character

figural narrative situation
through figures acting in
the story

Texts with an **authorial narrative situation** refer to the acting figures in the third person and present the action from an omniscient (all-knowing), godlike perspective. (Be careful to avoid the misleading term "third-person narration," since it does not sufficiently distinguish omniscient from figural narrative situations, as we will see later.) Using a narrator who is not an acting figure in the story easily allows for changes in setting, time, and action, while simultaneously providing various items of information beyond the range and knowledge of the characters. Leo Tolstoy (1828–1910), for example, introduces an omniscient narrator of this sort in his novel *War and Peace* (1869):

> . . . on a July evening in 1805 the well-known Anna Pavlovna Scherer, maid of honor and confidential friend of the Empress

Maria Feodorovna, greeted the influential statesman Prince Vasili Kuragin, who was the first to arrive at her reception.

Anna Pavlovna had been coughing for several days; she had the grippe, as she called it – grippe being then a new word used only by a few.

Her notes of invitation, distributed that morning by a footman in red livery, had been written all alike to all:

Count (or prince), if you have nothing better to do, and if the prospect of an evening with a poor invalid is not too frightful, I shall be very glad to see you tonight between seven and ten.

(1–2)

As is evident from this example, an omniscient narrator can go back in time ("Anna Pavlovna had been coughing for several days; she had the grippe"), know the content of personal letters ("Her notes of invitation [. . .] had been written all alike to all"), and possess exact information about different figures of the novel ("Anna Pavlovna Scherer [. . .] Empress Maria Feodorovna [. . .] Vasili Kuragin"). This omniscient narrative situation was particularly popular in the traditional epic but was also widely used in the early novel.

In contrast to omniscient narrative situations, **first-person narration** renders the action as seen through a participating figure who refers to himself or herself in the first person. First-person narrations can adopt the point of view either of the protagonist or of a minor figure. The majority of novels in first-person narration use, of course, the **protagonist** (main character) as narrator, such as, for example, Laurence Sterne's *Tristram Shandy* (1759–1767) or Charles Dickens's *David Copperfield* (1849–1850). J. D. Salinger's *Catcher in the Rye* (1951) self-consciously evokes this tradition of first-person narration when the adolescent protagonist Holden Caulfield addresses the reader:

If you really want to hear about it, the first thing you'll probably want to know is where I was born, and what my lousy childhood was like, and how my parents were occupied and all before they had me, and all that David Copperfield kind of crap, but I don't feel like going into it.

(3)

Another famous example of a first-person narrative by the protagonist is in the opening lines of Marcel Proust's (1871–1922) French novel *In Search of Lost Time* (1913–1927):

> For a long time I would go to bed early. Sometimes, the candle barely out, my eyes closed so quickly that I did not have time to tell myself: "I'm falling asleep." And half an hour later the thought that it was time to look for sleep would awaken me;

(1)

These first-person narrations by protagonists aim at a supposedly authentic representation of the subjective experiences and feelings of the narrator. The autobiography specifically relies on this particular aspect, as, for example, St. Augustine's (AD 354–430) *Confessions* (*c.* AD 397–398) or Benjamin Franklin's (1706–1790) *Autobiography* (1771–1788).

This proximity to the protagonist can be avoided by introducing a **minor character** as first-person narrator. By depicting events as seen through the eyes of another person, the character of the protagonist remains less transparent. A number of novels that focus on a main figure, for instance Herman Melville's (1819–1891) *Moby Dick* (1851) and F. Scott Fitzgerald's (1896–1940) *The Great Gatsby* (1925), mystify the protagonist by using this technique. The opening words of *Moby Dick*, "Call me Ishmael" (21), are uttered by the minor character Ishmael, who subsequently describes the mysterious protagonist Captain Ahab. In Fitzgerald's *The Great Gatsby*, Nick Carraway relates the events around the enigmatic Gatsby from the periphery of the action.

In the **figural narrative situation**, the narrator moves into the background, suggesting that the plot is revealed solely through the actions of the characters in the text. This literary technique is a relatively recent phenomenon, which has developed with the rise of the modern novel, mostly in order to encourage the reader to judge the action without an intervening commentator. The following example from Fyodor Dostoyevsky's (1821–1881) *Crime and Punishment* (1866) renders the action through the figural perspective of the protagonist. The main character, Raskolnikov, has just killed an old woman and her sister with an axe, when he suddenly hears approaching footsteps:

When he first heard them, the steps were far away, at the very bottom of the staircase, but he afterwards remembered clearly and distinctly that from the very first sound he guessed that they were certainly coming *here*, to the fourth floor, to the old woman's flat. Why? Was there something special, something significant, about them? The steps were heavy, regular, unhurrying. Already they had reached the first floor, they were coming on, their sound was clearer and clearer. He could hear the newcomer's heavy breathing. Already the steps had passed the second floor . . . They were coming here!

(78)

In the above passage, we as readers almost feel as if we are literally in the murderer's shoes. We experience the nervousness, the tension, and the man's growing fear. Even though the author has chosen a third-person narrator, which often disrupts the reader's proximity to the characters, the figural situation makes for a very intense reading experience. Mental reflections, inner thoughts, and worries are artfully employed to reveal the action. In contrast to an omniscient point of view, this figural narrative situation is bound to the perspective of a figure that is also part of the action. Prime examples of this technique are the novels of Franz Kafka (1883–1924), who deliberately employed the limited perspective of the protagonist in order to highlight the high degree of alienation of his characters. Also, the restricted access to information, solely bound to the experiences of the protagonist, which this narrative situation entails, ultimately conveys the helplessness and isolation of Kafka's main characters. This becomes very apparent in the beginning of his novel *The Trial* (1925):

Someone must have been slandering Josef K., for one morning, without having done anything wrong, he was arrested. The cook, employed by his landlady Frau Grubach, who brought him his breakfast each morning at about eight o'clock, failed to appear. That had never happened before.

(3)

If a text shifts the emphasis from exterior aspects of the plot almost exclusively to the inner world of a character, we call this narrative mode **stream-of-consciousness technique**. Related narratological phenomena are **interior monologue** and **free indirect discourse**. The narrator disappears, leaving the thoughts and psychological reactions of a participating figure as the sole mediators of the action. Influenced by Sigmund Freud's psychoanalysis, these techniques found their way into modernist prose fiction after World War I. Based on associations in the subconscious of a fictional character, this reflects a groundbreaking shift in cultural paradigms during the first decades of the twentieth century. Literature, under the influence of psychoanalysis and related sciences, shifted its main focus from the sociologically descriptive goals of the nineteenth century to the psychic phenomena of the individual. A good example is Jean-Paul Sartre's (1905–1980) French novel *Nausea* (1938):

> here is a cardboard box holding my bottle of ink. I should try to tell how I saw it before and now [. . .] Well, it's a parallelopiped rectangle, it opens – that's stupid, there's nothing I can say about it. This is what I have to avoid, I must not put in strangeness where there is none. I think that is the big danger in keeping a diary: you exaggerate everything. You continually force the truth because you're always looking for something. On the other hand, it is certain that from one minute to the next – and precisely *à propos* of this box or any other object at all I can recapture this impression of day-before-yesterday. I must always be ready, otherwise it will slip through my fingers.
>
> (1–2)

James Joyce (1882–1941) is considered to be the inventor of this technique, best exemplified by the final section of his novel *Ulysses* (1922), which strings together mental associations of the character Molly Bloom. Joyce renders the associative thoughts of Molly, while she is falling asleep, in a long sequence of sentences without punctuation. The entire Chapter 18 of the novel recreates Molly's uninterrupted train of thought. These are the last few lines at the end of the book:

> and then I asked him with my eyes to ask again yes and then he asked me would I yes to say yes my mountain flower and first I put my arms around him yes and drew him down to me so he could

feel my breasts all perfume yes and his heart was going like mad and yes I said yes I will Yes.

(933)

A famous example in American literature is William Faulkner's (1897–1962) renderings of impressions and events through the inner perspective of a mentally handicapped character in *The Sound and the Fury* (1929). In the following example of an observation made by Benjy, the question arises: What is it that he witnesses in his limited perception? "It was red, flapping on the pasture. [. . .] I held to the fence. [. . .] Maybe we can find one of they balls" (12). Benjy is observing a game of golf, and neither the game nor its rules are known to him – he simply registers the red flags and the white balls. We as readers are as puzzled as he is and have to decipher his sensory perceptions rendered through his interior monologues.

Virginia Woolf's (1882–1941) novel *Mrs Dalloway* (1925) also serves as an excellent example for this new focus on the mind, as it presents events not only through the thoughts of *one* person, but also through a number of other figures. As indicated by the title, the character Clarissa Dalloway is at the center of the novel, yet Woolf depicts her protagonist through the psyches of different personae. These figures cross paths with Clarissa Dalloway, reacting to her and thus revealing new character traits of the protagonist. Through the interaction between the different mental reflections, as well as a number of other structural elements, the novel achieves a closed and unified form. It is a striking example of how the use of narrative situation, character presentation, setting, and plot structure can create an interdependent network of elements that work toward a common goal. These experimental narrative techniques became the major structural features of modernism, thereby characterizing an entire literary era at the beginning of the twentieth century.

In order to better cope with modernist and postmodernist writings, which tend to be less straightforward in their use of narrative situations, the French literary theorist Gérard Genette (1930–) introduces a different set of terms, namely "homodiegetic" and "heterodiegetic". This distinction identifies whether or not the narrator is part of the diegetic world. A **homodiegetic narrator** is a character in the story who, consequently, has only a limited view of the action and particularly of the other characters' thoughts. A **heterodiegetic narrator**, on the other hand, is not part of the story world and, therefore, has unlimited knowledge and authority. It follows that all first-person narrative situations employ a homodiegetic narrator, who tells a story that he or she participates in, whereas all authorial as well as figural narrative situations feature a heterodiegetic narrator, who is not involved in the action rendered.

Another useful distinction that many narratologists make relates to how the presence of the narrator is indicated in the text. An **overt narrator** refers to himself or herself, speaks to the addressee, and often provides explanations of and comments on the action and the characters. The reader can clearly recognize the presence of a narrator figure as is the case in J. D. Salinger's *Catcher in the Rye* cited above. All first-person as well as authorial narratives employ overt narrators. **Covert narrators**, however, are barely noticeable. They never address themselves or the narratee, and do not comment or explain but adopt the point of view of a character from which they render the action seemingly unmediated as is always the case in figural narrative situations.

A covert narrator, and, in turn, the figural narrative situation, requires internal **focalization**. Focalization, another term coined by Genette, deals with the question of "who sees?" rather than "who speaks?"; in other words, the perspective from which the action is rendered. The character through whose eyes the reader sees the action is called the focalizer or reflector. Focalization also relates to the amount of information that is provided by the narrator. A narrative with **internal focalization** assumes a character's point of view and therefore has the same (limited) knowledge as the character (e.g., Kafka). In **externally focalized** narratives, the narrator is less knowledgeable than the characters (e.g., Hemingway). Finally, **zero focalization** corresponds to an omniscient point of view; in other words, the narrator knows more than the characters (e.g., Tolstoy).

Modernist and postmodernist novels often experiment with **changes of narrative situations** within one text in order to highlight decisive shifts in the course of action or narrative. The Dominican novelist Jean Rhys (1890–1979), for example, renders the first section of her novel *Wide Sargasso Sea* (1966) in first-person narration by the protagonist Antoinette. The story starts in the woman's childhood in the Caribbean: "'I was bridesmaid when my mother married Mr Mason in Spanish Town,' she tells. 'Christophine curled my hair. I carried a bouquet and everything I wore was new – even my beautiful slippers'" (28–29). Part 2 is different and tells the story from the point of view of Antoinette's husband, Mr. Rochester, while Antoinette is first drifting off into despair, then seemingly into madness: "She lifted her eyes. Blank lovely eyes. Mad eyes. A mad girl" (171). By suddenly switching perspectives, Rhys relates the story to the reader from several angles, never giving only one, ultimate truth. In the third and last part, when Antoinette is in England, locked up in the Rochester house, Rhys switches back to the original first-person narration, and back to Antoinette's point of view, which creates compassion for the imprisoned woman: "There is one window high up – you cannot see out of it. My bed had doors but they have been taken away" (180). Rhys's novel is an obvious example of how thematic aspects of a text, in this case the protagonist's loss of identity and control, can be emphasized on a structural level by means of narrative techniques, such as point of view.

The Canadian novelist Margaret Atwood (1939–) also applies this technique. However, although she changes the narrative situation, she stays with the same (main) character. Atwood renders the first section of her novel *The Edible Woman* (1969) in first-person narration by the protagonist. In the second part, she then uses a figural narrative situation in order to emphasize the woman's alienation: "Marian was sitting listlessly at her desk. She was doodling on the pad for telephone messages" (105). When Marian regains her identity at the end of the novel, Atwood switches back to the original first-person narration: "I was cleaning up the apartment. It had taken me two days to gather the strength to face it, but I had finally started" (289). Later on, Marian even reflects about these narratological changes when she says: "Now that I was thinking of myself in the first person singular again I found my own situation much more interesting" (290).

Setting

Setting is another aspect that is traditionally included in analyses of prose fiction, although it is relevant to discussions of other genres, too. The term setting denotes the location, historical period, and social surroundings in which the action of a text develops. In James Joyce's *Ulysses*, for example, the setting is clearly defined as Dublin, June 16, 1904. In other cases, for example William Shakespeare's *Hamlet* (c.1601), all we know is that the action takes place in medieval

Denmark. Authors hardly ever choose a setting for its own sake, but rather embed a story in a particular context of time and place in order to support action, characters, and narrative situation on an additional level.

For the first part of his Italian *Divine Comedy* (*c.*1307–1321), Dante Alighieri (1265–1321) uses the setting of a labyrinth to express the agonies of hell. In this epic, the *Inferno* is a tapered funnel, made of concentric terraces. The narrator follows these rings down into the gates of hell. The deeper he goes, the worse the sins as well as the punishment get. By employing this kind of labyrinth-like setting, offering an intertwined but clear path, Dante follows his role model Virgil, who, for his epic *Aeneid*, used a maze-like structure for the journeys of his hero Aeneas. Italo Calvino's (1923–1985) Italian novel *The Baron in the Trees* (1957) is set in the branches and tops of trees, as the protagonist decides as a child never to set foot on the earth again. Choosing this unusual environment, Calvino creates a kind of castle in the air for the baron, clearly distinguishing it from other, more traditional settings.

In the gothic novel and certain other forms of prose fiction, setting is one of the crucial elements of the genre as such. In the opening section of "The Fall of the House of Usher" (1840), Edgar Allan Poe (1809–1849) gives a detailed description of the building in which the uncanny short story will evolve. Interestingly, Poe's setting, the House of Usher, indirectly resembles Roderick Usher, the main character of the narrative and lord of the house:

> I know not how it was – but, with the first glimpse of the building, a sense of insufferable gloom pervaded my spirit. [. . .] I looked upon the scene before me – upon the mere house, and the simple landscape features of the domain – upon the bleak walls – upon the vacant eye-like windows – upon a few rank sedges – and upon a few white trunks of decayed trees – with an utter depression of soul which I can compare to no earthly sensation [. . .]. Perhaps the eye of a scrutinising observer might have discovered a barely perceptible fissure, which, extending from the roof of the building in front, made its way down the wall in a zigzag direction, until its way down became lost in the sullen waters of the tarn.
>
> (128–130)

The description of the facade of the house uses words such as "features," "eye-like," and "depression" that are reminiscent of the characterization of a human face. "White trunks of decayed trees" refers to the end of Roderick Usher's family tree – he will die without heirs, the last of his line. The crack in the front of the building mirrors the divided psyche of the lord of the house. At the end of the story, Poe juxtaposes the death of Usher with the collapse of the building, thereby creating an interdependence between setting, characters, and plot.

The modernist novel *Mrs Dalloway* (1925) by Virginia Woolf also relies heavily on setting to unite the fragmentary narrative perspectives into a single framework. As mentioned above, Woolf employs the mental reflections of a number of figures in her novel, ultimately to characterize her protagonist, Mrs Dalloway. Only through her carefully chosen use of setting can Virginia Woolf create the impression that the different perspectives or thoughts of the characters occur simultaneously. A variety of indicators in the text specifically grounds all events at a particular time and in a certain location. The action is situated in the city of London, which provides the grid in which the various reflections of the characters are intricately interwoven with street names and well-known sights. Temporal references, such as the tolling of Big Ben, a sky-writing plane, and the Prime Minister's car, appear in a number of episodes and thereby characterize them as simultaneous events that occur within different sections in the general setting of the city of London. At the outset of the novel, Woolf introduces temporal and spatial elements into the setting (see the italicized phrases in the following passage), which will later resurface in the subjective narratives of the respective mental reflections of the characters:

Mrs Dalloway said she would buy the flowers herself. [. . .]

For having lived in *Westminster* – how many years now? over twenty, – one feels even in the midst of the traffic, or walking at night, Clarissa was positive, a particular hush, or solemnity; an indiscernible pause; a suspense (but that might be her heart, affected, they said, by influenza) before *Big Ben strikes*. There! Out it boomed. First a warning, musical; then the hour, irrevocable. The leaden Circles dissolved in the air. Such fools we are, she thought, crossing *Victoria Street*. [. . . I]n the triumph and the jingle and the strange high singing of some *aeroplane* overhead was what she loved; life; *London*; this moment of June.

For it was the *middle of June*. The *War was over* [. . .]

(5–6, emphasis added)

Virginia Woolf consciously borrows from the visual arts, attempting to integrate formal elements of cubism into literary practice. The simultaneous projection of different perspectives in the characterization of a figure is a central concern of cubist art, which also tries to represent an object as seen from a number of perspectives in space simultaneously.

This example once again highlights the fact that the various levels of fiction, including plot, setting, point of view, and characters, tend to receive full meaning through their interaction with one another. In the interpretation of literary texts, it is therefore important to see these structural elements not as self-contained and isolated entities, but rather as interdependent elements whose full meaning is only revealed in the context of the other features and overall content of the text. Ideally, the structural analysis of these levels in literary texts should not stop at the mere description of these features, but rather show to what ends they are employed.

POETRY

Poetry is one of the oldest genres in literary history. Its earliest examples go back to ancient Greek literature. In spite of this long tradition, it is harder to define than any other genre. Poetry is closely related to the term lyric, which derives etymologically from the Greek musical instrument *lyra* ("lyre" or "harp") and points to an origin in the sphere of music. In classical antiquity as well as in the Middle Ages, minstrels recited poetry, accompanied by the lyre or other musical instrument. The term poetry, however, goes back to the Greek word *poieo* ("to make," "to produce"), indicating that the poet is the person who "makes" verse. Although etymology sheds light on some of the aspects of the lyric and the poetic, it cannot offer a satisfactory explanation of the phenomenon as such.

Most traditional attempts to define poetry juxtapose poetry with prose. The majority of these definitions are limited to characteristics, such as verse, rhyme, and meter, which are traditionally regarded as the classical elements that distinguish poetry from prose. These criteria, however, are already problematic with respect to the traditional epic and do not apply to modern prose poetry or experimental poetry. Explanations of the genre that combine poetic language with linguistic elements other than rhyme and meter do more justice to nontraditional forms, such as free verse or prose poems. These approaches examine lyric phenomena with respect to the choice of words as well as the use of syntactic structures and rhetorical figures. Although these elements dominate in some forms of poetry, they also appear in drama or fiction. In spite of the difficulties associated with the definition of poetry, the above-mentioned heterogeneous criteria outline the major qualities that are conventionally attributed to poetry.

The genre of poetry is often subdivided into the two major categories of narrative and lyric poetry. **Narrative poetry** includes genres, such as the epic long poem, the romance, and the ballad, all of which tell stories with clearly developed and structured plots (see the section on "Fiction" in this chapter). The shorter **lyric poetry**, the focus of the following comments, is mainly concerned with one event, impression, or idea.

Some of the precursors of modern lyric poetry can be found in Old English riddles and **charms**. These cultic and magic texts, for example the following charm "Against Wens," which is supposed to help to get rid of boils, seem strange today, but were common in that period.

Wen, wen, little wen,
Here you must not build, nor have any abode.
But thou must pass forth to the hill hard by,
Where thou hast a brother in misery.
He shall lay a leaf at thy head.

Under the foot of the wolf, under the wing of the eagle,
Under the claw of the eagle, ever mayest thou fade.
Shrivel as coal on the hearth,
Shrink as muck in the wall,
And waste away like water in a bucket.
Become as small as a grain of linseed,
And far smaller also than a hand-worm's hip-bone,
And become even so small that thou become naught.

These religious or magic charms form the beginning of many national literatures, and the magic-cultic dimension contributed decisively to the preservation of texts in early cultural history.

In addition to charms, **riddles** are another early manifestation of poetry, characterized by a playful approach to language. At the end of the *Exeter Book* (tenth century AD), one of the most important Anglo-Saxon manuscripts, more than 100 riddles have survived from the Old English period. Often, they suggest an obscene answer, as, for example, Riddle 44:

> A curiosity hangs by the thigh of a man, under its master's cloak. It is pierced through in the front; it is stiff and hard and it has a good standing-place. When the man pulls up his own robe above his knee, he means to poke with the head of his hanging thing that familiar hole of matching length which he has often filled before.
>
> (204–205)

Of course, the answer to this object "which hangs by the thigh of a man" is a key. It is clear how these riddles deliberately use a double-voiced discourse, only hinting at a second sexual content rather than explicitly stating it.

The next step in poetic expression abandons these overtly cultic origins and uses music as a medium, creating songs, as for example the Middle English anonymous "Cuckoo Song" (c.1250), which could be accompanied by an instrument.

Cuccu	*Cuckoo*
Sumer is icumen in,	Summer has come,
Lhude sing, cuccu!	Sing loud, cuckoo!
Groweþ sed and bloweþ med	The seed grows and the meadow blossoms,
And springþ the wde nu;	And the wood springs;
Sing cuccu!	Sing, cuckoo!

(1–5)

In this Middle English example, the **onomatopoeia** (verbal imitation of natural sounds) of the cuckoo's calling is clearly audible. The acoustic dimension is a typical feature of poetry, one that continues in modern pop songs.

In the Middle Ages, lyrical short forms, focusing on love, were also very popular; they were sung as lyrics and accompanied by a musical instrument. This kind of poetry is closely related to the Provençal troubadours (eleventh to fourteenth centuries), who influenced European lyric poetry, such as the German *minnesong*. Walther von der Vogelweide's (*c.*1170–1230) Middle High German poem "Under the Lime Tree" exemplifies this mutual relationship between love, poetry, and music. In contrast to the highly stylized courtly love, this particular poem introduces bodily issues, such as the sexual act:

Under the lime tree
On the heather,
Where we had shared a place of rest,
Still you may find there,
Lovely together,
Flowers crushed and grass down-pressed.
Beside the forest in the vale,
Tándaradéi,
 Sweetly sang the nightingale.

I came to meet him
At the green:
There was my truelove come before.
Such was I greeted—
Heaven's Queen!—
That I am glad for evermore.
Had he kisses? A thousand some:
Tándaradéi,
 See how red my mouth's become.

(1–18)

In this example, a woman tells about an encounter with her lover under a lime tree. Interestingly, the physical act itself is only referred to indirectly – namely, through the traces that were left: clearly, the crushed grass and flowers and the reddened mouth hint at the passion that was expressed in the encounter. In the chorus "Tándaradéi" (a kind of refrain), Walther von der Vogelweide tries to use onomatopoeia to imitate the nightingale's call. This phonetic choice is a typical lyric element. Modern song lyrics still represent this unity of music and language. Singers such as Bob Dylan (1941–) are often counted among the poets of the late 1950s and 1960s because the lyrics of their songs are comparable with poems.

The Old English period adopts ancient forms of poetry, such as the **elegy**, which laments the death of a dear person. Pierre de Ronsard's (1524–1585) *Élégies* (1556) revived the antique form for the French Renaissance. Examples from later periods include Thomas Gray's (1716–1771) "Elegy Written in a Country Church-Yard" (1751) or Walt Whitman's (1819–1892) "When Lilacs Last in the Dooryard Bloom'd" (1865–1866), lamenting the death of Abraham Lincoln. Goethe's *Roman Elegies* (1795) introduced the form to German romanticism, combining the topic of loss with sexual themes, inspired by erotic fantasies of Latin poets.

The **ode**, which was also known in classical antiquity, re-emerged in the Renaissance and remained in use in the subsequent literary periods. As John Keats's (1795–1821) "Ode on a Grecian Urn" (1820) demonstrates, it consists of several stanzas with a serious, mostly classical theme. However, the most important English literary form with a consistent rhyming pattern is the **sonnet**, which, from the Renaissance onward, has been used in poetry primarily to deal with the theme of "worldly love" (see the section on "Rhythmic-acoustic dimension" in this chapter).

Although some elements discussed earlier in this chapter on fiction also apply to the analysis of poetry, there are, of course, idiosyncratic features associated with the genre of poetry in particular. The following dimensions are not restricted to poetry alone, but nevertheless stand at the center of attention in analyses of this genre.

An important and controversial term is "image" or **imagery**, which is pertinent to a number of divergent issues discussed in subsequent sections of this chapter. The word itself derives from the Latin *imago* ("picture") and refers to a predominantly visual component of a text that can, however, also include other sensory impressions. Imagery is often regarded as the most common manifestation of the "concrete" character of poetry. Even if an abstract theme is at the center of the poem, the poet still uses concrete imagery in order to make this theme more accessible. The concrete character of poetic language can be achieved on three distinct but interrelated levels:

verbal dimension
diction
rhetorical figures
theme

visual dimension
concrete poetry
emblem

rhythmic–acoustic dimension
rhyme and meter
onomatopoeia

Verbal dimension

The concept of the narrator, which in fiction coincides with issues of narrative situation and character presentation, is usually referred to in poetry with the terms "voice" or "speaker." Since poetry is often a medium for the expression of subjective, personal events – an assumption that does not always correspond to the facts – the issue of the **speaker** is central to the analysis of poems. The question of whether the speaker and the author are one and the same person is, of course, also relevant to fiction. In the novel and the short story, however, a distinctive use of point-of-view techniques easily creates a distance between the narrator and the author.

In longer poetic forms, the narrative situation can be as complex as that of the novel or the short story. A good example is Samuel Taylor Coleridge's (1772–1834) **ballad** "The Rime of the Ancient Mariner" (1798). Here, a frame narrative in a figural narrative situation relates an incident in which a wedding guest is addressed by an uncanny mariner. "It is an ancient Mariner, / And he stoppeth one of three" (1–2). The mariner then recounts his adventures in a detailed first-person narration: "Listen, Stranger! Storm and Wind, / A Wind and Tempest strong! / For days and weeks it play'd us freaks" (40–42). By placing the story of the "Mariner" within a frame narrative, Coleridge presents the plot of the ballad on two levels (frame narrative and actual plot) as well as in two narrative situations (figural and first-person narration). The ballad assumes a position between the epic long forms and the lyric short forms. In spite of a well-developed plot and complex narrative perspective, the ballad, however, falls behind the epic and the romance in size and complexity.

The use of poetic language, more than the use of complex narrative situations, distinguishes poetry from other literary genres. Concrete nouns and scenes support this particular effect. In his "Elegy Written in a Country Church-Yard," which deals with human transitoriness, Thomas Gray uses concrete images, such as a cemetery, the ringing of a bell, a farmer returning from tilling, darkness, and tombstones. Gray describes objects and employs expressive scenes in order to make the poem concrete, although the actual theme of transitoriness is abstract. An elegy by W. H. Auden (1907–1973) uses a similar technique.

> Stop all the clocks, cut off the telephone,
> Prevent the dog from barking with a juicy bone,
> Silence the pianos and with a muffled drum
> Bring out the coffin, let the mourners come.
>
> [. . .]
>
> He was my North, my South, my East and West,
> My working week and my Sunday rest,
> My noon, my midnight, my talk, my song;
> I thought that love would last for ever: I was wrong.
>
> The stars are not wanted now: put out every one;
> Pack up the moon and dismantle the sun;
> Pour away the ocean and sweep up the wood;
> For nothing now can ever come to any good.
>
> (1–4, 9–16)

As this 1936 poem shows, Auden consciously introduces concrete objects ("juicy bone," "sun") and everyday situations ("working week," "Sunday rest") in order to treat the theme of mourning on a level that is familiar to the reader and therefore emotionally loaded. In contrast to philosophical texts, which remain abstract in their expression, poetry tries to convey themes in a concrete language of images.

Images and concrete objects often serve the additional function of **symbols** if they refer to a meaning beyond the material object. A cross in Christian thinking is, for example, much more than two crossed wooden bars. The poet can either use a commonly known, conventional symbol or create his or her own private symbol that develops its symbolic function only in its particular context. The albatross in

Coleridge's "The Rime of the Ancient Mariner," for example, is a private symbol. In the course of the poem, the murdered bird becomes a symbol of natural order that has been destroyed by man. It is only in the context of Coleridge's ballad that the albatross takes on this far-reaching symbolic meaning.

Further stylistic features include **rhetorical figures**, or figures of speech. These classified stylistic forms are characterized by their "nonliteral" meanings. Rhetorical handbooks distinguish more than 200 different figures, of which simile and metaphor are those most commonly used in poetry. A **simile** is a comparison between two different things that are connected by "like," "than," "as," or "compare," as in Robert Burns's (1759–1796) poem "A Red, Red Rose" (1796):

> O my Luve's like a red, red rose,
>   That's newly sprung in June,
> O my Luve's like the melodie
>   That's sweetly play'd in tune.
>
> (1–4)

Similes are also one of the main features of ancient epic poetry. The *Iliad* (seventh century BC) abounds in long rows of similes, as, for example, when Homer compares a fight between Hector and Achilles to the futile struggle of a defenseless pigeon attacked by a fierce hawk:

> Forward, with flying foot, Pelides [= Achilles] rush'd.
> As when a falcon, bird of swiftest flight,
> From some high mountain-top, on tim'rous dove
> Swoops fiercely down; she, from beneath, in fear,
> Evades the stroke; he, dashing through the brake,
> Shrill-shrieking, pounces on his destin'd prey;
> So, wing'd with desp'rate hate, Achilles flew,
> So Hector, flying from his keen pursuit,
> Beneath the walls his active sinews plied.
>
> (22.138–144)

What is most striking about this passage is that it creates in literature an effect that is reminiscent of morphing in animated film, highlighting the action in an almost graphic manner. Hector and Achilles transform within one line from humans into animals. First, a simile is used to make Achilles appear like a bird of prey ("as [. . .] a falcon"). But, ultimately, the fighter actually becomes the animal, as he, literally, "flew." This equation of one thing with another without actual comparison is called **metaphor**. If Burns, in the example above, had said "My love *is* a red, red rose," instead of "Oh, my love is *like* a red, red rose," the simile would be transformed into a metaphor. In his play *As You Like It* (*c.*1599), William Shakespeare, for example, uses a different metaphor in each stanza:

> All the world's a stage,
> And all the men and women merely players;
> They have their exits and their entrances;

(2.7)

A stage is used as a metaphor for the world, players for men and women, and so on. The metaphor and the simile juxtapose two elements: the *tenor* (the person, object, or idea) to which the *vehicle* (or image) is equated or compared. In "Oh, my love is like a red, red rose," "my love" functions as the tenor and "red rose" as the vehicle. Rhetorical figures are widely used in poetry because they produce a "nonliteral" meaning and reduce abstract or complex tenors to concrete vehicles, which again enhance the concrete character that poetry ought to achieve.

Literary theory often evokes the "concreteness" or closed form of poetry by calling the poem a "verbal icon" or "verbal picture." A frequently quoted example is the poem "Ode on a Grecian Urn," in which the romantic poet John Keats describes a painted Greek vase. It is an example of the use of imagery to achieve a pictorial effect. In the detailed description of various pictorial scenes, the poem is likened to a vase and is thus supposed to become part of the closed, harmonious form of the artifact.

> Thou still unravish'd bride of quietness,
> 　Thou foster-child of silence and slow time,
> Sylvan historian, who canst thus express
> 　A flowery tale more sweetly than our rhyme

(1–4)

The line "Thou foster-child of silence and slow time" indicates that on the vase – as in any work of plastic art – time stands still. People are thus able – through artistic production – to overcome their own transitoriness, evoked by the urn as a container for the ashes of the dead. Even 2,000 years after the artist's death, this work of art has the same power it had at the time of its creation. Keats juxtaposes and compares the pictorial portrayal on the vase with the lines of the poem, "who canst thus express / A flowery tale more sweetly than our rhyme." In the last stanza, Keats directly refers to the round, closed shape of the vase as a model for poetry:

> O Attic shape! Fair attitude! with brede
>   Of marble men and maidens overwrought,
> With forest branches and the trodden weed;
>   Thou, silent form, dost tease us out of thought
> As doth eternity: Cold Pastoral!

(50–55)

The "silent form" of the Attic vase is the poem's dominant concrete image, one that is not used for its own sake but rather to refer beyond the object to the form of poetry as such. In the description of the visual images on the vase, Keats juxtaposes pictorial art with literature; the closed and self-contained structure of the vase becomes a model for poetry. The durability of the work of art praises and contrasts man's ephemeral existence. The image of the vase therefore serves a triple function: as a symbol of pictorial art, as a model for the form of poetry, and as a concrete object that refers to the abstract theme of transitoriness and eternal fame. Despite its canonical status, or maybe precisely because of it, Keats's evocation of an urn or vase prompted parodies, as, for example, Wallace Stevens's (1879–1955) American modernist poem "Anecdote of the Jar" (1919):

> I placed a jar in Tennessee,
> And round it was, upon a hill.
> It made the slovenly wilderness
> Surround that hill.

(1–4)

Already the two opening verses seem to mock John Keats's "Ode on a Grecian Urn." Substituting Keats's urn with a mass-produced glass jar, Stevens not only makes fun of the ode as an outdated poetic genre, but also ridicules everything that the urn – as we have seen above – could symbolize as a metaphor for poetry as such. At the same time, he claims that the modernist period needs to distance itself from classical models as well as the spirit of the romantic period in order to find its own genuine voice.

In order to achieve this renewal of poetry, a number of movements in the first two decades of the twentieth century set forth their credos in manifesto-like statements. The movement of **imagism**, for example, continued the tradition of pictorial expression in poetry by stylizing the "image" as a key concept. The theoretical program of this literary "school," which is closely associated with the American poet Ezra Pound (1885–1972), focused on the "condensation" of poetry into powerful, essential images. The German word for poetry, *Dichtung*, was considered to mean the same as the Latin *condensare* ("to condense"), thus fitting very well the imagists' preoccupation with the reduction of poetry to essential pictures or images. According to Pound, poetry should achieve the utmost clarity of expression without the use of adornment. Pound voices this opinion in one of his manifestos (1913): "An 'Image' is that which presents an intellectual and emotional complex in an instant of time. [. . .] It is better to present one Image in a lifetime than to produce voluminous works" (4). The following poem from 1916 is a practical example of Pound's imagism:

IN A STATION OF THE METRO

The apparition of these faces in the crowd;
Petals on a wet, black bough.

Several longer versions preceded this poem before Pound reduced it to three lines by using an expressionistic word-picture for the portrayal of the crowds in a metro station. He starts with the people in the darkness of the station and then equates them with "Petals on a wet, black bough" (see metaphor, above). By using a pictorial element that is at the same time a common theme in Chinese nature painting, Pound emphasizes the pictorial character of his poem.

Pound drew on the Japanese poetic form of **haiku** as an example of this "condensing" form of poetry. They, too, contain three lines (and seventeen syllables) and on a thematic level refer to times of the day or seasons. The most famous example is a haiku from 1686 by the Japanese poet Matsuo Bashō (1644–1694):

an ancient pond	古池や
a frog jumps in	蛙飛び込む
the splash of water	水の音

These Japanese short poems are rendered in adaptions of Chinese written characters, which are far more suitable than our alphabetical writing for conveying the concrete and pictorial dimension that fascinated the imagist poets. The Chinese ideogram, which combines writing and picture, greatly influenced the imagists, whose main goal was to present pure verbal images to their readers. They intended to compensate for the lack of the pictorial dimension in alphabetical writing by condensing language as much as possible.

Visual dimension

While imagery in traditional poetry revolves around a transformation of objects into language, **concrete poetry** takes a further step toward the visual arts, concentrating on the poem's shape or visual appearance. This visual poetic genre also goes by the name "picture poem" (Latin **carmen figuratum**), famous examples of which are the Latin arrangements of the Carolingian abbot Rabanus Maurus (AD 780–856). Every page of his *De laudibus sanctae crucis* consists of verses in hexameter. Drawn into this text are figures – mostly crosses – that highlight certain parts of the text. Similar to contemporary crossword puzzles, these highlighted passages can be read from top to bottom or from left to right. Rabanus thereby indicates that the cross is omnipresent, shining through the hexameter text just as redemption is part of everyday life. The whole poem thus becomes an ode to the cross, both on the verbal and the visual level.

Picture poems, which were revived in the twentieth century, have a long tradition, reaching from classical antiquity to the Latin Middle Ages and on to the Baroque age. Among the best-known specimens of this "genre" in English literature are George Herbert's (1593–1633) "The Altar" (1633) and "Easter Wings" (1633):

Lord, who createdst man in wealth and store,
　　Though foolishly he lost the same,
　　　Decaying more and more,
　　　　Till he became
　　　　　Most poore:
　　　　　With Thee
　　　　O let me rise,
　　　As larks, harmoniously,
　　And sing this day Thy victories:
Then shall the fall further the flight in me.

My tender age in sorrow did beginne;
　　And still with sicknesses and shame
　　　Thou didst so punish sinne,
　　　　That I became
　　　　　Most thinne.
　　　　　With Thee
　　　　Let me combine,
　　　And feel this day Thy victorie;
　　For, if I imp my wing on Thine,
Affliction shall advance the flight in me.

Herbert's religious poem "Easter Wings" is about spiritual wings that prevent the soul of man from falling into perdition. At the same time, the visual appearance of the words on the page spells out a pair of wings. In the first half of each stanza, the individual lines get gradually shorter, thereby indicating the fall of man into evil, while in the second half the lines increase in length again in order to show the redemptive power of God. The individual "feathers" of these spiritual wings (i.e., the lines of the poem) become shorter the more man moves away from God, and increase in length the closer man comes to God. In both stanzas, man distances himself and eventually returns to God through a fall down from God and a flight up to God.

These pattern poems were extremely popular with the English metaphysical poets of the seventeenth century and a common feature of European poetry in the Baroque age. Another variant of this pictorial inclination of poetry in the seventeenth and eighteenth centuries are emblem books, which combine a few lines of poetry with an allegorical visual image rendered as an engraved picture, as in this sample page from Francis Quarles's (1592–1644) *Emblems* (1635):

[42]

XXXXXXXXXXXXXXXXXXXXXXXXX

EMBLEM II.

How eagerly the World we grafp?
Its Riches how we fondly clafp!.
But could we get all we can crave,
Death lays us naked in the Grave.

As outlandish as these visual poetic genres might seem to us today, emblem books such as Quarles's, went through countless editions and rank among the best-selling literary texts of the seventeenth century. In their attempt to combine word and image on one page, they appear as forerunners of contemporary forms, such as comic books or graphic novels.

Modernist authors developed new and unconventional forms of picture poems in the twentieth century. The following concrete poem by e. e. cummings (1894–1962) is a modern example of an abstract visual-verbal arrangement, which – despite its particular characteristics – works according to structural principles similar to those seen in George Herbert's text:

l(a

le
af
fa

ll

s)
one
l

iness

We can reconstruct the text of the poem as follows: "a leaf falls loneliness" or "l(a leaf falls)oneliness." e. e. cummings uses a single leaf falling from a tree as a motif for loneliness, arranging the letters vertically instead of horizontally in order to trace the leaf's movement visually. In the act of reading, the eye can follow the course of the leaf from top to bottom and also from left to right. The two parentheses almost resemble the material shape of a leaf when seen in profile: "(". When the parenthesis is closed a few lines down, ")", the "leaf" that it might represent has spun around also. In one instance, this movement is underlined by an arrangement in the form of a cross. The technical term for this cross-like placement of words or letters is **chiasmus**, which derives from the Greek letter *chi* (χ). Lord Byron

(1788–1824) uses a witty chiasmus in his satiric poem "Don Juan" (1819) when he writes "pleasure's a sin, and sometimes sin's a pleasure" (1.133). In cummings's example, the chiasmus is formed by a cross-like arrangement of only four letters in two consecutive lines:

    af
    fa

This poem contains further visual elements that form an interdependent network with levels of content. The double "l" of the word "falls" is at the center of the poem. These letters can easily be read as two "l"s for the first person singular or as the number "1" (one), thus underlining the fall from "two-someness" into loneliness. In "l-one-liness" only one "l" remains, or, as cummings expresses it:

    one
    l

This experimental poem, like a traditional elegy, laments the loss of companionship. While more traditional poems, such as Gray's or Auden's cited above, render loss through concrete names and imagery, cummings uses the smallest level of the materiality of words and letters to achieve this goal. As these examples show, traditional and experimental poetry often works with the pictorial aspects of language and writing or aim at combining these aspects. Attempts to turn a poem into a quasi-material object, however, can be achieved not only on a thematic level through the use of concrete nouns or scenes, and on the visual level through a particular layout of letters, words, or stanzas, but also through rhythmic and acoustic qualities.

Rhythmic–acoustic dimension

In order to achieve the concrete quality of poetic language, poems employ sound and tone as elements with their own levels of meaning. By choosing certain words in a line or stanza, a poet can produce a sound or tone that is directly related to the content of the statement. The acoustic element, like a poem's visual appearance in concrete poetry, can enhance the meaning of a poem. The following passage from Alexander Pope's (1688–1744) "An Essay on Criticism" (1711) is a self-reflexive example of this technique:

> True Ease in Writing comes from Art, not Chance,
> As those move easiest who have learn'd to dance.
> 'Tis not enough no Harshness gives Offence,
> The *Sound* must seem an *Eccho* to the *Sense*.
> *Soft* is the Strain when *Zephyr* gently blows,
> And the *smooth Stream* in *smoother Numbers* flows;
> But when loud Surges lash the sounding Shore,
> The *hoarse, rough Verse* shou'd like the *Torrent* roar.
>
> (362–369)

In these lines, Pope points out that, in what he considers a good poem, content and sound harmonize and form a unity ("The sound must seem an echo to the sense"). In lines 5 and 6 of our quotation, he mentions the west wind (Zephyr) and suggests its natural sound through the deliberate choice of words whose sounds ("z," "ph," "w," "oo," "th") are reminiscent of a gentle breeze. In lines 7 and 8, the harsh noise of the sea breaking on the shore is imitated by words with less gentle sounds ("sh," "gh," "v," "rr"). This unifying principle of sound and sense is of course not a goal for every poet, and modern examples often work against this more traditional attitude toward unity.

Meter and rhyme are further devices in the acoustic dimension of poetry that hold a dominant position in the analysis of poems, partly because they are relatively easy to objectify and measure. The smallest elements of meter are syllables, which can be either stressed or unstressed. According to the sequence of stressed and unstressed syllables, it is possible to distinguish between various metrical feet, whose number consequently indicates the meter. In the analysis of the meter, we first divide a line into syllables. The example here is the line "The woods are lovely, dark and deep" from Robert Frost's (1874–1963) poem "Stopping by Woods on a Snowy Evening" (1923):

The – woods – are – love – ly, – dark – and – deep

After the division into syllables, **stressed** syllables (´) and **unstressed** syllables (˘) are identified. The technical term for this process is **scansion**. In English, long vowels become stressed and short vowels are unstressed:

Thĕ – woóds – ăre – lóve – lў, – dárk – ănd – deép

According to the sequence of stressed and unstressed syllables, the line can be divided into **feet**:

Thĕ – woóds | – ăre – lóve | – lў, – dárk | – ănd – deép.

Here is a list of the five most important feet. The first three are disyllabic feet (based on two syllables) and the last two are trisyllabic feet (based on three syllables):

1 **Iambus**, or iambic foot: an unstressed syllable followed by a stressed syllable (˘´)
   Thĕ cúr | fĕw tólls | thĕ knéll | ŏf pár | tĭng dáy.
   (Thomas Gray, "Elegy Written in a Country Church-Yard" 1)
2 **Trochee**, or trochaic foot: a stressed syllable followed by an unstressed syllable (´˘)
   Thére thĕy | áre, mў | fíftў | mén ănd | wómĕn.
   (Robert Browning, "One Word More" 1)
3 **Spondee**, or spondaic foot: two stressed syllables (´´)
   Góod stróng | thíck stú | pé fў | íng ín | cénse smóke.
   (Robert Browning, "The Bishop Orders His Tomb at Saint Praxed's Church" 84)
4 **Anapest**, or anapestic foot: two unstressed syllables followed by one stressed syllable (˘˘´)
   Ănd thĕ sheén | ŏf thĕir spéars | wăs lĭke stárs | ŏn thĕ seá.
   (Lord Byron, "The Destruction of Sennacherib" 3)
5 **Dactyl**, or dactylic foot: one stressed syllable followed by two unstressed syllables (´˘˘)
   Júst fŏr ă | hándfŭl ŏf | sílvĕr hĕ | léft ŭs.
   (Robert Browning, "The Lost Leader" 1)

In his poem "Metrical Feet: Lesson for a Boy" (1806), Samuel Taylor Coleridge (1772–1834), in a self-reflexive manner, illustrates the different meters together with long and short marks over the syllables as a mnemonic aid for his son:

Tróchĕe tríps frŏm lóng tŏ shórt;
From long to long in solemn sort
Slów Spóndée stálks; stróng fóot! yet ill able
Évĕr tŏ cóme ŭp wĭth Dáctўl trĭsýllăblĕ.

Ĭámbĭcs márch frŏm shórt tŏ lóng;–
Wĭth ă léap ănd ă bóund thĕ swĭft Ánăpĕsts thróng;

(1–6)

According to the number of feet, it is possible to distinguish between a monometer (1), dimeter (2), trimeter (3), tetrameter (4), pentameter (5), and hexameter (6). In the description of the meter of a line, the name of the foot and the number of feet are incorporated. For example, the first line of Thomas Gray's "Elegy Written in a Country Church-Yard" (1751) ("Thĕ cúr | fĕw tólls | thĕ knéll | ŏf pár | tĭng dáy"), which consists of five iambic feet, is thus termed *iambic pentameter*. This meter, which is close to the rhythm of natural speech and therefore very popular in poetry and drama, is also referred to as **blank verse**. Another popular meter in English is the iambic hexameter, which is also called Alexandrine.

Alongside meter, **rhyme** also adds to the dimension of sound and rhythm in a poem. It is possible to distinguish internal, end, and eye rhymes. **Internal rhymes** are alliteration and assonance. **Alliteration** is the repetition of the same consonant at the beginning of words in a single line ("*r*ound and *r*ound the *r*ugged *r*ock the *r*agged *r*ascal *r*an"). If a vowel is repeated instead (either at the beginning or in the middle of words) it is called **assonance** ("Thou foster ch*i*ld of s*i*lence and slow t*i*me"). Alliteration was the most common rhyming pattern in Old English poetry, as this example from the Anglo-Saxon epic poem *Beowulf* (*c.* eighth century) illustrates:

Oft *Sc*yld *Sc*efing // *sc*eaþena þreatum
(There was *Sh*ield *Sh*eafson // *sc*ourge of many tribes)

(4, emphasis added)

The opening lines of William Langland's (*c.*1332–1387) Middle English "long poem" *Piers Plowman* (*c.*1360–1386) are also a good example of a meter in which alliteration and stress complement each other:

In a somer seson // whan soft was the sonne
I shope me in shroudes // as I a shepe were;
In habite as an heremite // vnholy of workes
Went wyde in þis world // wondres to here.

(1–4)

In this meter, every line contains four stressed syllables with additional alliterations (e.g., "sómer" – "séson" – "sóft" – "sónne"), while the number of unstressed syllables varies. In the middle, the line is split into two halves by a *caesura*, which marks the beginning of a new unit of thought. Langland's use of alliteration as an archaic rhyme scheme, centuries after its heyday in Anglo-Saxon times, turns out to be a political statement. After the occupation of England by the French-speaking Normans, the Old English indigenous traditions gave way to imported French forms, including end rhymes. The "alliterative revival" in the fourteenth century thus deliberately returns to indigenous, older forms in order to stress a revived English poetic self-consciousness that wants to celebrate its roots in a Germanic rather than Romance language tradition.

The most common rhyming scheme in modern poems is **end rhyme**, which is based on identical syllables at the end of certain lines. To describe rhyme schemes, letters of the alphabet are used to represent identical syllables at the end of a line, as, for example, in Robert Frost's (1874–1963) poem "Stopping by Woods on a Snowy Evening" (1923):

Whose woods these are I think I know	a
His house is in the village though;	a
He will not see me stopping here	b
To watch his woods fill up with snow.	a

(1–4)

Eye rhymes, however, stand between the visual and the acoustic dimensions of a poem, playing with the spelling and the pronunciation of words, as in these lines from Samuel Taylor Coleridge's "Kubla Khan" (1816):

Then reached the caverns measureless to m*an*,
And sank in tumult to a lifeless oce*an*:
And 'mid this tumult Kubla heard from far
Ancestral voices prophesying war!

(27–30, emphasis added)

The syllables "an" at the end of the first two lines are examples of eye rhyme, as the sequence of the letters "a" and "n" is identical, but pronounced differently in the two verses. Eye rhymes play with the reader's expectations. When reading the two lines in Coleridge's poem, one is tempted to pronounce the syllable "an" in "man" and "ocean" in such a way that the two words rhyme. By the time one gets to the word "ocean," however, it has become clear that they only rhyme visually and have to be pronounced differently. Eye rhymes permit authors to highlight certain words by creating a tension between visual and acoustic levels and thus to direct the reader's attention to specific elements of the poem.

The multitude of different **stanzas** in English poetry can be reduced to a few basic forms. Most poems are composed of **couplets** (two lines), **tercets** (three lines), or **quatrains** (four lines). The sonnet is an example of the combination of different stanzas. According to the rhyming scheme and the kind of stanzas, we can distinguish between "Shakespearean," "Spenserian," and "Italian" (or "Petrarchan") sonnets. In the Renaissance, sonnet cycles – consisting of a number of thematically related poems – became popular as a result of Italian influence. These cycles enabled poets to deal with certain topics in greater detail while working within the sonnet form.

The **English** or **Shakespearean sonnet**, which holds a privileged position in the English tradition, deserves a more detailed explanation. It consists of three quatrains and one couplet. The fourteen lines are in iambic pentameter and follow the rhyme scheme *abab cdcd efef gg*. Shakespeare's "Sonnet 73," "That time of year thou may'st in me behold" (1609), fulfills these criteria:

That time of year thou may'st in me behold	a
When yellow leaves, or none, or few, do hang	b
Upon those boughs which shake against the cold,	a
Bared ruined choirs, where late the sweet birds sang.	b
In me thou see'st the twilight of such day	c
As after sunset fadeth in the west;	d
Which by-and-by black night doth take away,	c
Death's second self that seals up all in rest.	d
In me thou see'st the glowing of such fire	e
That on the ashes of his youth doth lie,	f
As the deathbed whereon it must expire,	e
Consumed with that which it was nourished by.	f
This thou perceiv'st, which makes thy love more strong,	g
To love that well which thou must leave ere long.	g

Each segment of this sonnet (the three quatrains and the couplet) consists of a coherent sentence. The four sentences are connected on a thematic level by repetition: "in me behold" in the first line, "In me thou see'st" in the fifth and the ninth, and "This thou perceiv'st" in the thirteenth. Each quatrain introduces an image or metaphor that fits into the theme of the sonnet as a whole and works toward the couplet. The first stanza mentions boughs without leaves, followed by the setting sun and darkness in the second, and a dying fire in the third. Images from various areas all function as signs of mortality. The couplet draws a connection between these signs, which are visible in the speaker's face, and the overall theme of love. Shakespeare sees human love as arising out of the certainty of man's death.

This sonnet shows a very clear connection between formal and thematic elements. Such an intricate interdependence between form and content is typical of traditional poetry. Ideally, the verbal, visual, and rhythmic–acoustic dimensions – used here to illustrate the most important elements of the genre – should form an interdependent whole. However, modern prose poems often deliberately violate these rather rigid forms of unity on a formal level, as, for example, William Carlos Williams's (1883–1963) prose poem "This Is Just to Say" (1934):

I have eaten
the plums
that were in
the icebox

and which
you were probably
saving
for breakfast

Forgive me
they were delicious
so sweet
and so cold

At first sight, the three-stanza organization suggests a poem, but, on closer inspection, it appears more like a Post-it note on a refrigerator than a poem. No recognizable meter or rhyme supports the first impression of a traditional poem that the stanza format misleadingly suggested. The idea of unity, according to which several levels of expression connect, is most dominant in traditional forms of poetry. However, not every poem subscribes to the concept of unity as its main structural goal, as the above example shows. Experimental poetry, in particular, abandons these seemingly rigid structures in order to explore new "open forms," such as poems in prose or free verse. The degree to which the different levels of a work of art interconnect and support one another in order to create an effect of unity is of course not restricted to poetry alone. Similar mechanisms also apply to other genres.

DRAMA

So far, we have identified distinct features belonging to fiction and poetry, two genres that rely on the written or spoken word as their primary means of expression. The dramatic or performing arts, however, combine the verbal with a number of nonverbal or optical-visual means, including stage, scenery, shifting of scenes, facial expressions, gestures, make-up, props, and lighting. This emphasis is also reflected in the word drama itself, which derives from the Greek *draō* ("to do," "to act"), thereby referring to a performance or representation by actors.

Drama has its roots in cultic and ritual practice, some features of which were still present in stylized form in the classical Greek drama of the fifth century BC. Ancient tragedies and comedies were performed during festivals in honor of Dionysus, the god of wine and fertility. Tragedies by Aeschylus (c.525–456 BC), Euripides (c.480–406 BC), and Sophocles (497–406 BC), as well as comedies by Aristophanes (445–385 BC), mark the beginning of drama in Western culture.

While classical literary theory overlooks the nature of comedy, Aristotle deals extensively with the general elements and features of **tragedy**. In the sixth book of *The Poetics* (fourth century BC), he characterizes tragedy as "an imitation of an action which is serious, complete [. . .] with persons performing the action rather than through narrative [. . .], through a course of events involving pity and fear, the purification of those painful or fatal acts which have that quality" (25, 26–29). By watching the tragic events onstage, the audience is meant to experience a **catharsis** or spiritual cleansing. **Comedy**, on the other hand, has humorous themes that are intended to entertain the audience. It is often regarded as the stylized continuation of primitive regeneration cults, such as the symbolic expulsion of winter by spring. This fertility symbolism culminates in the form of weddings, which comprise standard happy endings in traditional comedies.

Drama was one of the main genres in classical antiquity, but its importance waned with the dawning of the Middle Ages. After the turn of the millennium, however, simple forms of drama re-emerged. **Mystery** and **miracle plays** adapted religious, allegorical, or biblical themes from Christian liturgy for performance in front of churches and in the yards of inns. The majority of the mystery plays known today have survived in four large cycles that were put down in the early fifteenth century in York, Chester, Wakefield, and another unknown city. The number of plays in each cycle ranges from 25 to 48, and in their entirety they cover all of the important biblical episodes, from Lucifer's downfall, the expulsion from Paradise, the birth and crucifixion of Christ to the Last Judgment.

Although these mystery plays primarily convey religious content, there are several very innovative ones that defamiliarize the mostly serious biblical plot by means of comical interludes. Such techniques clearly point toward the secular drama of the modern age. A particularly impressive instance of burlesque comedy within a religious frame is the *Second Shepherds' Play* (c.1425). Thematically, it revolves around the birth of Christ but only uses it to trigger its parodistic plot. The focus of the play is on Mak, a shepherd who cleverly steals a lamb from another flock. The comic climax occurs when the robbed shepherds search Mak's house. To distract them, Mak puts the lamb in a cradle and passes it off as his own newborn child. Although Mak is very skillful in making up all kinds of stories and excuses, the shepherds eventually recognize their lamb by its earmark and find the thief guilty. At the close of the play, the author reintroduces the actual topic (i.e., the birth of Christ) when the shepherds are called to the stable in Bethlehem. Once again, they amazedly look at a lamb, Jesus as the Lamb of God. So, in the first burlesque part, a real lamb passes for a child; in the second, more serious part, the savior child becomes the symbolic lamb that takes away our sins. Thus, the comedy that had no apparent religious content up to this point turns out to be a biblical mystery play after all. The *Second Shepherds' Play* clearly demonstrates how successfully and skillfully these plays reconcile individual comedy and original content with a religious framework. These medieval dramatic forms, together with the classical Roman comedies by Plautus (c.254–184 BC) and tragedies by Seneca (c.4 BC–AD 65), influenced later Renaissance drama, which reached its first peak in England with Shakespeare and his contemporaries.

William Shakespeare (1564–1616) and Christopher Marlowe (1564–1593) revived and developed classical forms of drama, and were among the first to reflect on different dramatic genres. A passage in Shakespeare's *Hamlet* (c.1601) wittily testifies to this reflection: "The best actors in the world, either for tragedy, comedy, history, pastoral, pastoral-comical, historical-pastoral, tragical-historical, tragical-comical-historical-pastoral, scene undividable, or poem unlimited" (2.2.378–381). Shakespeare parodies various mixed forms that, roughly speaking, can be reduced to the three basic forms of tragedy, comedy, and history play. Renaissance **history plays**, such as Shakespeare's *Richard II* (1597) or *Henry V* (c.1600), adapt classical English history for stage performance. These plays portray a historical event or figure but, through the addition of contemporary references, transcend the historical dimension and make general statements about human weaknesses and virtues. In many cases, the author chooses a historical pretext in order to comment on contemporary socio-political misery while minimizing the risk of censorship.

When the Puritans under the rule of Oliver Cromwell (1599–1658) and his Commonwealth (1649–1660) shut down the English theaters on moral and religious grounds, drama lost its status as a major genre. Although religion exercised only a brief influence on drama in England in this drastic way (until the Restoration of monarchy), it had far-reaching consequences in America. Because of the prominent position of Puritanism in American history, drama was almost nonexistent in the early phases of American literature. Also, after the *Declaration of Independence* in 1776, America distanced itself from England both politically and intellectually, which resulted in a ban on imported British plays for the American market. This hostile climate for theater prevented the development of an indigenous dramatic tradition in the United States until the first decades of the twentieth century.

During the Restoration period in late seventeenth-century England, drama, such as the **comedy of manners**, or **Restoration comedy**, portraying citizens from the upper echelons of society in witty dialogues, was very popular. William Congreve's (1670–1729) *The Way of the World* (1700) and William Wycherley's (1641–1715) *The Country Wife* (c.1675) are well-known examples. The **heroic drama** of the time – such as John Dryden's (1631–1700) *All for Love* (1677) – tries to recreate and adapt epic themes onstage. In the romantic period of the early nineteenth century, England produced the **closet drama**, a special form of drama that was not meant to be performed onstage but rather to be read in private. Percy Bysshe Shelley's (1792–1822) *Prometheus Unbound* (1820) is a well-known example of this unusual form of drama.

In the early modern era, the tragedy is, again, the focus of literary theory. Apart from the reception of Aristotle with respect to the three unities, which we will discuss in detail later, the *Ständeklausel* (estates-clause) is central to early-modern dramatic theory. According to this rule, expressed in the theoretical treatises of the Renaissance and Baroque eras, a tragedy should only feature people of a high class, such as kings or princes. Propagated especially by Martin Opitz (1597–1639), this concept was valid throughout the German-speaking world until the late eighteenth century.

In the eighteenth century, drama changed significantly due to the rise of the middle class, which gained a new kind of confidence throughout Europe in the Enlightenment. During this time, the **bourgeois tragedy** developed, ignoring the *Ständeklausel* and putting the common people in the spotlight. In Germany, notable examples are Gotthold Ephraim Lessing's (1729–1781) *Emilia Galotti* (1772) and Friedrich Schiller's (1759–1805) *Intrigue and Love* (1784).

The trend toward a more realistic presentation of reality onstage was epitomized by realism and naturalism in the late nineteenth century. These movements dealt with social misery on a broader scale and drama regained its importance as a major genre, albeit one that is intricately interwoven with developments in fiction. George Bernard Shaw (1856–1950) and Oscar Wilde (1854–1900) were among the most important English playwrights of this period. All major developments in the theater of the twentieth century can be seen as reactions to this early movement. For instance, **expressionist theater** and the **theater of the absurd** do away with the illusion that reality can be truthfully portrayed onstage, and emphasize more abstract and stylized modes of presentation. As with the postmodernist novel, the parody of conventional forms and elements has become a striking feature in many plays of the second half of the twentieth century, such as Samuel Beckett's (1906–1989) *Waiting for Godot* (1952) or Tom Stoppard's (1937–) *Travesties* (1974) and *Rosencrantz and Guildenstern Are Dead* (1966). Political theater, characterized by social criticism, together with the movements that have already been mentioned, has become very influential. Important American examples are Clifford Odets's (1906–1963) Marxist workers' play *Waiting for Lefty* (1935) and Arthur Miller's (1915–2005) parable *The Crucible* (1953) about the political persecutions during the McCarthy era.

Because of the element of performance, drama generally transcends the textual dimension of the other two major literary genres, fiction and poetry. Although the written word serves as the basis of drama, it is, in the end, intended to be transformed into a performance before an audience. In order to do justice to this change of medium, we ought to consider *text*, *transformation*, and *performance* as three interdependent levels of a play.

text
dialogue
monologue
plot
setting
stage directions

transformation
directing
stage
props
lighting

performance
actors
methods
gestures
facial expressions
voice

Text

Since many textual areas of drama – character, plot, and setting – overlap with aspects of fiction that have already been explained, the following section will only deal with those elements that are specifically relevant to drama per se. Within the **textual dimension** of drama, the spoken word serves as the foundation for dialogue (verbal communication between two or more characters) and **monologue** (**soliloquy**). The **aside** is a special form of verbal communication onstage in which the actor "passes on" to the audience information that remains unknown to the rest of the characters in the play.

The basic elements of plot, including exposition, complication, climax, and denouement, have already been explained in the context of fiction. They have their origin in classical descriptions of the ideal course of a play and were only later adopted for analyses of other genres. In connection with plot, the **three unities** of time, place, and action are of primary significance. These unities prescribe that the time span of the action should roughly resemble the duration of the play (or a day at the most) and that the place where the action unfolds should always remain the same. Furthermore, the action should be consistent and have a linear plot (see the section on "Fiction" in this chapter). The three unities, which were supposed to characterize the structure of a "good" play, have been falsely ascribed to Aristotle. They are, however, for the most part based on misreadings of his *Poetics* in the sixteenth and seventeenth centuries. These rigid rules for the presentation of time, setting, and plot were designed to produce the greatest possible dramatic effect. Shakespeare's plays, which have always held a very prominent position in English literature, only very rarely conformed to these rules. This is why English playwrights never respected the three unities as much as dramatists did elsewhere in Europe.

Indirectly related to the three unities is the division of a play into **acts** and **scenes**. Elizabethan theater adopted this structure from classical antiquity, which divided the drama into five acts. In the nineteenth century, the number of acts in a play was reduced to four and in the twentieth century generally to three. With the help of act and scene changes, the setting, time, and action of a play can be altered, thereby allowing the traditional unity of place, time, and action to be maintained within a scene or an act.

The theater of the absurd, like its counterpart in fiction, consciously does away with traditional plot structures and confronts the spectator with situations that often seem absurd or illogical. The complication often does not lead to a climax, resolution, or a logical ending. In this manner, the theater of the absurd, like many postmodernist novels or films, attempts artistically to portray the general feeling of uncertainty of the post-war era. Samuel Beckett, whose play *Waiting for Godot* contributed to the fame of the theater of the absurd, is the best-known representative in the English-speaking world. Comparing Beckett's

Waiting for Godot with a traditional plot, containing exposition, complication, climax, and denouement, we find few similarities. The title of Beckett's play gives away the situation of the two main characters, Vladimir and Estragon, who wait for a mysterious Godot, who never appears. Godot himself receives no further characterization in the course of the play. The entrance of other characters briefly distracts from – but does not really change – the initial situation. The two main characters do not pass through the main stages of a classical plot and do not undergo any development by the end of the play. Offering neither logical messages nor a conventional climax, Beckett's play consciously violates the expectations of audiences who are only familiar with traditional theater.

However, absurd and unconventional plot structures or plotlines are not only features of modern and postmodernist drama. We do find puzzling narrative strategies as early as in classical Greek drama of the late fifth century BC. A unique example in this respect is Sophocles's tragedy *Oedipus the King* (*c*.425 BC), which uses the plotline of a modern detective story. The action begins in medias res (in the middle of the plot), when Oedipus, the new king of Thebes, is forced by the oracle of Apollo to resolve the murder of his predecessor. Gradually, Oedipus uncovers the facts about the murder and realizes that he himself is the culprit he is so desperately trying to find. In the end, Oedipus has to accept that he unknowingly killed his own father, married his mother, and fathered children with her. Since Sophocles uses a popular myth for his play, contemporary audiences, right from the beginning, knew all of this. Therefore, what makes this play special is that the suspense for the audience does not reside in the plotline; rather, suspense is created by the clues presented in the course of the play, which Oedipus fails to interpret adequately. Consequently, the play almost becomes a play about reading and interpreting. When Oedipus, in the end, has full knowledge of his deeds, he realizes how he misread all the signs that could have pointed him in the right direction all along. With this moment of epiphany that presents the preceding action in a completely new light, *Oedipus the King* shares narratological features with recent "mind-tricking" films with a twist ending, such as *The Sixth Sense* (1999) (see the section on "Film" in this chapter).

In the twentieth century, with the innovations of the experimental theater and the theater of the absurd, nontextual aspects of drama move to the foreground. Nonverbal features, which traditionally functioned as connecting devices between text and performance, abandon their supporting role and achieve an artistic status equal to that of the text.

Transformation

Transformation, an important part of dramatic productions in the twentieth century, refers to the connecting phase between text and performance. It comprises all logistic and conceptual steps that precede the performance, which can be subsumed under the heading **directing**. This transformation is not directly accessible to the audience; nevertheless, it influences almost all elements of the performance. The task of the contemporary director includes choosing the script, making cuts in the text, working out a general concept, casting, adapting the stage, and selecting props, costumes and makeup, as well as guiding the actors through rehearsals. The director is therefore responsible for the entire artistic coordination that guides the text into performance.

The profession of the director began to evolve in the late nineteenth century and is thus a relatively new phenomenon in the development of drama. Although directing, as a coordinating principle, is as old as drama itself, the boundaries separating the actors, authors, and coordinators of a performance were, up to the nineteenth century, very vague. Every so often, the author himself would lead a production, or a more experienced actor would take on the task of directing. It was not until the second half of the nineteenth century that, with the development of realism, the requirements of productions grew more demanding and the profession of the director established itself as a mediator between authors and actors. Among the early directors, the Russian Konstantin Stanislavsky (1863–1938) is probably the most famous. Building on his ideas and methods, the prestigious Lee Strasberg (1901–1982) school of acting in New York greatly influenced the American theater tradition. The Austrian director Max Reinhardt (1873–1943) also caused an uproar in the American theater world with some spectacular productions in the early twentieth century.

Since its earliest days as a profession, directing has been closely connected with all of the various movements in drama. In the beginning, directing centered mostly on realistic or historically authentic productions in which the director remained inconspicuous. In the twentieth and twenty-first centuries, the artistic fame of the director has been growing as a result of innovative ideas arising from expressionist theater, the theater of the absurd, and experimental theater, which, together with the public's demand for an individual touch, increased the director's responsibility. With the focus shifting to production in modern drama, the director has moved from the sidelines of the theater in the nineteenth century to the forefront, shaping a performance in his or her own unique style.

A good (dramatic) example of the importance of the director is Samuel Beckett's *Catastrophe* (1982), a short play with a comparatively large number of stage directions, whose self-reflexive subject is the production of a play. The highly stylized drama revolves around a director, an actor, and a helper, who all engage in the production of a performance. In this respect, *Catastrophe* is a highly postmodernist work; the several levels of the play, including the transformation from text to performance, are already an integral part of Beckett's text, thereby laying bare the principles of drama per se.

Every step in the transformation of a text – the choice of the play, the cuts in the script, the accentuation of the play, the casting, the requirements of props, stage design, and rehearsal – has a specific audience in mind. What counts at this point is the director's conceptual idea. It resembles the interpretation of a score by a conductor, who emphasizes certain aspects of the "text" in order to convey an individual impression of a piece. This interpretive accentuation of a production is closely related to the trends of the time. Successful productions such as Ellis Rabb's (1930–1998) homoerotic interpretation (1970) of Shakespeare's *The Merchant of Venice* (c.1596–1598), or the many feminist adaptations of *The Taming of the Shrew* (c.1592), require a specific cultural background of the audience. Productions need not necessarily be in tune with the obvious trends of the time to be successful – quite to the contrary, as proven by the productions of the American Robert Wilson (1941–), who borrows techniques from architecture and painting. Whatever the approach, the director needs to decide what kinds of "tools" he or she is going to use in a production for a specific audience. All steps of the transformation – all verbal and nonverbal means of expression – are, ideally, included in the conceptual idea, which runs like a main theme through the entire production.

One of the aspects underlying every production is the spatial dimension. Traditional fiction expresses space primarily through description, whereas drama, for this purpose, uses dialogue, monologue, body language, and, above all, stage design, scenery, props, and lighting. Many elements of space in the theater are subject to historical conditions, but directors freely adapt older features for modern productions. The arrangement of the theater in a circle, for example, is an old concept dating back to ancient theater and is now being reused in modern productions to create a special interaction between the spectators and the actors.

The open-air structure of the classical Greek **amphitheater** included a space called the *orchestra* in the center of the theater and a stage building, or *skene*. The seating was arranged in semicircles around the orchestra. Similar to today's movie theaters, the rows for the audience increased in height with their distance from the orchestra. The actors could move between the *skene* and the orchestra while the chorus was positioned between the audience and the actors. In classical Greek drama, a mask was worn by every character or "person" – a term that can be traced back to the Latin word *persona*, meaning "mask."

Elizabethan theater differs greatly from its classical precursors. A Greek theater could hold up to 15,000 spectators while an Elizabethan theater, like the Globe, could only contain a maximum of 2,000 people. The Shakespearean Globe Theatre in London was an octagonal building that had an uncovered courtyard with cheap seats. The more expensive seats were situated on three levels, in covered balconies that surrounded the inner courtyard. The stage stretched out into the courtyard on its lowest level, but also included an upper level that was directly adjacent to the balconies. In this manner, balcony scenes, such as the one in *Romeo and Juliet,* could be staged by making use of the lower and upper levels of the stage. Because of the spatial separation of the stage areas, it was possible to stress thematic aspects of a play on a spatial level as well. In Shakespeare's *Richard II* (1597), for example, the submission of the king is not only highlighted in the dialogue but also visually and spatially as a change from an upper to a lower level: "Down, down I come, like glist'ring Phaeton . . . In the base court? Base court, where kings grow base" (3.3.178–180).

Elizabethan theater, like classical theater, worked without elaborate props. Many aspects that modern realistic drama renders through scenery and other means were left to the spectator's imagination. Dimensions of the setting that from the Baroque period onward were conveyed on a nonverbal level through painted scenery had to be expressed by the spoken word in Renaissance theater. In this manner, the dawning of a new day in *Romeo and Juliet* is expressed verbally: "The grey-eyed morn smiles on the frowning night, / Check'ring the eastern clouds with streaks of light; / And fleckéd darkness like a drunkard reels / From forth day's path and Titan's burning wheels" (2.3.1–4).

A parodic example of verbal "stage design" due to a lack of props can be found in the short "play within the play" in the last act of Shakespeare's *A Midsummer Night's Dream* (1595), in which amateur performers create a stage on the stage. The "Prologue" to the performance not only introduces the characters of the play, but also the props, which in this scene are also represented by actors:

> This man with lime and roughcast doth present
> Wall, that vile Wall which did these lovers sunder;
> And through Wall's chink, poor souls, they are content
> To whisper. At the which let no man wonder.
> This man, with the lantern, dog, and bush of thorn,
> Presenteth Moonshine.

(1.130–135)

Shakespeare draws our attention to the imaginary world that is created by the actors onstage, when an actor "plays" a wall in the moonshine. Shakespeare does more than merely parody the theater of his day – he also sheds light on the world of theater, showing it to be an illusion created by the interaction between actors, text, and the imagination of the audience.

"Modern" theater after the Renaissance, on the other hand, attempted a kind of realism that required stage, scenery, and props to be redesigned. The stage took on the basic shape of a "box" with three walls and a ceiling, separating the audience from the actors more than in any of the preceding architectural shapes. Watching the performance onstage is like looking through an invisible fourth wall, the impression being one of a self-contained and independent world onstage. This **proscenium stage** was established in the eighteenth and nineteenth centuries and has remained the dominant form of stage design to this day. This new architectural shape of the theater is part of the development of realism in literature, which stresses the importance of a supposedly truthful portrayal of reality. George Bernard Shaw's plays are among the most important English contributions to this European movement. The plot of the drawing-room comedy is an extreme example of the fusion of the proscenium stage and realistic drama of that time. The play is staged in an almost authentic reconstruction of a drawing room and closely follows the three unities of place, time, and action, as in Oscar Wilde's *The Importance of Being Earnest* (1895). This tradition is continued in the twentieth century, as, for example, in Eugene O'Neill's (1888–1953) *Long Day's Journey into Night* (c.1941; published 1956), which is also designed for a drawing-room setting.

In reaction to the movement of realism, there are a number of modern developments that, paralleling trends in poetry and prose, try to find new modes of presentation. A major impulse of innovation came from German expressionist drama and film of the 1920s and 1930s. Heavy, exaggerated makeup, costumes, and settings characterized **expressionism**. Elmer Rice's (1892–1967) *The Adding Machine* (1923) is an American example of the departure from realist-naturalist theater. The main character of the play is Mr. Zero. After 25 years of good work, his company wants to replace him with an adding machine. Beside himself with rage, Mr. Zero kills his boss, for which he is sentenced to death and ultimately executed. In the afterlife in the Elysian Fields, however, he gets reemployed – working again on an adding machine. Rice uses expressionist elements to point out the estrangement of American city life, which is dominated by alienation in an increasingly industrialized environment.

It is interesting that expressionist theater and the theater of the absurd both return to simple, abstract scenery and props. Expressionist makeup (which recreates the effect of the mask) and the empty stage of the theater of the absurd resemble older forms that privileged the spoken word and the actor. In Beckett's *Waiting for Godot*, the scenery consists merely of a park bench and a stylized tree; the stage design thus mirrors the emptiness of the dialogue. In 1958, Edward Albee (1928–) finished his play *The Zoo Story*, one of the first examples of the theater of the absurd in America. The one-act play centers around a bizarre murder on a park bench. Six years later, the African American playwright Amiri Baraka (1934–) in *Dutchman* (1964) took on this idea, but changed the bench into a seat on the New York Subway. Here, the seductive white Lula approaches the African American Clay in order to engage him in a flirtatious conversation. However, Lula goes on to insult Clay, continuously mocking him for his assimilated lifestyle, which, according to her, does not conform with his racial identity. In the end, she stabs him in front of all the other passengers, who do nothing to stop her. The play ends with Lula turning toward another well-dressed African American, her next victim. Tom Stoppard's *After Magritte* (1971) uses scenery and props in a slightly different way. On a nonverbal level of the play, Stoppard re-enacts onstage the surrealist paintings of René Magritte (1898–1967), which are preoccupied with philosophical problems of language.

Since many experimental pieces were not originally designed for performance in large established theaters, it was possible to experiment with stage forms. In particular, abandoning the traditional proscenium stage allowed for the discovery of new modes of interaction between actors and audience. The gap between stage and auditorium became less obvious and the audience could be included in the performance. In England, these experimental forms are referred to under the heading "fringe theatre," in America under "off-Broadway" and "off-off-Broadway theater," as they are not staged at the established theaters on Broadway.

As these examples show, the various elements of transformation and text influence each other. Plays designed for an unconventional stage generally differ from traditional plays in form and content, which in turn indirectly affects the performance and requires special qualifications on the part of the actors.

Performance

The last phase, the **performance**, focuses on the actor, who conveys the combined intents of author and director. It has only been during the last hundred years that the methodological training of **actors** has established itself as a theatrical phenomenon alongside directing. Until the end of the nineteenth century, the transformation of the text was almost entirely in the hands of the actor. Since the quality of acting in a play differed immensely between individual performances, methods had to be found that ensured constant results. Training in breathing, posture, body movement, and psychological mechanisms facilitated the repeated reproduction of certain moods and attitudes onstage.

There are two basic theoretical approaches to modern acting: the external or technical method and the internal or realistic method. In the **external method**, the actor is supposed to be able to imitate the moods required in his or her part by using certain techniques, but without actually feeling these moods. It relies on impersonation and simulation. The **internal method**, however, builds on the individual identification of the actor with his or her part. Personal experience of feelings and the internalization of emotions and situations that are required in the part underlie the internal method. It was internal identification with the role, rather than impersonation, that became the main goal of the school of acting in the United States under the Russian director Konstantin Stanislavsky, mentioned above, and his pupil Lee Strasberg. This technique, known as "The Method," stresses "being" rather than "showing." It has produced a number of famous actors, such as Marlon Brando (1924–2004), James Dean (1931–1955), Paul Newman (1925–2008), and Julie Harris (1925–). Of the two approaches, method acting, with its emphasis on being, is the one most widely applied in theaters. Most of today's acting schools, however, borrow from both traditions, according to the requirements of the specific play to be performed.

We have already discussed many aspects relating to figures in drama with regard to fiction. However, more than other genres, drama relies on acting characters (*dramatis personae*) and thereby gives rise to aspects that apply only to this genre. For instance, we cannot take for granted the interaction of several characters within a play. Originally, the **chorus** was the centerpiece of classical Greek drama; only later, in the fifth century BC, the addition of more characters created the conditions for a dialogue between the figures and the chorus. In classical Greek drama, the number of actors onstage at a specific moment was restricted to three persons besides the chorus. The latter was originally a conveyor of lyrical poems that partly commented on the action of the play and partly addressed the actors in a didactic manner. The choir also had a special status in Elizabethan theater, filling time gaps and informing the audience about new situations, as in Shakespeare's *Henry V* (*c.*1600).

Also, the terms "flat" and "round" for characters are as valid for drama as they are for fiction. Some types of drama, such as comedy, have recurring character types, called **stock characters**, including the boastful soldier, the cranky old man, or the crafty servant. At first sight, the figures in classical Greek drama resemble flat characters, since all actors wear masks onstage. On the one hand, the immobile mask stresses one particular or distinctive feature of the character; on the other, it allows one actor to represent more than one figure in a play, which helps to contain production efforts and costs.

As far as gender is concerned, it is important to realize that in classical Greek theater as well as in Elizabethan theater, women were banned from the stage, thus leaving all female roles to be played by young men (cross-dressing). At times, this tradition led to complicated situations in comedies, as in Shakespeare's *As You Like It*, where female characters played by men suddenly dress up as men. The female character Rosalind, who, according to the conventions of Elizabethan theater, was played by a young man, dresses up as a man in the course of the play. At the end of the play the character reveals his/her true female identity and marries Orlando. This tradition of casting men as women continued until the seventeenth century, and was only abolished in Restoration drama. In modern drama, the term **breeches role** applies to a part in which a woman dresses like a man in order to pass as a man. However, contrary to the legal reasons for cross-dressing in previous periods, this modern kind of gender masquerade is motivated solely by the plot of the play.

Text, transformation, and performance are central aspects not only of theater productions, but, by analogy, they also apply to the medium of film, bearing in mind film's specific characteristics. Film scripts differ from drama in that they take into account the visual, acoustic, and spatial possibilities of the medium. Transformation in film is quite different from transformation in drama, where it leads to a single, continuous performance. In film, only short sequences at a time are prepared for shooting, thus requiring that the actors work in ways that differ drastically from acting onstage. In theater, actors have to make themselves intelligible to the last row of the audience through heightened verbal expression, exaggerated facial expressions, gestures, make-up, and voice projection. In film, camera and sound techniques can create these effects, giving the medium its specific quality and granting it the status of an independent genre, despite its strong connections with the traditional performing arts and its links with fiction.

FILM

At the beginning of the twenty-first century, it is impossible to neglect **film** as a semi-textual genre both influenced by and exerting influence on literature and literary criticism. Film is still strongly predetermined by literary techniques; conversely, literary practice developed particular features under the impact of film. Many of the dramatic forms in the twentieth century, for example, have evolved in interaction with film, whose means of photographic depiction challenged the means of realistic portrayal in the theater. Drama could therefore abandon its claim to realism and develop other, more stylized or abstract forms of presentation. Photography and film have also had a major influence on the fine arts; innovative, more abstract approaches to painting have been taken in response to these new media. The same can be said for postmodern fiction, which also derives some of its structural features from film.

Film's idiosyncratic modes of presentation – such as camera angle, editing, montage, slow and fast motion – often parallel features of literary texts or can be explained within a textual framework. Although film has its own specific characteristics and terminology, it is possible to analyze film by drawing on methods of literary criticism, as film criticism closely relates to the traditional approaches of textual studies. The most important of these methodologies coincide with the ones that we will discuss in the next chapter on literary theory. There are, for example, approaches similar to text-oriented literary criticism that deal with the material aspects of film, such as film stock, montage, editing, and sound. Methodologies that are informed by reception aesthetics focus on the effect on the spectator, and approaches, such as psycho-analytical theory or feminist film theory, regard film within a larger contextual framework. The major developments of literary theory have therefore also been borrowed or adapted by film studies.

In spite of their differing forms and media, drama and film are often categorized under the heading **performing arts** because they use actors as their major means of expression. The visualization of the action is not left merely to the imagination of the reader, but rather comes to life in the performance, independent of the audience. In both genres, a performance (in the sense of a visual representation by people) stands at the center of attention. It is misleading, however, to deal with film exclusively in the context of drama, since categorizing it under the performing arts does not do justice to the entire genre, which also includes non-narrative subgenres without performing actors.

The study of film has existed for quite some time now as an independent discipline, especially in the Anglo-American world. Since its invention more than 100 years ago, film has also produced diverse cinematic genres and forms that no longer permit the classification of film as a mere by-product of drama. Because of its visual power – the visual element plays only a minor role in fiction – film is hastily classified as a dramatic genre. If we deal with film from a formalist-structuralist point of view, however, its affinity to the novel often overshadows its links to drama. Typical narratological elements of the novel – varied narrative techniques, experimental structuring of the plot, foreshadowing and flashback, the change of setting and time structure – are commonly used in film. The stage offers only limited space for the realization of many of these techniques.

The most obvious difference between film and drama is the fact that a film is recorded and preserved rather than individually staged in the unique and unrepeatable manner of a theater performance. Films, and particularly DVDs and blu-ray Discs, are like novels, which in theory can be repeatedly read or viewed. In this sense, a play is an archaic work of art, placing the ideal of uniqueness on a pedestal. Every theatrical performance – involving a particular director, specific actors, and scenery – is a unique event that eludes exact repetition. A film, on the other hand, can be shown in different cities at the same time, and it would be impossible to judge one screening as better or worse than any other one since the film always remains the same in its thousands of identical copies. In sum, we can say that, although performance is at the heart of both drama and movies, it takes on a completely different character in film, due to the characteristics of a mechanically reproducible medium.

In order to fully understand the medium, it is necessary to look at the **physiological principles** of film. The history of film in the nineteenth century is closely connected with that of photography. A quick succession of individual shots produces for the human eye the impression of a moving picture. To create this illusion, 24 pictures per second have to be connected. Within every second of a film, the motion of the projector is interrupted 24 times. Each picture appears on the screen for only a fraction of a second. The quick projections of images are too rapid for the human eye, which does not pick up individual pictures, but rather sees a continuous motion. As early as the late nineteenth century, inventors exploited this physiological phenomenon to carry out the first successful cinematic experiments.

In America, early cinematic adaptations of narrative literature were carried out at the turn of the century. Among the first narrative films were children's stories, such as Georges Méliès's (1861–1938) *Cinderella* (1899), or adaptations of novels, such as Edwin S. Porter's

(1870–1941) *Uncle Tom's Cabin* (1903) and J. Stuart Blackton's (1874–1941) *Adventures of Sherlock Holmes* (1905). While the early films simply adopted the rigid perspective of the proscenium stage, the genre clearly departed from drama immediately prior to and during World War I. New techniques, such as camera movement and editing, were invented. An early American example that applied these new techniques is D. W. Griffith's (1875–1948) *The Birth of a Nation* (1915), an epic narrative film about the American Civil War and its aftermath. Many of the major genres, such as the Western, slapstick comedies, and love stories, already existed in the early American silent movie. By World War I, Hollywood had become the center of the film industry, with a widespread network of cinemas all over America.

Outside America, the Russian filmmaker Sergei Eisenstein (1898–1948) was one of the key figures in film history, inventing new techniques in the field of film editing in the years after the Russian Revolution. In Germany, between the wars, Robert Wiene's (1881–1938) *The Cabinet of Dr Caligari* (1919) and Fritz Lang's (1890–1976) *Metropolis* (1926) were famous contributions to expressionist film. Influenced by psychoanalysis, expressionist film added a new dimension to the medium, attempting, for example, to visualize dreams and other psychological phenomena.

When **sound** was introduced to film in the mid-1920s, some of the progressive visual techniques of the silent era were abandoned for a brief period in favor of sound and recorded music. The sheer weight of sound equipment initially hampered camera mobility. The acoustic dimension enabled the development of action through dialogue and not merely through the visual means of the preceding decades. By the 1930s, Hollywood's **genres** included the Western, the musical, gangster and adventure movies, science fiction, the horror film, and opulent costume epics. During and after World War II, film noir (literally, "black film") developed as a new genre dealing with corruption in the disillusioned world of the American metropolis. Billy Wilder's (1906–2002) *Double Indemnity* (1944) and Robert Siodmak's (1900–1973) *The Killers* (1946) are well-known examples.

The post-war era saw an increased interest in European productions. Italian neorealist film became internationally renowned through directors such as Roberto Rossellini (1906–1977) and Vittorio de Sica (1901–1974), who treated realistic topics in authentic surroundings. In these films, the directors tried to capture the everyday life of post-war

Italy by breaking away from the artificiality of the "closed" studio set and thereby founding novel cinematic forms. In the early 1960s, French directors, such as Jean-Luc Godard (1930–) and François Truffaut (1932–1984), gained international fame for their innovations in film. Thanks to the *Neuer Deutscher Film* (new German cinema), including the directors Rainer Werner Fassbinder (1946–1982), Werner Herzog (1942–), and Wim Wenders (1945–), German film enjoyed new international fame, which it had lost for some time. In the last decades of the twentieth century, ethnic voices also established themselves in film, including African American director Spike Lee (1957–) with *Do the Right Thing* (1989), Asian American filmmaker Wayne Wang (1949–) with *The Joy Luck Club* (1993), and Mexican American director Robert Rodriguez (1968–) with *El Mariachi* (1992).

In film, as in other genres, various levels contribute to the overall artistic impression. This medium, which strongly relies on technical aspects, has several important, uniquely cinematic features with their own terminology. The most essential elements of film can be subsumed under the dimensions of *space*, *time*, and *sound*.

spatial dimension	temporal dimension
film stock	slow and fast motion
lighting	plot time
camera angle	length of film
camera movement	flashback
point of view	foreshadowing
editing/montage	

acoustic dimension
dialogue
music
sound effects

Spatial dimension

The deliberate choice of **film stock**, including black-and-white or color, high-contrast or low-contrast, sensitive or less sensitive material, produces effects that directly influence the content of a film. The insertion of black-and-white material in a contemporary color movie, for example, can create the impression of a historical flashback. Steven Spielberg (1946–), for example, reduced the colors of his movie *Saving*

Private Ryan (1998), thus creating the aesthetic impression of a movie from the era of World War II. Conversely, the sudden use of a color image in an otherwise black-and-white film draws special attention to the scene. In Spielberg's Holocaust film *Schindler's List* (1993), one of the very few instances of color is a little girl in a red coat – the color of blood. This sudden visual change makes the image stand out in an extraordinary way. A similar effect can be achieved through the use of old newsreels from an earlier era of film. It is also possible to convey certain moods or to create specific settings by varying the choice of film stock. As early as 1939, Victor Fleming (1883–1949) used color passages in *The Wizard of Oz* (1939) as a contrast to black-and-white film stock. Spike Lee also inserts a short color passage into his black-and-white film *She's Gotta Have It* (1986) and thereby contrasts the feelings of the female protagonist in this particular scene with other scenes, all of which are conveyed in black-and-white film stock.

Lighting is indirectly connected to film stock since certain light conditions have to be fulfilled corresponding to the sensitivity of the film. A famous experiment in this respect is Stanley Kubrick's (1928–1999) *Barry Lyndon* (1975), which uses only natural or candlelight instead of electric light. Lighting is also employed to obtain certain visual effects, as, for example, in Orson Welles's (1915–1985) *Citizen Kane* (1941), where the director changes the lighting pattern parallel to the personal development of the protagonist, Charles Foster Kane. While the young, idealistic Kane appears without shadows, later in the film his face is partially covered by shadows in order to point out the development of darker sides in his character. This low-key lighting is also a typical feature of film noir, a popular genre around the time of World War II.

Part of the spatial dimension is also the **framing** or composition of the scene, whose elements are summarized under the French term *mise en scène*, literally meaning "to place on stage," and referring to the arrangement of all visual elements in a theater production. In film, it serves as an umbrella term for the various elements that constitute the frame, including camera distance, camera angles, lenses, and lighting, as well as the positioning of persons and objects in relation to each other.

Terms such as *close-up*, *medium* and *long shot* refer to the distance between camera and object or to the choice of a particular section of that object or person to be represented. With the aid of an extreme long shot in a Western classic, a character almost completely vanishes in the landscape. The choice of this shot may stress vastness and human helplessness in a wilderness where the character has to stand his or her ground. The use of wide-angle lenses can achieve similar effects. Telephoto lenses create the opposite impression, either bringing the object closer to the foreground or making the background appear closer. A related technique is the use of distortions of the entire frame so that the image appears as if it were reflected in a curved mirror. A whole episode in Spike Lee's *Crooklyn* (1994) uses a vertical distortion in order to make the characters look like elongated Barbie dolls. Lee thereby evokes the experience of the child protagonist while visiting her relatives, whose worldview and role models are equally distorted.

An important consideration is the **camera angle** from which a certain scene is filmed. It is possible to distinguish between high angle, straight-on angle, and low angle shots, depending on the position of the camera. For example, if a character is supposed to appear tall, the camera is positioned low and aimed high (low angle). In this manner, stylized distortions of size can be achieved. It is also possible to even out real disproportions. When filming his fantasy-epic *The Lord of the Rings* (2001–2003), director Peter Jackson (1961–) used special camera angles in order to make certain actors seemingly shrink to the size of a Hobbit, while others appeared taller in the same shot. Placing one actor in the background and the other one in the foreground, the camera is locked down, creating a "forced perspective." This optical illusion tricks viewers into believing that the actors are indeed smaller, and not just farther away. One downside of the technique was that it restricted the camera in its movements, or did not work at all. However, for the movie trilogy, the visual effects team employed motion control and two different cameras that moved relative to each other, but in different directions. The two images were later combined into one, keeping up the illusion of disproportion, while, at the same time, offering a dynamic feel.

As this example shows, **camera movement** is linked to the camera angle and allows for a change of perspective. In the early days of film, the camera was too heavy to be moved during a scene. When lighter and more mobile equipment was developed, however, cameras could be moved more freely. A very striking example is Robert Zemeckis's (1952–) *Forrest Gump* (1994). Here, the camera meticulously follows a computer-animated feather that is seemingly carried by the wind.

The camera angle is also related to issues of point of view in literature and poses similar questions. In the majority of films, the perspective is that of an omniscient "narrator" who at times borrows subjective points of view of characters in the film. Only a few rare cases consistently maintain a subjective perspective or point of view. In Robert Montgomery's (1904–1981) *Lady in the Lake* (1946), almost the entire plot is filmed from the perspective of the protagonist. The main character only becomes visible to the viewer when he looks into a mirror. This technique forces the viewer to identify with the protagonist, through whose eyes we see the action.

Editing is one of the major cinematic techniques that have contributed to the flexibility of the medium. In Edwin S. Porter's (1870–1941) *The Great Train Robbery* (1903), the final version of the film was cut and rearranged in a separate process. The early Russian film developed **montage** as a filmic technique that creates effects similar to the use of the rhetorical figures of metaphor and simile in literature. Two images or objects that are in no way directly connected can be joined on a figurative level through montage. In his film *Strike* (1924), for example, Sergei Eisenstein juxtaposes a massacre of workers with scenes from a slaughterhouse, thereby comparing the workers' fate with the slaughter of animals.

Most of the early cinematic experiments, using a rigid camera angle, simply adapted the setting of the proscenium stage. However, the technical innovations that followed enabled the medium to develop independently and led to the discovery of new forms of artistic expression. With the use of a mobile camera, editing, and montage, film definitely departed from its roots in the theater.

Temporal dimension

Film, like literature, can employ the dimension of time in a variety of ways. Aspects of plot that have already been mentioned, such as **foreshadowing** and **flashback**, or interwoven levels of action and time, can be translated into film. The specific qualities of the medium enable the treatment of time in ways that do not exist in other genres. Simple examples of these techniques are fast motion and slow motion, which defamiliarize the action. In the film *Koyaanisqatsi* (1983), Godfrey Reggio (1940–) uses fast motion and slow motion to draw attention to everyday situations, such as city traffic or the changing of the seasons, stressing the importance of an ecological awareness on an endangered planet.

It is, however, not absolutely necessary to resort to special speeds in order to lengthen or shorten the temporal dimension. The cinema has other ways to create a discrepancy between the plot time and the **running time** of a film. Stanley Kubrick's *2001: A Space Odyssey* (1968), for example, covers several million years of human evolution by cutting from a bone tool, thrown into the air by a caveman, to a futuristic spaceship. At the end of Marc Forster's (1969–) film *Stay* (2005), the entire plot turns out to have been the dream of a dying car-crash victim. The film, however, stretches these moments to what appears to be a much longer time. In his project *Dimension* (1991–1997), Danish director Lars von Trier (1956–) attempted something similar by showing the passage of over 30 years in only approximately 90 minutes of screen-time, and – this would have been a first – without the help of make-up or special effects. In 1991, he began filming his actors every year, reducing the collected material to three-minute snippets a year. However, von Trier abandoned the project in the late 1990s.

In contrast to the above examples, films such as Fred Zinnemann's (1907–1997) Western *High Noon* (1952) make the actual length of the film (i.e., its running time) more or less correspond to the 90-minute time span of the action. The plot of *High Noon* revolves around the elapsing time during which the protagonist takes precautions against a dangerous criminal, who is set to arrive in town on the twelve o'clock (high noon) train. By equating real time and plot time, Zinnemann is able to emphasize the major feature of the film's content on a formal level, thus creating a powerful impression on the viewer. The American television series *24* (2001–2010) works with the same concept: each season is made up of 24 hour-long episodes, each also portraying the exact time span of an hour. Consequently, one season tells the events of a whole day (i.e., 24 hours). Several inserts that indicate the time of day appear throughout the episodes. Some other devices that can indicate the passage of time in film are clocks, calendars, newspapers, signs of aging, or changing fashion styles.

In the discussion of character presentation and plot, the use of time indicators in Virginia Woolf's novel *Mrs Dalloway* (1925) has already been pointed out. The novel consists of a number of simultaneously occurring episodes. Jim Jarmusch (1953–) uses a similar narrative technique in his film *Mystery Train* (1989), in which he presents events in the lives of three groups of people in Memphis, Tennessee. The film consists of three independent episodes, all of which connect through a number of time indicators. A revolver shot, a radio announcement, and a passing train are recurring features in all three episodes, making it clear for the viewer that the episodes are taking place simultaneously. Like Virginia Woolf, Jarmusch, here, tries to present a picture from diverse, fragmented perspectives, which are nevertheless held together by a number of unifying elements. While *Mrs Dalloway* places the character of Clarissa at its center, *Mystery Train* revolves around the mystic figure of Elvis Presley, who is viewed from three different perspectives in three different episodes. As in Woolf's novel, multilayered modes of character presentation correlate with complex narrative and temporal structures.

The more complex a film becomes, and the more **discontinuous** its **narrative** is, the more important it is to structure the plot with time indicators. Popular solutions are written inserts or the use of a narrator. Quentin Tarantino (1963–), for instance, incorporates chapter titles into his movie *Pulp Fiction* (1994), and, in this way, marks the beginnings and endings of three different episodes. In contrast, Steven Soderbergh (1963–) chooses color filters for the different episodes in his film *Traffic* (2000). In Stephen Daldry's (1961–) film *The Hours* (2002), the viewer meets three parallel, female characters in different cities and decades, all, however, united by recurring match cuts and montage sequences. For *Memento* (2000), director Christopher Nolan (1970–) repeats crucial links between the individual segments of the plot that is partially told backward. For his biographical film *I'm Not There* (2007), Todd Haynes (1961–) choses different actors to portray singer Bob Dylan in the different stages of his life, which in turn offers temporal guidance for the viewers.

In mainstream cinema, nonlinear plots, along with "mind-tricking narratives," (i.e., films with a twist ending) such as *The Sixth Sense* (1999), have been rapidly gaining popularity since the 1990s. In these kinds of movies, the viewers are misled by the clever way the plot is presented – only to realize in the end, when the real solution is revealed, that things were not as they seemed. Only when watching the movie a second time and analyzing it are these tricks made obvious to the viewers. Consequently, narratological approaches created for the analysis of novels are now increasingly being applied to film studies.

Acoustic dimension

It was not until the 1920s that the **acoustic dimension** was added to film, bringing about a radical change of the medium. Information was no longer conveyed merely by means of visual elements, such as facial expressions, gestures, or subtitles, but also through language (**dialogue, monologue, voice-over**), recorded music, and sound effects.

A number of movies deal with the transition from silent film to sound film, a famous example being Billy Wilder's (1906–2002) *Sunset Boulevard* (1950). He plays with the concepts of verbal and nonverbal expression as the two basic dimensions of film. The two main characters – a scriptwriter of the new sound film and a diva from the silent era – personify the distinction between "word" and "image." While the diva embodies the visual dimension of the medium, the acoustic dimension comes to life in the character of the scriptwriter. In order to give an even sharper picture of the two underlying principles of verbal (dialogue) and nonverbal (facial expressions, gestures) communication, Wilder adds subjective voice-over commentary by the male protagonist which is built in as an interior monologue and acts as a defamiliarizing element. Wilder's *Sunset Boulevard* is representative of a group of self-reflecting films that are concerned with the problems posed by the medium of film. More than 60 years later, Michel Hazanavicius's (1967–) *The Artist* (2011) pursued a similar goal. In a time when sound films are standard, the director deliberately embraced anachronism by producing a silent movie, which, in turn, also dealt with the downfall of this kind of film. Here, the resulting alienation effect manages to highlight basic mechanisms of film aesthetics and narratology.

Along with dialogue and sound effects, the film score assumes a special position and usually supports the plot. The volume, sound, rhythm, and pace of the music change according to the situation and underscore levels of meaning with acoustic effects. Film music can also contrast with the plot and create ironic or parodic effects. An important distinction has to be made between the **diegetic score** (i.e., music that is literally part of the plot), and **extradiegetic score** (i.e., music outside of the plot). A good example for diegetic music is George Lucas's (1944–) *American Graffiti* (1973). In this portrayal of small-town American life from the point of view of young people, the music of the 1960s is constantly playing on the teenagers' car radios.

The happy songs, however, stand in sharp contrast to the feel of the plot. The youngsters are frustrated and bored as they cruise through town in their cars at night. The music from the loudspeakers, laden with the typical themes of the American dream of freedom, fulfillment, and love, creates an almost humorous effect, serving as a counterpoint to the actual disillusionment of the teenagers. Their reality is the monotonous recurrence of daily events, reflected in the circular movement of driving around town.

In addition to diegetic music, a film's plot is usually supported by the conventional and inconspicuous use of music and sound effects. Romantic scenes are underlined with harmonious music, and threatening sounds back up scenes of danger and violence. In Spielberg's *Jaws* (1975), for instance, exactly the same melody plays each time the great white shark approaches. In horror films, this is a very popular strategy for suggesting danger or suspense to the audience. In certain instances, of course, the action may also be defamiliarized by contrasting the level of meaning and content with the acoustic level. In both cases, the acoustic dimension acts as an integral element of film, intricately interwoven with features of the spatial and temporal dimensions. It should be mentioned, however, that this practice is not without controversy. Since the beginning of the sound film, many filmmakers have opposed the use of music as an extradiegetic tool. In 1995, for example, Lars von Trier and other Danish filmmakers created the *Dogme 95* movement, which demanded more honesty in film, and which, among other things, banned all music added in postproduction. A recent example is Michael Haneke's (1942–) *The White Ribbon* (2009), which does completely without extradiegetic music, focusing instead on visual composition and language.

While the study of film as a "literary" phenomenon has finally come into its own, a more recent and emerging field is the study of popular television. Television had long been considered cinema's unwelcome and inferior stepbrother, but in the past two decades a veritable flood of "quality TV" series, such as *Twin Peaks* (1990–1991), *The Sopranos* (1999–2007), *Dexter* (2006–), and *Mad Men* (2007–), greatly helped to emancipate the genre. While in many ways similar to film on a formal level (spatial, temporal, and acoustic dimensions discussed in this chapter all apply to television as well), what mainly sets TV apart from its older brother are the different conditions of production, distribution (broadcast), and its serial structure. A series is fragmented into seasons and episodes, each with a fixed length designed to fit a set time slot in a TV-channel's weekly program. Such rigid programming automatically influences and arguably limits the structure of the narrative. On the other hand, it also allows more elaborate character development and a more complex web of character interrelations than we might be accustomed to in films.

In addition to television, in recent years literary scholars have also begun to pay attention to texts that go beyond the printed word, the theater, and filmed storytelling. Approaches of literary theory can be applied to such manifold and recent phenomena as video games, comic books, or various forms of online narration such as fan fiction and daily blogs. Each of these phenomena possesses its own idiosyncratic mechanisms and narrative techniques, and consequently challenges the old patterns and narratological approaches. In a world of rapidly growing and complex mass media – and *new* media – analysis of these genres has gained considerable significance. Therefore, literary theory and **media studies**, whose task it is to get a theoretical grasp on human expression through all media, are becoming increasingly interconnected.

As with the individual elements treated in connection with the genres of fiction, poetry, and drama, the different dimensions of film can hardly be seen as self-contained entities. The isolation of elements is only a helpful tool for approaching a complex work of art and can never fully account for all of its interdependent subtleties. We should also be aware that the very act of differentiating levels and elements of a genre is inevitably arbitrary and always remains subject to current trends, methodological approaches, and the subjective preferences of the person who compiles them. The dichotomies and classifications mentioned above are, therefore, meant to facilitate first encounters with texts, but should by no means be taken as general patterns according to which texts have to be interpreted. On the contrary, they should ideally yield to combinations with other suitable systems or eventually be selectively incorporated into one's personal methods of analysis.

PERIODS OF LITERATURE

Literary history attempts to group various texts, based on similarities in structure, content, or narrative characteristics, and attribute them to a specific historical period. The following basic overview focuses primarily on English and American literature, but also weaves in movements, authors, and works of international significance from world literature, in order to provide a wider background. This chapter makes no claim to be complete and can only give a summary, not a concise list of all the works and authors that have shaped literature to this day.

Ancient world	3000 BC–AD 400
Old English	400–1066
Middle English	1066–1450
Renaissance and humanism	1450–1660
Colonial period	seventeenth and eighteenth centuries
Eighteenth century	eighteenth century
Romanticism and transcendentalism	1800–1850
Realism and naturalism	1850–1900
Modernism	World War I–World War II
Postmodernism	second half of the twentieth century
Ethnic voices	
Postcolonial literature	

In **classical antiquity**, Egyptian and Mesopotamian writing date back as far as 3000 BC. One of the earliest literary benchmarks is the Mesopotamian *Epic of Gilgamesh*, whose different parts evolved between 2100 and 600 BC. This epic poem recounts the adventures of the mythological King Gilgamesh and his futile search for eternal life. In Western culture, writing and literature only re-emerge in the eighth century BC in **Ancient Greece**. Two of these early works are the epic poems the *Iliad* and the *Odyssey* (seventh century BC), which depict the siege of Troy by the Greek army, the city's fall, and the journeys of Odysseus. In the sixth century BC, epic poetry gives way to shorter poetic forms, including the love poems by the female poet Sappho (*c.*600 BC), as well as the drinking songs by Anakreon (*c.*580–495 BC). With the rise of Athenian democracy in the fifth century BC, drama evolves as a new, powerful voice, including Sophocles's (497–406 BC) tragedy *Oedipus the King* (*c.*425 BC) and Aristophanes's (445–385 BC) comedy *The Frogs* (405 BC). In the wake of classical Greek culture, late antiquity produces a number of prose texts, for example Achilles Tatius's romance *Leucippe and Clitophon* (late second century AD). These kinds of protonovels present themselves as a mixture of travel, adventure, and love story, being popular examples of light fiction in the ancient world. In many ways, they anticipate elements and features of the modern novel.

The majority of popular genres of Greek Antiquity continue as Latin adaptations in **Roman literature**. This includes, for example, the comedies of Plautus (*c.*250–184 BC) and Terence (*c.*185–159 BC), Catullus's (84–54 BC) love poetry, and Horace's (65–8 BC) satires. All of these works exert a dominating influence on later periods. While the Middle Ages knew Greek texts only by their Latin paraphrases, the grand works of Roman Antiquity form the basis of medieval literary understanding in the West. Especially, Virgil's (70–19 BC) national epic the *Aeneid* (*c.*31–19 BC), and Ovid's (43 BC–AD 17/18) *Metamorphoses* (1 BC–AD 10) – an extensive collection of myths in verse – influence and inspire medieval authors as literary models. St. Augustine of Hippo (AD 354–430) establishes another "bridge" between classical antiquity and the Middle Ages. His *Confessions* (*c.* AD 397–398) mark the beginning of the genre of the autobiography.

The **Middle Ages** develop directly out of the culture and literature of the Western Roman Empire. Following its downfall in the fifth century AD, a number of nations adopt the legacy of the ancient world.

Despite the progressing development of national languages, Latin continues to function as a lingua franca (a supranational language) throughout the Middle Ages and into early modern times: it dominates literature, administration, and the sciences. Medieval literature is, therefore, primarily a pan-European, Latin literature that escapes narrow national boundaries. Nevertheless, apart from Latin works, medieval authors also produce literary texts in regional vernacular languages.

The **Old English** or **Anglo-Saxon period**, the earliest period of English literature, is considered to begin with the invasion of Britain by Germanic (Anglo-Saxon) tribes in the fifth century AD, and lasts until the French invasion under William the Conqueror (c. 1028–1087) in 1066. The true beginnings of literature in England, however, are to be found in the Latin Middle Ages, when monasteries are the main institutions that preserve classical culture. Among the most important Latin literary texts of this period is the *Ecclesiastical History of the English People* (AD 731) by the monk Beda Venerabilis (673–735). As in other parts of Europe, national literatures develop in the vernacular, parallel to Latin literature. The earliest of these texts, written between the eighth and eleventh centuries, are called "Old English" or "Anglo-Saxon." The number of texts that have been handed down from this period is very small, comprising anonymous charms, riddles, and poems, such as "The Seafarer" (c. ninth century) or "The Wanderer" (c. ninth to tenth century), as well as epic works, such as the mythological *Beowulf* (c. eighth century) or *The Battle of Maldon* (c. 1000), which is based on historical facts.

When the French-speaking Normans conquer England in the eleventh century, a definite rupture occurs in culture and literature. From the latter half of this **Middle English period**, a number of texts from various literary genres have been preserved. The long list includes lyric poetry and epic long poems with religious content, such as *Piers Plowman* (c. 1360–1386), which has been attributed to William Langland (c. 1332–1387). The romance, a new genre of a secular kind, develops in this period and includes the anonymous *Sir Gawain and the Green Knight* (fourteenth century) and Thomas Malory's (c. 1408–1471) *Le Morte d'Arthur* (1470). This form indirectly anticipates and influences the development of the novel in the eighteenth century. Middle English literature also produces cycles of narratives, such as Geoffrey Chaucer's (c. 1343–1400) *Canterbury Tales* (c. 1387), similar to Giovanni Boccaccio's

(1313–1375) *Decameron* (*c.*1349–1351) in Italy and comparable works of other national literatures. Throughout the Middle Ages, all important literary genres are present. The only exception is drama, which develops very late in the fourteenth and fifteenth centuries, when mystery and miracle plays adapt religious topics for theater audiences. Drama is therefore one of the most striking literary innovations of the later Middle English period. After almost an entire millennium in which theater had little or no significance, drama re-emerges in these religiously inspired plays toward the end of the Middle Ages, and thus prefigures the development of modern drama in the Renaissance.

In the evolving national literatures outside of England, we find similar trends and genres, including charms, riddles, and epic poetry, as in the Old High German *Lay of Hildebrand* (*c.*840). After the turn of the millennium, French Arthurian romances (*c.*1170) by Chrétien de Troyes (*c.*1140–1190), as well as their manifold adaptations in other languages, such as Hartmann von Aue's (*c.*1165–1215) German *Erec* (late twelfth century), influence or parallel similar works in Middle English literature. In fourteenth-century Italy, Dante Alighieri's (1265–1321) religious epic *The Divine Comedy* (*c.*1307–1321) marks the beginning of a new age in literature and culture (i.e., the dawning of the Renaissance). Apart from significant achievements in the visual arts, Italy also sets the standard in literature, influencing the rest of Europe. For example, Francesco Petrarca's (1304–1374) poetry collection, *Canzoniere* (1370), as well as his sonnets, will dominate modern European love poetry for centuries.

In the early fifteenth century, **Renaissance** ideas begin to spread from Italy all over Europe. Unlike the Middle Ages, the Renaissance fully explores and revives all of classical literature, including ancient Greek texts. The term "Renaissance," meaning rebirth, expresses this basic concern of the period. Byzantine scholars, who disseminate the command of the classical Greek language in Western Europe, enable access to a hitherto neglected area of cultural history. This first phase of the Renaissance is known as **humanism** and focuses especially on aspects of classical languages, literatures, and rhetoric. Important editors and translators, such as Erasmus of Rotterdam (*c.*1466–1536), indirectly fuel the reformation with editions of the Greek Bible. In England, Thomas More's (*c.*1477–1535) travel fantasy *Utopia* (1516) marks the beginning of the genre of modern utopian literature. In a similar vein, humanism produces hybrid prose texts, displaying features of a philosophical as well as a literary nature. The most significant examples of this genre are the essays of the French writer Michel de Montaigne (1533–1592) and of the English author Francis Bacon (1561–1626).

In linguistics, the English Renaissance is also called the Early Modern English period, a term that focuses on the history of the language. Literary history usually subdivides the English Renaissance according to political rulers into the **Elizabethan age** (Queen Elizabeth I, 1533–1603) or the Jacobean age (King James, 1566–1625). Particularly notable in these periods is the revival of classical genres, such as the epic with Edmund Spenser's (c.1552–1599) *Faerie Queene* (published in two installments, 1590 and 1596), and modern drama with William Shakespeare (1564–1616), Christopher Marlowe (1564–1593), and others. Their renewal of Greco-Roman genres was to influence and dominate the further course of English literary history. Besides the adaptation of drama and epic, the English Renaissance also produces relatively independent prose genres, as, for example, John Lyly's (c.1554–1606) romance *Euphues* (1578) or Philip Sidney's (1554–1586) *Arcadia* (c.1580). A quite unusual literary form that shows an affinity to the drama of the time is the *court masque*, which relies on elaborate architectural designs. This period comes to a close with the establishment of the Commonwealth (1649–1660) under the guidance of the Puritan Oliver Cromwell (1599–1658). The prohibition of drama for religious reasons and the enforced shutdown of public theaters during the *Puritan interregnum* greatly influenced English literary history. The outstanding literary oeuvres of this time are written by John Milton (1608–1674), whose political pamphlets and religious epics (*Paradise Lost*, 1667, and *Paradise Regained*, 1671) mark both the climax and the end of the English Renaissance. In literary history, the era after the Puritan Commonwealth is also referred to as the *Restoration* or sometimes – rather vaguely – as *Baroque*. After more than a decade without theater in England, drama remerges in this era with popular genres, such as the Restoration comedy.

Early modern England in many respects follows literary trends that are popular on the Continent, including Italian epics such as Lodovico Aristo's (1474–1535) *Orlando Furioso* (1532), Torquato Tasso's (1544–1595) *Gerusalemme Liberata* (1581), and Luís Vaz de Camões (1524–80) *The Lusiads* (1572), Portugal's national epic. In the Renaissance, the genre of narrative prose literature is, somewhat unjustly, overshadowed by these other genres. Nevertheless, it does exist, as is apparent in France with works such as François Rabelais's (c.1494–1553) grotesque *The Life of Gargantua and of Pantagruel* (1532–1564), which, together with a large number of narrative prose texts in the Elizabethan age, paves the way for the modern novel.

Only in the transitional period between the late Renaissance and Baroque does prose fiction (i.e., the novel) become a new, driving force outside of England. During the Spanish *siglo de oro*, the golden age (1550–1680), Miguel de Cervantes's (1547–1616) *Don Quixote* (1605–1615), which is generally considered to be the first modern novel, immediately influences European literature through numerous translations. In German-speaking countries, the most famous early example of prose fiction is Hans Jacob Christoph von Grimmelshausen's (c.1621–1676) novel of education *Simplicissimus* (1669). In contrast to these early Continental examples, the English novel lags behind considerably and will only fully emerge as late as the eighteenth century.

In the Renaissance, drama also experiences a heyday outside of England with authors such as Lope de Vega (1562–1635) and Pedro Calderón (1600–1681) in Spain, Jean Racine (1639–1699) and Molière (1622–1673) in France, and Jost van den Vondel's (1587–1679) Neo-Latin tragedies in the Netherlands. In German-speaking countries, drama develops more slowly than throughout the rest of Europe. Professional actors emerge, but drama is still strongly influenced by religion, due to the prominent position of the Jesuit drama in schools.

Concerning poetry, old styles survive in the Renaissance; throughout Europe, however, newer forms, such as concrete poetry and emblems, gain wide popularity. A famous example of concrete poetry is George Herbert's (1593–1633) "Easter Wings," in which the letters are grouped into unconventional typographic arrangements, in order to also carry meaning on a visual level. The emblem, on the other hand, exhibits image and text as two separate but mutually interdependent dimensions. Originating in Italy with Andreas Alciatus's (1492–1559) *Emblemata* (1531), this religious, moralizing genre will remain very popular throughout Europe until the eighteenth century.

Much of the literary writing in America in the seventeenth century and the first half of the eighteenth century is religiously motivated and therefore may be subsumed under the rubric **Puritan** or **colonial literature**. This period can be seen as the first literary phenomenon on the North American continent. Early American texts reflect, in their historiographic and theological orientation, the religious roots of American colonial times. John Winthrop (1588–1649) and Cotton Mather's (1663–1728) notes in diary form and Anne Bradstreet's (c.1612–1672) poetry are among the most important sources for an understanding of the early colonies. In recent years, there has been an increased interest in works by African American slaves, such as Phillis Wheatley's (c.1753–1784) *Poems on Various Subjects* (1773). These texts provide new insights into the social conditions of the period from a non-European perspective.

The next major period in English literary history is the **eighteenth century**, which is also referred to as the "neoclassical," "golden," or **Augustan age**. This period adapts classical literature and literary theory to suit contemporary culture. Authors such as John Dryden (1631–1700), Alexander Pope (1688–1744), Joseph Addison (1672–1719), and Jonathan Swift (1667–1745) write translations, theoretical essays, and literary texts in a variety of genres. This is also a time of influential changes in the distribution of texts, including the development of the novel as a new genre and the introduction of newspapers and literary magazines, such as the *Tatler* (1709–1711) and the *Spectator* (1711–1714). Daniel Defoe's (c.1660–1731) *Robinson Crusoe* (1719), Samuel Richardson's (1689–1761) *Pamela* (1740–1741) and *Clarissa* (1748–1749), Henry Fielding's (1707–1754) *Tom Jones* (1749), and Laurence Sterne's (1713–1768) *Tristram Shandy* (1759–1768) mark the beginning of the novel as a new literary genre in England. It soon assumes the privileged position previously held by the epic or romance and becomes one of the most productive genres of modern literary history. This English influence is clearly visible in Johann Wolfgang von Goethe's (1749–1832) German epistolary novel *The Sorrows of Young Werther* (1774) or the coming-of-age story *Wilhelm Meister's Apprenticeship* (1795–1796).

From a philosophical perspective, the eighteenth century is also called the **Enlightenment**, responding to the strongly religious and dogmatic period of the Baroque. The term embodies several different trends in the various national literatures of the eighteenth century, which are all defined by their critical stance toward traditional values and concepts. A central aspect of this period is reason, which imposes a strong sense of personal responsibility on humans as self-regulating beings. The movement is causally connected to the works of the French philosopher René Descartes (1596–1650). Theorists such as John Locke (1632–1704) in England, Immanuel Kant (1724–1804) in Germany, and Voltaire (1694–1778) in France transform the Enlightenment into a global phenomenon, spreading it as far as North America. In England, it intersects with the emergence of regularly published journals, a new medium of the eighteenth century. In German literature, the spirit of reason and tolerance is especially evident in Gotthold Ephraim Lessing's (1729–1781) dramatic output. He challenges the rigid, neo-classical rules of drama in his theoretical works and also breaks new ground in his own plays. Lessing's *Emilia Galotti* (1772) marks the beginning of the genre of the bourgeois tragedy in the German-speaking world, while his later work *Nathan the Wise* (1779) is a vivid example of the enlightened idea of tolerance.

In Germany, the late eighteenth century is also referred to as *Sturm und Drang*, mostly connected with names such as Johann Gottfried Herder (1744–1803), Friedrich Schiller (1759–1805), and Goethe. Even though their work is generally based on the principles of the Enlightenment, the poets of *Sturm und Drang* explore new possibilities through the poetry of folk songs, as well as Jean-Jacques Rosseau's (1712–1778) concepts of nature. Both aspects – folk songs as well as admiration of nature – anticipate features of romanticism as the next supraregional trend.

In literary history, the term **romanticism** refers to the time between the end of the eighteenth century and the first decades of the nineteenth century. The first edition of the *Lyrical Ballads* (1798) by the British poets William Wordsworth (1770–1850) and Samuel Taylor Coleridge (1772–1834) marks the beginning of a new period in which nature and individual experience play important roles. Romanticism may be seen as a reaction to the Enlightenment and the political changes taking place throughout Europe and America at the end of the eighteenth century. In addition to Wordsworth and Coleridge, the most important representatives of English romanticism include the poets William Blake (1757–1827), John Keats (1795–1821), and Percy Bysshe Shelley (1792–1822), as well as Mary Shelley (1797–1851) with her novel *Frankenstein* (1818). The tension between nature and the individual self, or the violation of natural order in Shelley's *Frankenstein*, resemble some of the key concepts at work in romantic literature in general.

In America, romanticism largely coincides with the movement of **transcendentalism** in the first half of the nineteenth century. In his philosophical essays, Ralph Waldo Emerson (1803–1882) pleads for a culture of self-reliance that questions authority and privileges the individual. "Nature" – which is also the title of one of his most famous essays – becomes the umbrella term for an unobstructed encounter with the natural world, a goal that is also pursued by Henry David Thoreau (1817–1862) with his autobiographical novel *Walden* (1854). Walt Whitman (1819–1892), in his extroverted poetic incantation of the material world, and Emily Dickinson (1830–1886), with her introspective poetry, are indebted to Emerson's ideas as well. In this worldview, the individual transcends his or her surroundings (i.e., nature) in order to arrive at a deeper philosophical understanding. Nathaniel Hawthorne's (1804–1864) self-reliant female protagonist in the novel *The Scarlet Letter* (1850) and Herman Melville's (1819–1891) highly individualistic Captain Ahab in *Moby Dick* (1851) also follow this transcendental logic. Even Edgar Allan Poe's (1809–1849) abject characters can be seen as an extreme form of this transcendentalist notion of self-realization.

The next important supraregional period in literary history begins in the second half of the nineteenth century with **realism** and **naturalism**. Both movements attempt to paint realistic images through literature. Often, realism is defined as a trend that translates reality into language. By contrast, naturalism is seen as an attempt to portray the effects of social and environmental influences on literary characters. Both movements affect all literary genres, but above all they manifest themselves in novels and plays. This movement can be seen as a reaction to romanticism and as a means for coming to terms with the threat of the booming industrialization of the Victorian period.

Early examples of this trend in England are George Eliot's (1819–1880) novel *Middlemarch* (1871–1872) and Charles Dickens's (1812–1870) *David Copperfield* (1849–1850). In the United States, William Dean Howells (1837–1920) is a major theorist of realism whose popular novel *The Rise of Silas Lapham* (1885) also initiates an American realist literary tradition. One of the most successful authors of this period is the American Mark Twain (1835–1910) with his novel *The Adventures of Huckleberry Finn* (1884). Twain's use of Huck Finn as narrator is groundbreaking, as the story is told from the unconventional first-person perspective of a social outcast whereby Twain realistically reproduces the protagonist's sociolect. Despite his temporal distance from the transcendentalists, Twain's protagonist Huck functions as a hidden voice for Emerson's fresh, unobstructed, and natural view of the world. He is not weighed down by any burdens of civilization, and thus is able to approach his environment with unspoiled immediacy. While Twain explores realism via American regionalism, the American author Henry James (1843–1916) is very much influenced by European realism and Continental settings. His narratological innovations, such as the figural point of view imposed on his expatriate American protagonists, rank among the major contributions to this international movement.

For the European novel, important examples of realism and naturalism include Stendhal's (1783–1842) *The Red and the Black* (1830) and Gustave Flaubert's (1821–1880) *Madame Bovary* (1857) in France, and Fyodor Dostoyevsky's (1821–1881) *The Brothers Karamazov* (1879–1880) in Russia. In drama, the pace is set in Scandinavia with authors such as Henrik Ibsen (1828–1906) and his play *A Doll's House* (1879). In the German-speaking world, Gerhart Hauptmann (1862–1946) is known for plays with high social awareness such as *The Weavers* (1893), whereas in England, George Bernard Shaw (1856–1950) is associated with this movement.

While realism and naturalism strive for a truthful representation of reality in literature, **modernism**, in the first decades of the twentieth century, reacts directly to the realistic trends of the previous century. Modernism discovers innovative narrative modes, such as the stream-of-consciousness technique, and structural forms, such as collage and literary cubism. Modernism is a blanket term, encompassing the extensive literary innovations in all genres, which manifest themselves under the influence of psychoanalysis and other cultural-historical phenomena of the early twentieth century. Because of its experimental and innovative use of the temporal and spatial dimensions in the arts, the movement is also often referred to as the period of "time and space." A famous early example is Ambrose Bierce's (1842–1913) short story "An Occurrence at Owl Creek Bridge" (1890). In this short story, Bierce experiments with objective time and time as experienced sub-jectively by the protagonist, who is being hanged on a railway bridge during the American Civil War. While the convict is falling, he imagines that the rope snaps and allows him to escape. What follows is the detailed description of his imaginary escape. The story ends abruptly with the death of the convict as his neck breaks. Only then does the reader realize that the man's escape took place entirely in his imagination, the duration of the scene encompassing only the interval between his fall and his death.

One of the key figures of modernism is the American writer Gertrude Stein (1874–1946), whose apartment in Paris becomes a meeting point for a number of expatriate writers and artists, including Pablo Picasso (1881–1973), Ezra Pound (1885–1972), and Ernest Hemingway (1899–1961). Stein's unconventional style takes elements from modern paintings, as, for example, in her novel *Three Lives* (1909), and thereby functions as a model and catalyst for younger writers. The main works in England and America include James Joyce's (1882–1941) novels *Ulysses* (1922) and *Finnegans Wake* (1939), Virginia Woolf's (1882–1941) *Mrs Dalloway* (1925) and *To the Lighthouse* (1927), Ezra Pound's epic-like *The Cantos* (1915–1962), and T. S. Eliot's (1888–1965) long poem *The Waste Land* (1922).

One of the most internationally renowned writers is the American southern author William Faulkner (1897–1962). With his novel *The Sound and the Fury* (1929), Faulkner simultaneously continues in and departs from the realist tradition of Mark Twain's *Huckleberry Finn*. Faulkner takes Twain's limited perspective of a social outcast even further, telling part of the story from the point of view of a severely mentally handicapped person. In order to make sense out of the unfiltered and idiosyncratic perspective of the mentally challenged protagonist, the reader is continuously forced into guesswork about the significance and meaning of his observations.

Among the major innovations in American literature during the modernist period, however, is the emergence of drama as a productive, indigenous genre. Throughout the centuries, drama in America not only lagged behind European forms, but was virtually nonexistent. With Eugene O'Neill's (1888–1953) expressionist play *The Emperor Jones* (1920), American drama enters the international arena for the first time and soon develops into an important global player.

Outside of the English-speaking world, major proponents of German modernism are Rainer Maria Rilke (1875–1926) with his poems and prose, Robert Musil's (1880–1942) novel *The Man Without Qualities* (1930–1942), and Hermann Broch's (1886–1951) novel trilogy *The Sleepwalkers* (1931–1932). In Spanish and Latin American literature, this period is referred to as *Modernismo* and reaches international significance through the works of the Spanish authors Miguel de Unamuno (1864–1936) and Federico García Lorca (1898–1936), as well as the Portuguese writer Fernando Pessoa (1888–1935). France becomes another center of modernism, largely due to many English-speaking expatriates in Paris, who support an influential circle of writers and artists. During the modernist period, many different movements form, such as Dadaism, Italian Futurism, and German expressionism.

After World War II, **postmodernism** revives modernist efforts regarding innovative narrative techniques by adapting them in an academic, sometimes formulaic way. This literary movement of the second half of the twentieth century indirectly deals with Nazi crimes and the nuclear destruction during World War II, while structurally continuing and building on the approaches of modernism. Narrative techniques with multiple perspectives, interwoven plot strands, and experiments in typography characterize the texts of this era. American novels, such as John Barth's (1930–) *Lost in the Funhouse* (1968), Thomas Pynchon's (1937–) *The Crying of Lot 49* (1966), Raymond Federman's (1928–2009) *Double or Nothing* (1971), and British novelist John Fowles's (1926–2005) *The French Lieutenant's Woman* (1969) help the movement to attain a strong recognition in literary criticism.

The theater of the absurd, including works such as Samuel Beckett's (1906–89) *Waiting for Godot* (1952) and Tom Stoppard's (1937–) *Travesties* (1974) in England, as well as its American counterparts, such as Edward Albee's (1928–) *The Zoo Story* (1958), have become milestones of postmodernist international theater. In Latin America, postmodernism develops an independent format through the works of the Argentinian authors Jorge Luis Borges (1899–1986) and Julio Cortázar (1914–1984), Columbian novelist Gabriel García Márques (1927–), and Mexican author Carlos Fuentes (1928–2012). In the German-speaking world, Peter Handke's (1942–) novels and plays, as well as Max Frisch's (1911–1991) works, are important contributions to this international phenomenon.

Partly parallel to postmodernist writing, but also independent of the major strand, authors of various ethnic backgrounds position themselves as part of mainstream literature for the first time in literary history. In the 1980s, the avant-garde works of postmodernism, many of which seem exaggerated today, are overshadowed by women's and **"minority" literatures** (i.e., literature written by marginalized groups, including women, gays, or ethnic minorities such as African

Americans, Chicanos, and Chicanas). These literatures, which have gained considerably in importance over the last few decades, sometimes return to more traditional narrative techniques and genres, often privileging socio-political messages over academic, structural playfulness. Works such as Sylvia Plath's (1932–63) *The Bell Jar* (1963), Erica Jong's (1942–) *Fear of Flying* (1973), Doris Lessing's (1919–) *The Grass Is Singing* (1950), or Margaret Atwood's (1939–) *The Handmaid's Tale* (1985) are major representatives of female voices in English, American, and Canadian literature. Parallel to this gender-specific trend in mainstream literature, ethnic writers ensure the influential status of texts by hitherto neglected voices in the literary landscape of the late twentieth century. This includes works by African American writers such as Richard Wright's (1908–1960) *Native Son* (1940), Alice Walker's (1944–) *The Color Purple* (1982), and Toni Morrison's (1931–) *Beloved* (1987), as well as the works of Chinese American authors, such as Maxine Hong Kingston's (1940–) *The Woman Warrior* (1976).

In addition to women's literature and ethnic voices, **postcolonial literature** has become another center of attention. This vast body of texts is also categorized under "Commonwealth literature" or "Anglophone literatures." These works from former British colonies in the Caribbean, Africa, India, and Australia have significantly contributed to a change in contemporary literature. In many cases – but by no means in all – dimensions of content have regained dominance and act to counterbalance the academic playfulness of modernism and postmodernism. Salman Rushdie's (1947–) *Satanic Verses* (1988), Derek Walcott's (1930–) *Omeros* (1990), Chinua Achebe's (1930–2013) *Things Fall Apart* (1958), and Janet Frame's (1924–2004) *An Angel at My Table* (1984) are respective examples of **Anglophone literatures** from Asia, the Caribbean, Africa, and New Zealand. Partly under these influences, the general trend seems to privilege less complicated and apparently more traditional narrative techniques, while, at the same time, focusing attention on content more than in earlier, exaggerated narrative forms.

The contemporary American writer Jonathan Franzen (1959–) continues this trend by breaking with postmodernist traditions in the vein of authors such as Vladimir Nabokov (1899–1977) or Thomas Pynchon (1937–). Franzen's realistic novel *The Corrections* (2001) portrays a genre picture of a family, converging three different story lines into one Christmas morning. His resistance against a postmodernist style, however, is not revolutionary. Even during the heyday of post-modernism, the successful US author John Updike (1932–2009) favored a more realistic way of writing, as is evident in his *Rabbit* (1960–2001) novel cycle. However, other young authors do still draw on established postmodernist techniques. David Foster Wallace's (1962–2008) last novel *Infinite Jest* (1996), for instance, employs various postmodernist elements, such as extra-long sentences, cryptic vocabulary, hundreds of footnotes and sub-footnotes, and several lines of action.

As these last examples show, the above suggestions for periodization are often difficult to maintain, since individual authors frequently escape these rigid classifications. From the earliest periods onward, there was also continuous exchange and mutual influencing. For instance, ancient Greek literature functioned as a model for Roman literature, which in turn shape medieval culture. Both Greek and Latin texts indirectly brought about the Renaissance, a new literary and cultural period in the early modern age. The Elizabethan age also revived genres, such as classical drama, while the eighteenth century adapted the late classical proto-novel and the medieval romance for the new genre of the modern novel. Romanticism and transcendentalism objected to classical norms and learning, whose orientation toward nature forced realists and naturalists to turn to industrialization and urban culture as a new focus. Modernism and postmodernism, on the other hand, defied realist claims to authenticity by exploring unconventional structural and narratological dimensions. Parallel to these trends in the twentieth century, voices of minorities have challenged these movements, while, at the same time, experimenting with some of their features. The closer we come to the present time, the more difficult it gets to define or demarcate the boundaries of periods or movements, since most of them only emerge in the course of time through a mutual agreement of readers and critics. Whether the contemporary developments will therefore have to be classified as a new literary period, or just as a continuation of postmodernism, remains to be seen.

THEORETICAL APPROACHES TO LITERATURE

As with the classification systems of genres and text types, the approaches to literary texts subscribe to a number of divergent methodologies. The following sections show that literary interpretations always reflect a particular institutional, cultural, and historical background. Consecutive or parallel schools represent the various trends in textual studies, at times competing with one another. On the one hand, the various scholarly approaches to literary texts partly overlap; on the other, they differ in their theoretical foundations. The abundance of competing methods in contemporary literary criticism requires a basic familiarity with at least the most important trends and their general approaches.

Historically speaking, the systematic analysis of texts developed in the magic or religious realm, and in legal discourse. At a very early date in cultural history, magic and religion indirectly furthered the preservation and interpretation of "texts" in the widest sense of the term. The interpretation of oracles and dreams forms the starting point of textual analysis and survives as the basic structure in the study of the holy texts of all major religions. The mechanisms at work are, however, most apparent in oracles. An ecstatic person or medium in a state of trance receives encoded information about future events from a divinity. These messages were often put into rhymed verse, which could preserve the exact words more easily than an oral prose text.

Oral utterances could thus be "stored" through rhyme and meter in a quasi-textual way, making it possible to later retrieve the data in unchanged form. An important aspect of this oral precursor of written textual phenomena is that the wording of an utterance was seen as a fixed text that could consequently be interpreted. Famous classical examples of the different possible interpretations of oracles can be found in Herodotus's (c.480–425 BC) *Histories* (second half of the fifth century BC). During the Persian Wars, the Athenians turned to the Delphic oracle, asking what they should do in order to prepare for the Persian attack. The oracle recommended that they "hide behind wooden walls." Some people interpreted these walls as the Acropolis, which was then surrounded by hedges. Others (and this turned out to be the better interpretation) read the "wooden walls" as ships they should build in order to compete with the Persians in a sea battle. As we are told by Herodotus, they won the battle at Salamis in 480 BC.

The interpretation of encoded information in a text is important to all religions; it usually centers on the analysis or *exegesis* of canonical texts, such as the Bible, the Qur'an, or other holy books. As with dream and oracle, the texts that interpretations consequently decode are considered to have originated from a divinity and are therefore highly privileged. It is important to observe that the interpretation of these kinds of texts deals with encoded information, which can only be retrieved and made intelligible through exegetic practices. We can trace these religious and magic origins of textual studies from preliterate eras all the way to contemporary theology, always exerting a major influence on literary studies.

Partly influenced by religion, legal discourse also had a decisive impact on textual studies. As with religious discourse, in law a fixed legal text had to precede jurisdiction. Juridical texts, like religious ones, are only indirectly accessible since by nature they demand interpretation with regard to a particular situation. The overall importance of legal texts in everyday life consequently led to an extensive body of literature concerning their application and interpretation. Even today, the exegesis of legal texts remains the form of interpretation that most of us deal with in everyday situations. Since most religions also include legal elements, such as Judaic law, Islamic law, or canon law in Christianity, religious and legal discourses have always interacted with one another. The approaches and methodologies associated with both (the exegesis of the Bible and the interpretation of legal texts) have always indirectly influenced literary studies. Literary criticism derived its central term **interpretation** from these two areas of textual study. Already in antiquity, scholars believed texts to have not only a literal meaning, but also a figurative or allegorical one. In the Middle Ages, it had become normal to read the Bible on several allegorical levels in addition to its literal meaning: This exegesis of religious and legal texts was based on the assumption that the meaning of a text could only be retrieved through the act of interpretation. The biblical Exodus could, for instance, be seen as an actual occurrence. It could, however, also be an allegory of God saving his people from hardship and misery. Biblical scholarship coined the term **hermeneutics** for this procedure, which has consequently fueled literary interpretation over the past several centuries. Since literary criticism as a discipline holds a variety of opinions – many of them contradictory – concerning the purpose and applicability of textual interpretation, a number of theoretical trends and methodological approaches characterize the field.

Although each academic discipline tries to define and legitimate its scholarly work by terms such as "general validity," "objectivity," and "truth," most disciplines are subject to a number of variable factors including ideologies, socio-political conditions, and fashions. The humanities in general and literary studies in particular are characterized by a multiplicity of approaches and methodologies. Within the field of literary studies, **literary theory** has developed as a distinct discipline influenced by philosophy. Literary theory analyzes the philosophical and methodological premises of literary criticism. While literary criticism is mostly interested in the analysis, interpretation, and evaluation of primary sources, literary theory tries to shed light on the very methods used in these readings of primary texts. Literary theory thus functions as the theoretical and philosophical consciousness of literary studies, constantly reflecting on its own development and methodology.

Among the many diverse methods of interpretation it is possible to isolate four basic approaches, which provide a grid according to which most schools or trends can be classified. Depending on the main focus of these major methodologies, we can distinguish between text-, author-, reader-, and context-oriented approaches. We can subsume the following theoretical schools under these four basic rubrics:

text
philology
rhetoric
formalism and structuralism
new criticism
semiotics and deconstruction

author
biographical criticism
psychoanalytic criticism
phenomenology

reader
reception theory
reader-response criticism
reception history

context
literary history
Marxist literary theory
gender theory
new historicism and cultural studies

The text-oriented approach is primarily concerned with questions of the "materiality" of texts, including editions of manuscripts, analyses of language and style, and the formal structure of literary works. Author-oriented schools put their main emphasis on the author, trying to establish connections between the work of art and the biography of its creator. Reader-oriented approaches focus on the reception of texts by their audiences and the texts' general impact on the reading public. Contextual approaches attempt to place literary texts against the background of historical, social, or political developments while, at the same time, attempting to classify texts according to genres as well as historical periods.

This classification inevitably results in a drastic reduction of highly complex theories to their most basic patterns. The following overview intends to depict the central tenets of these methodological approaches to texts, both as expressions of the cultural consciousness as well as the ideologies of the era in which they exerted their major impact. This simplified categorization should not mislead anyone into believing that each theoretical school subscribes to a single, invariable methodology. Despite overlaps between many of the schools, each school's general outlook is usually dominated by one particular approach. The following survey is meant to highlight and summarize the main emphases of the most popular schools and theoretical trends in literary studies.

TEXT-ORIENTED APPROACHES

Many of the modern schools and methodologies in literary criticism adhere to **text-oriented approaches** and thereby indirectly continue to apply mechanisms rooted in the above-mentioned primordial textual sciences of religion, legal practice, and divination. All of these traditions place the main emphasis on the internal textual aspects of a literary work. Extratextual factors concerning the author (his or her biography, other works), audiences (race, class, gender, age, education), or larger contexts (historical, social, or political conditions) are deliberately excluded from the analysis. Although the text serves as the focal point of every interpretive method, some schools privilege other aspects, such as biographical information concerning the author, problems of reception, and the like, which are only indirectly related to the literary work as such. Text-oriented traditions, however, center on the text per se, primarily investigating its formal or structural features. Traditional philology, for example, highlights "material" elements of language; rhetoric and stylistics analyze larger structures of meaning or means of expression; and the formalist-structuralist schools, including Russian formalism, the Prague school of structuralism, new criticism, semiotics, and deconstruction, attempt to trace general patterns in texts or illuminate the nature of "literariness."

Philology

In literary criticism, the term **philology** generally denotes approaches that focus on editorial problems and the reconstruction of texts. Philology, which experienced its heyday in the Renaissance with the rediscovery of ancient authors, the invention of the printing press, and the desire for correct editions of texts, remained one of the dominant schools into the nineteenth century. Informed by the rise of modern science, these philological approaches attempted to incorporate advanced empirical methodologies into the study of literature.

Central to this approach is **textual criticism**, which tries to reconstruct the physical basis of a literary text. Ancient texts pose a special challenge, such as the Mesopotamian *Epic of Gilgamesh* (c. 2100–600 BC), which exists, for instance, in a number of versions and fragments of cuneiform tablets. However, more "recent" texts, such the works of Shakespeare, also need to be edited, since their first printed editions in the Renaissance were very inconsistent. The materiality of texts, a major concern of traditional philology, is still relevant to today's literary scholarship, as is illustrated by the debate concerning the reliability of the generally accepted edition of James Joyce's *Ulysses* (1922). In the 1980s, a number of competing Joyce editions, all claiming to be the definitive text, revived the interest in questions of textual editions and philological methodologies.

This positivist spirit of textual criticism is also reflected in the major concordances (alphabetical lists of words) of nineteenth-century literary scholarship, which document the exact frequency and usage of words by a particular author. These empirical studies, for example, not only list all the words employed by Shakespeare in his dramas and poems, but also provide the exact line reference for each entry. Concordances, as the most extreme developments of these positivist approaches in philology, have been experiencing a revival due to current digital technologies. The possibility of transferring large amounts of textual data into electronic media, such as the complete works of an author or all texts of an entire period (as, for example, the *Thesaurus Linguae Graecae*, which stores all written documents in ancient Greek on one CD-ROM), has given rise to computer-assisted frequency analyses of words and similar quantitative or statistical investigations.

Rhetoric and stylistics

In addition to traditional editorial problems, today's text-oriented schools focus primarily on aspects of form (textual and narrative structure, point of view, plot patterns) and style (rhetorical figures, choice of words or diction, syntax, meter). Together with theology and grammar, **rhetoric** remained the dominant textual discipline for almost 2,000 years. Since ancient Greco-Roman culture treasured public speech, orators compiled a number of rules and techniques for efficient composition and powerful oratory. Although rhetoric was mainly concerned with teaching effectively how to influence the masses, it soon developed – as did the interpretation of holy and legal texts – into a theoretical academic discipline. In its attempt to systematically classify and investigate elements of human speech, rhetoric laid the foundation for current linguistics and literary criticism.

Rhetoric originally mediated rules concerning eloquence and perfect speech, and was hence primarily prescriptive. It offered guidelines for every phase of textual composition including *inventio* (selection of themes), *dispositio* (organization of material), *elocutio* (verbalization with the help of rhetorical figures), *memoria* (the technique of remembering the speech), and *actio* (delivery of the speech). Despite its prescriptive and practical inclination, rhetoric also introduced descriptive and analytical elements into textual studies. Even in its earliest phases, rhetoric analyzed concrete textual samples in order to delineate rules for the composition of a "perfect" text. In these theoretical investigations into textuality, structural and stylistic features – above all, *dispositio* and *elocutio* – eventually surfaced as the dominant areas of inquiry. Today's text-oriented literary criticism derives many of its fields from traditional rhetoric and still draws on its terminology.

In the nineteenth century, rhetoric eventually lost its influence and partially developed into **stylistics**, a field whose methodology was adopted by literary criticism and art history as well. With the aim of describing stylistic characteristics of individual authors, entire nations, or whole periods, stylistics focused in its analyses of texts on grammatical structures (lexis, syntax), acoustic elements (melody, rhyme, meter, rhythm), and overarching forms (rhetorical figures). Although stylistics experienced a slight revival a few decades ago, its main contribution to recent literary theory was as a precursor to formalist-structuralist schools of the early twentieth century.

Formalism and structuralism

The terms **formalism** and **structuralism** encompass a number of schools in the first half of the twentieth century whose main goal lies in the explication of the formal and structural patterns of literary texts. This emphasis on the intrinsic and structural aspects of a literary work deliberately distinguished itself from older traditions – above all, the biographical literary criticism of the nineteenth century – which were primarily concerned with extrinsic or extratextual features in their analysis of literature. The consecutive schools of Russian formalism, the Prague school of structuralism, new criticism, and poststructuralism find a common denominator – despite their respective characteristics – in their general attempts to explain levels of content in relation to formal and structural dimensions of texts.

In traditional philosophical and aesthetic discourse, *form* denotes the relationship between different elements within a specific system.

Questions concerning form and content, already discussed by ancient philosophers, lie at the heart of this approach. According to this traditional point of view, which goes back to the Greek philosopher Aristotle (384–322 BC), things in the world only exist because shapeless matter receives structure through superimposed form. Form thus functions as a container in which content is presented. This basic philosophical principle, which distinguishes between a level of structure and a level of content, was introduced into literary criticism as early as classical antiquity. Aristotle, for instance, in his *Poetics* (fourth century BC), adopts the notion of the determining function of form over matter for literary phenomena by using formal schemes to explain generic features of drama. With this structural approach, Aristotle lays the foundation for twentieth-century formalist movements in the study of literature and language. While a number of schools of literary criticism focus primarily on the level of content (the "what?" of a text), formalists and structuralists emphasize the level of form (the "how?" of a text).

During and after World War I, **Russian formalism** sought an objective discourse of literary criticism by foregrounding structural analyses, or, as Roman Jakobson (1896–1982) puts it, "The subject of literary scholarship is not literature in its totality, but literariness, i.e., that which makes of a given work a work of literature" (see Erlich 172). In its search for the typical features of *literariness*, Russian formalism rejects explanations that base their arguments on the spirit, intuition, imagination, or genius of the poet. This "morphological" method developed by the formalists deliberately neglects historical, sociological, biographical, or psychological dimensions of literary discourse, propagating instead an intrinsic approach that regards a work of art as an independent entity. In contrast to traditional, extrinsic methodologies, Russian formalism privileges phonetic structures, rhythm, rhyme, meter, and sound as independent meaningful elements of literary discourse.

According to Victor Shklovsky (1893–1984) and a number of other formalists, these structural elements in a literary text cause an effect called **defamiliarization**. This tendency, inherent in literary language, counteracts the reader's familiarity with everyday language and consequently offers a tool for distinguishing between literary and nonliterary discourse. Laurence Sterne's novel *Tristram Shandy* (1759–1767), which abounds in a variety of defamiliarizations of its own genre, serves as the classic example in formalist explanations of this concept.

The novel starts much like a traditional autobiography, which relates the life of the main character from his birth to his death. Defamiliarizing features already surface, however, in the fact that the narrative does not actually begin with the birth of the hero but rather with the sexual act of his conception, thus parodying traditional expositions in this genre. Subsequently, Sterne deliberately highlights and parodies traditional narrative structures and plot patterns when he, for example, inserts the preface and the dedication of the novel in the middle of the text and places Chapters 18 and 19 after Chapter 25. In addition, Sterne introduces *lacunae* (blank spaces) into the text, which have to be filled by the reader's imagination. These elements play with the familiar conventions of the early novel, while simultaneously laying bare the fundamental structures of the novel and reminding the reader of the artificiality of the literary text. In modern literary criticism, this self-reflexiveness is often labeled **metafiction** (fiction about fiction). This term denotes literary works that reflect on their own narrative elements, such as language, narrative structure, and plot development. In postmodern texts of the second half of the twentieth century, meta-fictional traits become so common that they almost function as *leitmotifs* (dominant features) of the period.

Russian formalism's central concept of defamiliarization in many respects anticipates the Brechtian notion of the **alienation effect**, which – leaving its characteristics aside – also attempts to foreground self-reflexive elements of a text or work of art. Like the proponents of Russian formalism, the playwright and theoretician Bertolt Brecht (1898–1956) was concerned with ways of demonstrating the artificiality of literary discourse. He demanded that, in dramatic performances, actors – and, above all, the audience – should maintain a critical distance from the play. Brecht carefully positioned alienating elements to remind the spectator of the artificial and illusory nature of a theatrical performance. In order to achieve this effect, an actor, during a dialogue onstage, for example, would unexpectedly address the audience, thereby breaking the illusion of the self-contained world of the play.

Formalism also attempts to analyze structurally such textual elements as characters in a plot, which older schools traditionally explain on a merely thematic level. Vladimir Propp's (1895–1970) character typology, which reduces the almost infinite number of characters in Russian fairy tales to a limited list of recurrent types, became one of the most influential contributions of Russian formalism to the general structuralist theories of the twentieth century. This kind of analysis attempts to narrow down the infinite number of possible literary characters to a finite number of basic structural agents, including villain, donor, helper, princess, hero, and false hero.

The principle of this procedure is based on **myth criticism**, which analogously tries to restrict thematic phenomena to formal structures. Similar to Propp's character typology, myth criticism exposes patterns of myth – for example, the mother–son relationship and patricide in the myth of Oedipus – as deep structures that underly a variety of texts. The most famous and influential example of this approach is J. G. Frazer's (1854–1941) voluminous work *The Golden Bough* (1890–1915), which tries to reveal the common structures of myths in different historical periods and geographical areas. A continuation of Propp's character typology and Frazer's myth analysis was carried out in the 1950s and 1960s by Claude Lévi-Strauss (1908–2009) in *Structural Anthropology* (1958), which also refers to basic mythological patterns in its descriptions and analyses of cultures. The most influential contribution offered by the mythological approach to literary criticism, however, is the work of Northrop Frye (1912–1991), who places structures of myth at the heart of what he considers to be the main literary genres. According to Frye, the forms of comedy, romance, tragedy, and irony (i.e., satire) resemble the patterns of the seasons (spring, summer, autumn, and winter, respectively) in primordial myth.

Archetypal criticism, based on C. G. Jung's (1875–1961) depth psychology, works along similar lines by searching texts for collective motifs of the human psyche, which supposedly are common to different historical periods and cultures. These archetypes represent primordial images of the human unconscious, which have retained their structures in various cultures and epochs. Archetypes such as shadow, fire, snake, garden of paradise, hell, or mother figure, constantly surface in myth and literature as a limited number of basic patterns of psychic images, which lend themselves to a structural model of explanation.

In line with this approach, one could, for example, interpret Edgar Allan Poe's short story "The Cask of Amontillado" (1846) with reference to collective archetypes. Poe tells the story of a man who is lured into a subterranean wine cellar by a friend under the pretext of wine tasting; instead, his friend buries him there alive. Having been tricked, he enjoys the wine and foolishly faces death with a laugh. When analyzing these images, it becomes evident that Poe reworked concepts that are deeply rooted in myth and religion: death as a crypt-like underground chamber, wine, which dulls the fear of approaching death, and laughter in the face of death. These images surface in the Christian Eucharist, too, which employs a stylized consumption of wine to symbolize resurrection, thus turning the grave into a womb from which the deceased is reborn.

As is evident from this example concerning death and resurrection, various cultures, religions, myths, and literatures have recourse to primordial images or archetypes that – like a subconscious language – express human hopes and fears. The aim of archetypal criticism is in line with the methodology of formalist schools, which delve beneath the surface of literary texts in their search for recurrent deep structures.

New criticism

Largely independent of European formalism and structuralism, **new criticism** established itself as the dominant school of literary criticism in the English-speaking academic community during the 1930s and 1940s. Literary critics such as William K. Wimsatt (1907–1975), Allen Tate (1899–1979), and J. C. Ransom (1888–1974) represented this school, which maintained its status as an orthodox method for more than three decades. The central features of new criticism – whose name deliberately negates preceding critical methods – are best understood in contrast to the academic approaches in literary studies that were prevalent in the preceding years. New criticism objects to evaluative critique, source studies, investigations of socio-historical background, and the history of motifs; it also counters author-centered biographical or psychological approaches as well as the history of reception. Its main concern is to free literary criticism of extrinsic factors and thereby shift the center of attention to the literary text itself.

New criticism disapproves of what are termed the affective fallacy and the intentional fallacy in traditional analyses of texts. The term **affective fallacy** stigmatizes interpretive procedures that take into account the emotional reaction of the reader as an analytical "tool." In this respect, new criticism does away with the use of ungrounded subjective emotional responses caused by lyrical texts. In order to maintain an objective stance, the critic must focus solely on textual characteristics. The term **intentional fallacy** applies to interpretive methods that attempt to recover the original intention or motivation of an author while writing a particular text. New criticism, therefore, does not try to match certain aspects of a literary work with biographical data or psychological conditions of the author; instead, its aim is the analysis of a text – seen as a kind of message in a bottle without a sender, date, or address – based solely on the text's intrinsic dimensions.

In its analyses, new criticism consequently focuses on phenomena such as multiple meanings, paradox, irony, wordplay, puns, or rhetorical figures, which – as the smallest distinguishable elements of a literary work – form interdependent links with the overall context. A central term often used synonymously with new criticism is **close reading**. It denotes the meticulous analysis of these elementary features, which mirror larger structures of a text. New criticism thus also objects to the common practice of paraphrase in literary studies since this technique does not do justice to such central elements of a work, as, for example, multiple meanings, paradox, or irony. Another recurrent term in new critical interpretations is unity, which goes back to Aristotle's *Poetics*. The elements mentioned above that underly close reading supposedly reflect or unearth the unified structure of the entire literary text.

Poetry, in particular, lends itself to this kind of interpretation since a number of genre-specific features such as rhyme, meter, and rhetorical figures call attention to the closed or unified character of this genre. This is why new criticism focuses predominantly on poems. Famous examples of new critical analyses are a number of readings of John Keats's "Ode on a Grecian Urn" (1819). In this poem, Keats describes an ancient vase whose round and self-contained form functions as a symbol of the closed unity of the ideal poem. A new critical interpretation therefore tries to explain the different metrical, rhetorical, stylistic, and thematic features as partial aspects of the poem's unity (see also Chapter 2's section on "Poetry").

Among the formalist schools, new criticism particularly distinguishes itself by the rigidity of its rules for textual analysis. Its applicable methodology and clear guidelines, however, are mainly responsible for the dominant position it held until the late 1960s in English and American universities. It was pushed into the background by reader-oriented approaches as well as by newer text-centered schools. These recent text-oriented trends are often subsumed under the term **post-structuralism**, not only because they come after the above-mentioned structuralist schools, but also because they adapt structuralist methodology for purposes that go beyond older approaches.

Semiotics and deconstruction

Semiotics and deconstruction belong to more recent trends in text-oriented literary theory of the 1970s and 1980s, approaching a text as a system of **signs**. One basis for these complex theoretical constructs is the linguistic model of Ferdinand de Saussure (1857–1913). The Swiss linguist starts from the assumption that language functions through representation, in which a mental image is verbally manifested or represented. Before a human being can, for example, use the word "tree," he or she has to envision a mental concept of a tree. Building on this notion, Saussure distinguishes between two fundamental levels of language by referring to the prelinguistic concept (in this case, the mental image of a tree) as the **signified** and its verbal manifestation (the sequence of the letters or sounds T-R-E-E) as the **signifier**.

mental concept or
signified (French *signifié*)

linguistic realization or
signifier (French *signifiant*)   T-R-E-E

Saussure introduces a similar dichotomy in his two-leveled structural explanation of language as a means of communication. The conceptual level of *langue* provides the necessary abstract rules and methods of combination that are eventually realized by *parole* in individual spoken or written utterances.

Semiotics and deconstruction use the verbal sign or *signifier* as the starting point of their analyses, arguing that nothing exists outside of the text (i.e., that our perception of the world is of a textual nature). According to these schools, language or texts function in a way that resembles a game of chess. A limited number of signs, like the figures on a chessboard, only make sense when they are in a closed system. Language and text are viewed as part of a system whose meaning is created by the interaction of its different signs as well as the internally distinct features of its elements. This model of explanation is based on the principle of *binary opposition*. The term refers to the elementary distinctness of linguistic signs that cause difference in meaning. In the minimal pairs "h*u*t"/"h*a*t" or "*p*ull"/"*b*ull," for example, only one letter or sound (phoneme) is responsible for differentiating between the meanings of similar combinations of letters.

A new and unconventional aspect of semiotics and deconstruction is their attempt to extend the traditional notion of textuality to non-literary or nonlinguistic sign systems. Semiotic methods of analysis that originated in literary criticism have been applied in anthropology, the study of popular culture (e.g., advertisements), geography, architecture, film, and art history. The majority of these approaches emphasize the systemic character of the object under analysis. Buildings, myths, or pictures are regarded as systems of signs in which elements interact in ways that are analogous to letters, words, and sentences. For this reason, these divergent disciplines are often subsumed under the umbrella term semiotics (the science of signs). Among the most famous semioticians is the Italian Umberto Eco (1932–), who, before becoming an internationally renowned novelist with *The Name of the Rose* (1980), had a career as a leading theorist in semiotics.

A practical example of the analysis of nonlinguistic sign systems is Roland Barthes's (1915–1980) semiotics of fashion. This French literary critic regards clothes or garments as systems of signs whose elements can be "read" just like the literary signs of texts. A few millimeters' width of a tie contains complex information. For example, a narrow leather tie conveys a completely different message than a short, wide tie or a bow tie. These textile signs – just like the words of a language – can only transmit meaning when they are seen in their particular context or sign system. Signs, therefore, only generate meaning when they interact with other signs. Fashion, as a manifestation of social relations, provides a good example of these mechanisms in a non-linguistic system. The signs as such remain the same over the years, but their meaning varies when the relationships between them change. Thus, wide pants, short skirts, or narrow ties convey messages that differ from those they conveyed a few years earlier.

Like semiotics, **deconstruction** also highlights the building-block character of texts whose elements consist of signs. This poststructuralist method of analysis starts with the assumption that a text can be analyzed (deconstructed) and reassembled in the course of analysis (constructed). The text, according to the theory, does not remain the same after its reconstruction, since the analysis of signs and their reorganization in the interpretive process is like a continuation of the text itself. Traditional divisions into primary and secondary literature therefore dissolve when one regards interpretation as a continuation or integral part of the text.

Deconstruction is intricately interwoven with the works of the French philosopher Jacques Derrida (1930–2004) and the literary theorist Paul de Man (1919–1983). This approach does not provide any clear-cut guidelines for the analysis of texts and does not consider itself to be a monolithic method or school. Despite the complexity of its philosophical bases, deconstruction developed into one of the most influential theoretical trends in literary criticism during the 1970s and 1980s and has continued to provide basic notions and terminology for recent publications on literature.

An important example is Derrida's concept of *différance*. While Saussure saw a "signified" (mental concept) behind every "signifier" (sign) in order to explain meaning, deconstruction deliberately does away with the signified by privileging the interaction between signifiers. Sometimes, the concept of an encyclopedia is used to explain how meaning is derived in this system of interdependent signs. Every entry or signifier is embedded in a network of cross-references, each of which in turn contains a number of further references. For example, if you look up the term "tree" in a dictionary, the given definition might be "plant bigger than a bush." We could consequently look up the explanation for "bush" and probably find it described as a "plant bigger than a houseplant" – and so on. The meaning of a specific term, therefore, evolves in the continuous process of referring to other terms or signifiers. The neologism *différance* conflates the words "to defer" and "to differ," thereby pointing out both the constant "deferral" to other signifiers and the "difference" that necessarily distinguishes the various signifiers in the system from each other. According to this model of explanation, meaning is generated through reference and difference on the level of the signifier only. This system of explaining the production of meaning in language does away completely with the notion of an elusive and immaterial signified, and focuses instead on the material level of the signifier.

Playful adaptations of this theory are postmodernist "dictionary novels," such as *The Dictionary of the Khazars* (1984) by the Serb author Milorad Pavić (1929–2009) or Walter Abish's (1931–) *Alphabetical*

Africa (1974). These texts adopt the external form and structure of a dictionary or encyclopedia in order to highlight the postmodern theoretical notions of text in their own literary medium. Dictionary novels can be read either from beginning to end in a linear way, or by starting somewhere in the middle of the text and moving back and forth from cross-reference to cross-reference. Precursors to this genre, however, existed a long time before postmodernism, as, for example, Ambrose Bierce's (1842–1914) *The Devil's Dictionary*, which used this format as early as 1906.

This cluster of text-oriented theories emphasizes intrinsic dimensions of literary works. Their main objective lies in the analysis of basic textual structures (narrative techniques, plot patterns, point of view, style, rhetorical figures) as well as in the differences between everyday and literary language or between prose and poetry. Semiotics and deconstruction represent the most extreme examples of text-oriented literary criticism, which, by extending the term "text" to nonliterary sign systems, provide textual modes of explanation for different cultural phenomena.

AUTHOR-ORIENTED APPROACHES

In the nineteenth century, before the major formalist-structuralist theories of the twentieth century, **biographical criticism** evolved as a dominant movement. This **author-oriented approach** established a direct link between the literary text and the biography of the author. Dates, facts, and events in an author's life are juxtaposed with literary elements of his or her works in order to find aspects that connect the biography of the author with the text. Research into the milieu and education of the author should ideally shed light on certain phenomena in the text. In addition, an author's library can provide insight into the author's background reading, or letters and diaries may reveal additional personal information.

Autobiographies are obviously suitable for this kind of approach, which compares the fictional portrayal with events and people from the author's life. In many cases, autobiographical material enters the fictional text in code. The American playwright Eugene O'Neill (1888–1953), for example, used veiled autobiographical elements in his play *Long Day's Journey into Night* (*c.*1941; published 1956). Although the characters and events in the play are supposedly fictional, they are based on real people and dramatize events from O'Neill's family life.

Fyodor Dostoyevsky's (1821–1881) novel *The Gambler* (1867) deliberately draws from autobiographical experiences. The protagonist's fateful gambling problem is reminiscent of Dostoyevsky's experiences when he became addicted to gambling during a trip to Germany, losing his entire advance for his new novel to the addiction. Franz Kafka's (1883–1924) work is often quite autobiographical. He had, for instance, a difficult relationship with his father, a fact that influenced many of his works. His issues with authorities and paternal omnipotence, for instance, are very evident in the novella *In The Penal Colony* (1919), as well as in the novels *The Trial* (1925) and *The Castle* (1926).

Many authors, however, wish to keep their texts fictional and their private spheres intact and, hence, oppose this approach. For example, the American author J. D. Salinger (1919–2010), who became famous with the publication of his novel *The Catcher in the Rye* (1951), strictly refused to make public any information about his private life during the last decades, taking legal action even against his own daughter when she revealed family details in a book. The postmodern author Thomas Pynchon (1937–) is also very protective of his private life. However, he gave a parodistic spin to this attitude when he appeared as a character in the television series *The Simpsons* (1989–), lending his voice to a cartoon figure with a paper bag over his head.

Canonical authors in particular – those who are highly regarded in literary criticism, such as Shakespeare, Milton, or Joyce – often tend to be mythologized. This leads to attempts to reconstruct the author's spirit through his or her work. Phenomenological approaches assume that the author is present in his or her text in encoded form and that his or her spirit can be revived by an intensive reading of his or her complete works.

As the example from Franz Kafka's life shows, many biographical approaches also tend to employ psychological explanations. This has led to **psychoanalytic literary criticism**, a movement that sometimes deals with the author, but primarily attempts to illuminate general psychological aspects in a text that do not necessarily relate to the author exclusively. Under the influence of Sigmund Freud (1856–1939), psychoanalytic literary criticism expanded the study of psychological features beyond the author to cover a variety of intrinsic textual aspects. In many instances, fictional characters of a text are subjected to a psychological analysis, almost as if they were real people. A frequently cited example in this context is the mental state of Hamlet in Shakespeare's drama; psychoanalytic critics ask whether Hamlet is mad and, if so, which psychological illness he is suffering from.

Sigmund Freud, too, borrowed from literary texts in his explanations of certain psychological phenomena. Some of his studies, among them the analysis of E. T. A. Hoffmann's (1776–1822) story "The Sandman" (1817), rank among the classic interpretations of literary texts. In the second half of the twentieth century, psycho-analytic literary criticism regained momentum under the influence of the French analyst Jacques Lacan (1901–1981), whose interpretation of Edgar Allan Poe's texts, for instance, had a major impact on Anglo-American literary theory. During the last decades of the twentieth century, Lacanian theory heavily influenced psychoanalytic film theory. The interest in psychological phenomena indirectly abetted the spread of the "reader-centered" approaches. Their focus on the reception of a text by a reader or on the reading process can, therefore, be seen as an investigation of psychological phenomena in the widest sense of the term.

READER-ORIENTED APPROACHES

As a reaction to the dominant position of text-oriented new criticism, a **reader-oriented approach** developed in the 1960s called **reception theory**, reader-response theory, or aesthetics of reception. All three terms are used almost synonymously to summarize those approaches that focus on the reader's point of view. Some of these approaches do not postulate a single objective text, but rather assume that there are as many texts as there are readers. This attitude implies that a new individual "text" evolves with every individual reading process.

With the focus on the effect of a text on the recipient or reader, reception theory opposes new criticism's dogma of the affective fallacy, which demands an interpretation free of subjective contributions by the reader. Reader-centered approaches examine the readership of a text and investigate why, where, and when a text is read. They also examine certain reading practices of social, ethnic, or national groups. Many of these investigations also deal with and try to explain the physiological aspect of the actual reading process. They aim at revealing certain mechanisms that are at work in the transformation of the visual signs on paper into a coherent, meaningful text in the mind of the reader.

The founder of reception aesthetics, the German literary theorist Wolfgang Iser (1926–2007) argues, for example, that every text has an **implied reader**. The author writes, according to this concept, an abstract reader into his or her text, thereby shifting the attention from the real reading individual to a disembodied dimension of reception, intricately interwoven with the text itself. Reception aesthetics assumes that a text creates certain expectations in the reader in every phase of reading. These expectations are then either fulfilled or left unfulfilled. Wolfgang Iser's term of the **blank** or "spot of indeterminacy" refers to the options stimulated by the text and consequently "filled" by the reader. This principle of the blank applies to the elementary level of the sentence as well as to more complex units of meaning. While reading even the first words of a sentence, the reader continually imagines how it might continue. In every phase, the reader attempts to complement what is missing through his or her own imagination and skill at combination. Similarly, we continually pick up open questions, which we then connect to various explanatory options. Filling the blanks, on the one hand, depends on subjective individual traits and, on the other, on more general features, such as education, age, gender, nationality, and the historical period of the reader.

In his movie *The Sixth Sense* (1999), for example, M. Night Shyamalan (1970–) uses intentional blanks to fuel the viewers' imagination. Only at the very end, however, can the viewer interpret these moments correctly. During a dinner scene for their wedding anniversary, for instance, the wife seems to be upset with her husband. She does not react to his apology for being late, and when he tries to grab her hand, she pulls it away. At the end of the movie, we realize that the husband is in fact a ghost, having died earlier. Now we know that her cold reaction was due to the simple fact that she could never see or hear him in any of those scenes, and that she was mourning her loss. Having this new knowledge, and replaying the movie in our mind's eye, we now interpret things very differently. We realize that we could have filled these spots of indeterminacy in another way, maybe even guessed that he was a ghost right there and then.

The reader's expectation plays a role in every sort of text, but it is most obvious in literary genres such as detective fiction, which depend very much on the interaction between text and recipient. Edgar Allan Poe's "The Murders in the Rue Morgue" (1841), for example, consists of several blanks of this sort, which consistently guide the reader's imagination and expectation in different directions. A viciously mutilated body is found in a Paris apartment. The reconstruction of the murder and the discovery of the culprit are founded on a number of contradictory testimonies and circumstantial evidence; the reader is continually forced to change his or her assumptions in order to identify the murderer's motive and identity. When the detective finally discloses that the culprit was not a human being, as we all assumed, but rather a violent orangutan, we all go back to certain scenes of the story in our minds, asking ourselves why we had not picked up the clues ourselves.

Playing with the reader's expectations is a main concern in detective fiction but is also present in any other literary genres, though in varying intensity and clarity. Expectations are at the basis of interpretation on every level of the reading process, from the deciphering of a single word or sentence to the analysis of thematic structures of texts. Reception theory, therefore, shifts the focus from the text to the interaction between reader and text. It argues that the interpretation of texts cannot and must not be detached from the reading individual or implied reader.

A further aspect that is closely connected with this movement is the investigation of the reception of texts by a particular readership. In **reception history**, sales figures are examined together with reviews in newspapers and magazines. These analyses can either look at the reception of texts in a particular period (synchronic analysis) or trace changes and developments in the reception of texts in literary history (diachronic analysis).

The reader-centered approaches of reception theory and reception history, particularly influential in the 1970s as reactions to the dogmas of new criticism, were pushed into the background in the 1980s by text-oriented semiotics and deconstruction, as well as by a variety of context-centered schools.

CONTEXT-ORIENTED APPROACHES

The term **context-oriented approach** refers here to a heterogeneous group of schools and methodologies that do not regard literary texts as self-contained, independent works of art, but try to place them within a larger context. Depending on the movement, this context can be history, social and political background, genre, nationality, or gender. The most influential movement to this day is **literary history**, which divides literary phenomena into periods, describes and groups texts with respect to historical backgrounds, dates texts and examines their mutual influence. This movement is associated with the discipline of history and is guided by historical methodology. The entire notion of literary history has become so familiar to us that it is difficult to distinguish it as an approach at all. This historically informed methodology, which organizes literary works in a variety of categories, is, of course, as arbitrary and dependent on conventions as any other approach.

An important school that places literary works in the context of larger socio-political mechanisms is **Marxist literary theory**. On the basis of the writings of Karl Marx (1818–1883) and literary theoreticians in his wake, including Georg Lukács (1885–1971) and Antonio Gramsci (1891–1937), texts become expressions of economic, sociological, and political factors. Conditions of production in certain literary periods, as well as their influence on the literary texts of the time, feature as key factors of interpretation. The critic Ian Watt (1917–1999), in his book *The Rise of the Novel* (1957), for example, argues that, compared with previous centuries, eighteenth-century England had a new material basis for literary production, dissemination, and reception of texts. A large and wealthy enough reading public, cheap printing presses, and efficient ways of spreading texts gave rise to a new mode of remunerating authors through a royalty system, and consequently produced the genre of the modern novel in England. The Elizabethan age, for example, lacked these material preconditions and was therefore still based on a patronage system, in which wealthy sponsors commissioned literary works. In such a climate, the novel would not have been able to evolve as it did in eighteenth-century England.

In Germany, the Frankfurt school, whose Marxist theoreticians include Theodor Adorno (1903–1969) and Jürgen Habermas (1929–), has exerted a major influence on English and American literary criticism. Independent of the fall of the Eastern Bloc, Marxist literary theory has lost much of its former impact over the last several decades. Since the mechanisms of class, on which Marxist theory focuses, often parallel the structural processes at work in "race" and "gender," the theoretical framework provided by Marxist criticism has been adapted by younger schools that focus on marginalized groups, including gender theory, African American and gay and lesbian literary criticism, or postcolonial literary studies. Text-oriented theoretical approaches such as deconstruction and new criticism are also indebted to Marxist thought, both for their terminology and philosophical foundations.

New historicism

One of the latest developments in the field of contextual approaches has been **new historicism**, which arose in the United States in the late 1980s. It builds on poststructuralism and deconstruction, with their focus on text and discourse, but adds a historical dimension to the discussion of literary texts. Such interpretations would, for instance, view certain works by Shakespeare together with historical documents on the discovery of America, and then treat discovery itself as a text. History, therefore, is not regarded as isolated from the literary text in the sense of a "historical background" but rather as a textual phenomenon in its own right. For example, one of the leading figures in new historicism, Stephen Greenblatt (1943–), has analyzed a colonial text of early American literature by Thomas Harriot (c.1560–1621), comparing the relationship between Europeans and Indians in this text with the structures of dependence in Shakespeare's play *The Tempest* (c.1611). As a result, the mechanisms of power prove to be deeply rooted cultural structures, which dominate the historical as well as the literary discourses of the time.

New historicism takes an approach similar to that of the poststructuralist schools, including nonliterary phenomena in the definition of "text" and thus treating historical phenomena as it would treat literary ones. A key term in new historicist analyses is "discourse," which becomes an umbrella term for mechanisms at work in both realms, the historical and the literary. The movement is comparatively new and, like deconstruction, opposed to rigid methods associated with a particular school.

Related to new historicism, although an independent movement, is the field of **cultural studies**, which has advanced in the 1990s to one of the most influential areas within literary studies, if not the humanities as such. Although firmly rooted in literary studies, this approach deliberately analyzes the different aspects of human self-expression, including the visual arts, film, TV, commercials, fashion, architecture, music, or popular culture as manifestations of a cultural whole. In contrast to semiotics, which is equally interested in isolating nonliterary phenomena from a text-oriented, structuralist approach, cultural studies adopts a comprehensive perspective, which attempts to grasp culture's multifaceted nature at large.

Even though there has been an increased interest in cultural studies recently, cultural approaches and methodologies have existed in the humanities for a long time. The Swiss art historian Jacob Burckhardt (1818–1897) in *The Civilization of the Renaissance in Italy* (1860), for instance, argued already in the nineteenth century that cultural production is a holistic phenomenon, spreading over different areas of art. In the twentieth century, English theorist Raymond Williams (1921–1988) in his book *Culture and Society* (1958) supported this view. His plea for an understanding of cultural differences takes into consideration the whole of cultural production rather than isolated details. This evidently context-oriented approach considers literature as an important, but not the only, manifestation of larger cultural mechanisms.

Most noticeably, all of these newer approaches focus on "the Other." In his book *Orientalism* (1978), for example, literary scholar Edward Said (1935–2003) analyzed the way Western culture sees the Orient as the stereotypical "Other." Recent scholarly interest is very much directed toward these national, regional, or ethnic "minorities" – the term "minorities" referring to a marginal group within a more dominant society. In past decades, **postcolonial theory** has put a strong focus on societies that have evolved out of former colonies. The Indian theorist Homi Bhabha (1949–) is an important scholar in this field, incorporating ideas of poststructuralism and deconstruction for his theory of culture and cultural identity. His notion of culture as a phenomenon, determined by discursive forces, shows striking structural analogies to recent trends in gender studies. These approaches regard cultural identity, similar to gender, as a construction process of numerous forces, rather than a biologically determined given.

Gender theory

The most productive and, at the same time, most revolutionary movement of the younger theories of literary criticism in general and the contextual approaches in particular is **gender theory**. This complex critical approach is part of a movement that has established itself in almost all academic disciplines and has become particularly strong in the various branches of modern literary criticism. Although gender is always at the center of attention in the different schools of gender theory, this particular movement may be used to demonstrate how different approaches in literary studies tend to overlap.

Feminist literary theory, for example, starts with the assumption that "gender difference" is an aspect that has been neglected in traditional literary criticism and, therefore, argues that traditional domains of literary criticism have to be re-examined from a gender-oriented perspective. At the beginning of this movement in the late 1960s, thematic issues such as the portrayal of women in literary texts by male authors stood in the foreground. These early attempts of feminist literary criticism concentrated on stereotypes or distorted portrayals of women in a literary tradition dominated by men. One of the main issues of this reader-centered attitude is the identification of the woman reader with fictional female characters in literary texts. For this reason, the early phase of feminist literary theory goes by the name of **images of women criticism.**

The next phase in feminist literary theory, the use of historical and author-centered approaches, can be described as feminist literary history and **canon revision**, whose primary goal was to establish a new set of standard primary texts by non-male authors. Feminist literary critics in the mid-1970s drew attention to neglected female authors in the literary canon and propagated a new literary history by focusing on an independent female literary tradition. This kind of feminist literary criticism with a focus on the revision of the canon remained the dominant movement up to the late 1970s, when it weakened and diversified under the influence of French feminists.

With the American reception of **French feminists** such as Hélène Cixous (1937–), Luce Irigaray (1932–), and Julia Kristeva (1941–), who have strong backgrounds in psychoanalysis and philosophy, the focus of feminist literary criticism shifted at the beginning of the 1980s to textual and stylistic reflections. Assuming that gender difference determines the act of writing (i.e., the style, narrative structure, content, and plot of a text) feminist literary criticism entered domains that are usually treated by text-oriented formalist-structuralist schools. This movement in feminism views the female physical anatomy as responsible for a specifically feminine kind of writing that manifests itself in plot, content, narrative structure, and textual logic. This theoretical assumption is commonly referred to by its French term *écriture féminine* ("female writing").

Later works of this movement, which endeavor to account for the position of men in literary criticism and in feminism, produced one of the most distinctive paradigm changes in this field by shifting the emphasis from feminist theory to gender theory. In **gender theory**, the object of analysis is no longer the female alone, but rather the interaction between the genders. An increasing number of male critics are now working on gender issues, thus integrating masculinity into gender studies. In accord with these latest developments, the role of male and female homosexuality in literature and literary criticism has received a great deal of attention. In the early 1990s, this led to the development of queer theory, which looks at society and culture not merely from a homosexual angle but includes all notions of sexual identity that deviate from the established "norm" of heterosexuality. In literature, proponents of queer theory might, for instance, point out homophilic undercurrents in works that had hitherto been taken for granted as "straight" writing.

The most recent trends in gender theory incorporate concepts of deconstruction, thus questioning the entire notion of a stable gender identity. This discussion, which was initiated by the American literary theorist Judith Butler (1956–), approaches gender identity in a manner reminiscent of deconstruction, explaining meaning in language. Gender is thus "constructed" through a number of interacting elements within a societal system. The key term is "gender construction" according to which "man" and "woman" adopt the role of signifiers whose meaning or identity is construed through an interdependent network of other signifiers.

In summary, we can point out a few tendencies that have developed in feminist literary theory since the end of the 1960s: the first cluster of publications in the field focused primarily on what is specifically female (protagonist, author, or canon), followed by poetic or aesthetic theories based on gender difference (*écriture féminine*). The latest development is toward a comprehensive view of the importance of both "genders" in literary production and reception, as well as the notion that gender is the result of a discursive practice. Although gender studies will always reflect its origins in feminism, recent dialogic trends indicate a shift toward a joint inquiry carried out by scholars of both genders. As feminist literary criticism shows, the distinction between textual, author-centered, reader-centered, or contextual approaches cannot always be strictly maintained. In practice, any movement in literary criticism makes use of a combination of a variety of approaches, although one aspect usually dominates and is therefore used to classify the work with a particular school. Although different philologies, such as English, German, or Romance Languages have contributed to the theoretical discourse in literary studies, traditionally comparative literature has been instrumental as a platform for discussing and disseminating literary theory within literary studies.

Comparative literature

Even though Johann Wolfgang von Goethe (1749–1832) had already coined the term "world literature" – and thus advocated a supraregional approach to literature – **comparative literature**, as a discipline devoted to this kind of scholarly inquiry, developed relatively late, at the beginning of the twentieth century. Comparative literature evolved as a reaction to the nationalist views on literature in the nineteenth century and subsequent National Socialist tendencies. Its main principle is to compare and contrast literary texts of different origins, languages, cultures, and periods. During the Nazi regime, many leading literary scholars went into exile, for example René Wellek (1903–1995), who moved from Prague to London, where he significantly helped to establish comparative literature as an independent discipline. However, also in Germany, National Socialism indirectly caused this approach to gain momentum. It is not surprising that one of the first important texts of the discipline originates as a reaction to the chauvinist view on German literature during the Third Reich. In his publication *European Literature and the Latin Middle Ages* (1948), Ernst Robert Curtius (1886–1956), a scholar from Alsatia, tried to implement a global view on Latin medieval texts as a pan-European phenomenon. Naturally, comparative literature has not always represented unifying concerns. Comparing literature from different origins has also been a means of privileging one's own national literature over others.

Despite ideological differences within the discipline, all areas and methods are based on the concept of comparison, as clearly implied by the name of the discipline. Generally, the two main areas of research are interliterary and transliterary comparison. **Interliterary comparison** denotes reciprocal influences between literatures of linguistically and culturally different areas. This includes the traditional search for ideas and motifs in various literatures with regards to content. **Transliterary comparison**, on the other hand, links literature with other media or ways of artistic expression, such as painting, music, dance, film, law, or natural sciences.

A good example for a comparativist approach at its best is the oeuvre of the Russian literary critic and theorist Mikhail Bakhtin (1895–1975). Although Bakhtin produced most of his works in the first half of the twentieth century, his writing did not receive adequate recognition in the West until the 1970s. Trained in a formalist tradition, Bakhtin uses texts from different literary periods and languages in order to trace common structural features. Next, he deduces theoretical concepts from his findings, thereby shedding light on general principles of literary discourse per se. Among these concepts is the "carnival-esque," which Bakhtin pinpoints as a staple of late medieval or early modern literature in its attempt to invert traditional hierarchies or orders of society. Other terms that dominate Bakhtin's research are the "chronotopos," devoted to the temporal and spatial dimensions of literary texts, as well as "dialogism" as a key feature of literary discourse. In his work, Bakhtin does not simply trace a particular motif in different literatures for its own sake, but rather instrumentalizes this motif in order to arrive at a deeper understanding of the workings of literature in general. In this sense, Bakhtin's comparativist approach contributed to what is called "general literature," another major focus of comparative literature that is more or less synonymous with the field of "literary theory."

Dealing with literature on a theoretical level and investigating multicultural aspects of literature tend to transcend national bound-aries. Consequently, comparative literature used to be a suitable forum for discussing and communicating these issues that are pertinent to all philologies. However, in the past few decades, most philologies have discovered and claimed literary theory and studies in multiculturalism as their own core competencies, thereby moving these discussions away from comparative literature into traditional literature departments.

So far, we have categorized the various approaches of the different schools according to their common methodological features. What follows is an attempt to list the various movements in the order of their historical succession. The dates given must not be taken as absolute figures; rather, they stand for the periods when the respective movements were at their peak:

Antiquity and Middle Ages	rhetoric
Renaissance	philology
nineteenth century	stylistics
	biographical criticism
first half of twentieth century	psychoanalytic criticism
	myth criticism
	comparative literature
c.1920–1930	Russian formalism
c.1940–1960	new criticism
c.1970–1980	reception theory
c.1970–	semiotics
	feminist literary theory and gender theory
	deconstruction
c.1980–	new historicism and cultural studies

The majority of the movements mentioned here existed simultaneously, with certain schools repeatedly reaching and relinquishing a position of dominance. The historical sequence of the various literary movements shows that there is a constant shifting of focus and an alternation between text-, author-, reader-, and context-oriented approaches. Especially over the last couple of decades, the various movements have changed quickly and have been short-lived, akin to fashions.

In the interpretation of literary texts, it is important to decide which approaches are suitable for the text at hand and can lead to new results. Although a text might imply a certain approach because of its thematic, historical, or structural qualities, unconventional approaches might often produce more original and rewarding results. Postmodernist texts work well with a structural approach as they deal with formal elements. Politically or ideologically motivated texts are ideal for a Marxist approach. Biographies or autobiographies lend themselves to a comparison with the life of the author. In addition, it seems uncommon today to interpret a text by a female author without referring to gender. However, these obvious approaches do not have to dominate the discussion of a text. On the contrary, the choice of methodological approach should be guided primarily by the originality of the results it might produce, while reflecting one's personal interests, the state of current research, or the trends of the time.

LITERARY CRITIQUE OR EVALUATION

In the English-speaking world, the term **literary criticism** can refer to the literary interpretation of texts as well as their evaluation. For that reason, "literary critique" is sometimes used to differentiate between the interpretation of a text and the evaluative criticism that often occurs in connection with literary awards and book reviews.

A significant forum for evaluative criticism is the weekend edition of major newspapers that introduce the latest in primary or secondary literature in the form of **book reviews**. Among the most distinguished papers in the English-speaking world that review both primary and secondary texts are the *New York Times Book Review* (since 1896), the *New York Review of Books* (since 1963), and the *Times Literary Supplement* (since 1902). Scholarly (secondary) literature is most often reviewed in special journals by literary critics who comment on new book publications in their respective fields of research.

Related to book reviews are **review articles**, which discuss a broader theme (such as "Latest publications in literary gender theory in English" or "The phenomenon of new historicism") or a number of secondary sources on a particular text or author. This kind of general survey offers a basic impression of the latest trends or publications in a certain field.

A similar text type is the reader's review in a publishing house, which is not meant for the general public. Readers evaluate manuscripts that have been submitted to a publisher. The tone and style of these evaluations are like book reviews. The following extract from a parodic text by the Italian literary critic and author Umberto Eco (1932–) points out the relativity and limitations of this kind of discourse. It also shows how certain literary methods and approaches are used not just for analysis and interpretation, but also for evaluation and critique. In his "Regretfully, We are Returning . . . Reader's Reports" (1972), Eco writes a series of fictitious negative reviews of texts belonging to the classical canon of literary history. Eco tries to insinuate what would happen if the classics of world literature were submitted to publishers today and rated with conventional methods. He particularly wants to illustrate the relativity of these evaluations by writing, for instance, a fictitious review of the Bible:

> I must say that the first hundred pages of this manuscript really hooked me. Action-packed, they have everything today's reader wants in a good story. Sex (lots of it, including adultery, sodomy, incest), also murder, war, massacres, and so on. [. . .]
>
> But as I kept on reading, I realized that this is actually an anthology, involving several writers, with many – too many – stretches of poetry, and passages that are downright mawkish and boring, and jeremiads that make no sense.
>
> The end is a monster omnibus. It seems to have something for everybody, but ends up appealing to nobody. And acquiring the rights from all these different authors will mean big headaches, unless the editor takes care of that himself. The editor's name, by the way, doesn't appear anywhere on the manuscript, not even in the table of contents. Is there some reason for keeping his identity a secret?
>
> I'd suggest trying to get the rights only to the first five chapters. We're on sure ground there. Also come up with a better title. How about *The Red Sea Desperadoes?*

(33)

Here, Eco parodies a reader-centered approach as he investigates the effect of the text on a potential bestseller-reading public with a strong desire for "sex and crime." The dominating reader-centered approach is, however, interrupted by biographical questions about the authorship of the text and by textual considerations that are pertinent to stylistic criticism.

Literary awards apply similarly dubious criteria. The question concerning the evaluation of texts is as old as literature itself. As early as classical antiquity, drama contests took place on set occasions to find the best playwright. A classical parody of "objective" criteria of evaluation is Aristophanes's (c.448–380 BC) comedy *The Frogs* (c.405 BC), in which Aeschylus and Euripides, the main representatives of Greek drama, engage in a contest. After a series of unsuccessful attempts at finding a winner, the god Dionysus, who is in charge of the contest, chooses an "empirical" method of evaluation: he uses scales to measure the "weight" of the verses. Aeschylus wins the contest because he mentions a river in his verse while Euripides only mentions a boat.

These parodies of literary critique show that the evaluation of texts in literary criticism is controversial, mostly because this process depends on too many variables. Some experimental texts receive bad reviews at the time of their publication yet prove to be highly valued and influential later on. Book reviews and bestseller lists are relatively short-lived; their importance lies primarily in the information they provide about the reception of a certain text in a specific historical period.

FILM THEORY

In the twentieth century, **film theory** has developed into an independent discipline, while still engaging in a constant exchange with literary theory. The following survey of theoretical developments in film studies therefore in many ways parallels approaches in the history of literary theory.

The first major book on film studies, Hugo Münsterberg's (1863–1916) *The Photoplay* (1916), inaugurates **psychological film theory** by analyzing mental reactions and processes that take place when one watches a movie. Münsterberg and early film theorists regarded the spatial and temporal freedom of filmic storytelling to be very similar to the processes of the human imagination. A crucial observation for future film studies was their belief that inner, human reality can best be expressed through the medium of film.

Even though essentially rooted in a formalist–structuralist methodology, the concept of **montage** by the Russian director Sergei Eisenstein (1898–1948) is connected to Münsterberg's psychological reception theory. Eisenstein does not focus primarily on the portrayal of accurate reality in film, but instead he argues that contrapuntal cuts can create specific scenes in a viewer's mind. According to this concept of montage, one should not aim for seamless cuts but for contrast and confrontation instead. Based on these ideas, proponents of Russian-formalist film studies expressed a strong aversion toward "talkies." They argued that a realistic soundtrack, including dialogue, noises, and music, does not fit the montage concept of dialectic antitheses. In a similar vein, the German Gestalt psychologist Rudolf Arnheim (1904–2007) in the 1930s also argued that sound corrupts the artistic qualities of film. In sum, this period is indebted to a formalist approach to film, as it does not emphasize realistic representations but the film's potential for abstractions and illusions.

In contrast to the Russian formalists, the **realism movement** after World War II regarded *mise-en-scène* and screen layout as the basis of illusionary, filmic reality. Critics like Siegfried Kracauer (1889–1966) and André Bazin (1918–1958) argued that illusion is not created by the photographic capture of reality but by the intentional composition of a shot. Examples are found especially in silent movies, as well as in the techniques of famous directors like Orson Welles (1915–1985).

The French **"auteur" theory**, created and advocated by Andrew Sarris (1928–2012) and François Truffaut (1932–1984), analyzes specific characteristics of great filmmakers. Like author-oriented approaches, it views a director's oeuvre as an expression of his or her style. This could be problematic when discussing film. While authors are usually solely responsible for their works, a director is only one of many people (screenwriter, actors, make-up artists, producer, and so on) who contribute to the creation of a movie.

Because of these limitations, auteur theory soon lost its momentum, giving way to more film-specific approaches. Similar to text-oriented studies in literature, they are among the most productive fields of research of the second half of the twentieth century. Christian Metz's (1931–1993) *Film Language* (1963), for example, is the major proponent of **film semiotics**, which tries to explain film as a language-like, semiotic system, restricted by a number of media-specific codes that create filmic narration. Since the 1980s, literary and **film narratology** have been closely interconnected, as books such as David Bordwell's (1947–) *Narration in Film* (1985) or the works of Seymour Chatman (1928–) illustrate. Their major achievement is that they adapt and question literary concepts such as point of view or the role of the narrator for film studies.

Semiotics, deconstruction, and Marxist theory, as well as the psycho-analytical works of Jacques Lacan (1901–1981), have been shaping literary studies as well as film studies since the 1970s. Special importance must also be attributed to **feminist film studies**. In 1975, Laura Mulvey's (1941–) essay "Visual Pleasure and Narrative Cinema" triggered an extensive discussion about the "male gaze" in film. According to Mulvey, traditional Hollywood cinema is based on the psychoanalytical processes of a male viewer, consequently fragmenting and objectifying the female body into eroticized objects of the male gaze. In recent years, this approach has been further explored through questions of filmic gender construction, based on Judith Butler's publications on gender theory. The latest developments in film and media theory focus on narrative aspects of recent digital phenomena such as computer games or augmented reality simulation.

As this concise synopsis shows, literary studies uses a combination of theoretical approaches, gravitating around the dimensions of text, author, reader, and context. Film studies more or less shares these four dimensions however, it tends to use the terms media, auteur, and viewer in order to do justice to film as a medium related to, but independent from literature. Literature and film are in a constant dialogue, not only practically, but also in their theoretical framework, and must therefore be viewed as two mutually dependent forces.

5

WHERE AND HOW TO FIND SECONDARY LITERATURE

In the age of the Internet, it is necessary to preface a chapter on secondary literature with a few words of caution. Without doubt, the Internet has revolutionized and simplified the search for information in many everyday situations. However, despite its obvious advantages, this new tool is of limited service for literary studies, and it is important to be aware of these limitations before using the Internet as a source for scholarly research. Only a very small percentage of scholarly works, such as certain primary texts, monographs, or articles, are accessible on the Internet; most are still published solely in print. Even though there are journals that appear in an additional electronic version, many of them are available online for registered users only (i.e., your university has to subscribe to the specific service). The same holds true for other large databases of primary literary texts. The consequence for literary scholars is that they still have to do the bulk of their research in libraries, not in cyberspace. If professors consider research papers with sources taken predominantly from the Internet to be amateurish and untrustworthy, this does not necessarily mean that they oppose current technological developments on principle. It is much more likely that their negative evaluation of a student's work is due to its lack of scholarly foundation and insufficient research into secondary sources for the paper.

Another mistake could be that you do not properly evaluate the quality of an Internet resource. Assessing online secondary material is difficult not only for the beginner but also for advanced students or researchers. In general, you can apply the following basic rules for evaluation: If the article you find on the Internet comes from a major database, such as *Project Muse* or *JSTOR*, you can be almost certain that the text you retrieve is, in principle, very likely to be a good source. These large databases give online access to several hundred scholarly journals in the field, most of which are also available in printed form from major university presses. Almost all of these journals are peer-reviewed, which means, first of all, they have a general editor and an editorial board vouching for the quality of the articles. If you find articles on the Internet outside of these major journal databases, look for the same criteria: an editor or editorial board, guaranteeing the quality and high standards of the publication, and, ideally, some indication that the article underwent a peer-reviewed process. In this case, the web source makes clear that the text passed through a process of evaluation by other scholars in the field before it was accepted for (online) publication. This information is usually stated prominently on the homepage, identifying the website or online journal as a "peer-reviewed" or "refereed" source.

Finding secondary material is one of the first steps in preparing to write a research or term paper. Such projects, like any scholarly analysis of literary works, should ideally open a new perspective, cast light on a hitherto neglected aspect of a text, and establish a connection with the state of current research in the field. In order to meet these requirements, it is necessary to consult the existing secondary literature for available material on a certain topic, text, or author. The works of previous researchers in a field influence your own work by providing insights related to your topic and thus possibly supporting your particular arguments, or by delineating the boundaries of your topic. In some cases, a certain topic may have been sufficiently dealt with or treated in much the same way as you have in mind. In such instances, it is necessary to rethink the entire approach or, in the worst case, abandon the project entirely.

But what are the characteristics of a well-researched scholarly paper? Most term papers for college or university courses require a clear-cut topic, focusing on a certain aspect of a text or author. When doing research for a lower-level seminar paper, it is usually sufficient to consult the subject index of the departmental or university library catalogue for the monographic (i.e., book-length) secondary literature on a certain topic. For more elaborate projects – such as master's theses, dissertations, and essays to be published in scholarly journals – it is necessary to compile as complete a list of secondary literature as possible. In these advanced research projects, it is important to incorporate the results of other researchers and to ensure that one's own findings are original and hitherto unpublished.

Secondary sources include articles and essays, and book reviews, as well as "notes" (very short essays on a narrowly defined topic), which are all predominantly published in scholarly journals. As with other academic fields of research, literature journals publish the latest and most up-to-date results in article form. Essays or articles are often collected in "anthologies," which focus on a specific topic, mostly compiled and published by an editor. A collection of essays in honor of a well-known scholar is called a *Festschrift*. A book-length publication, usually by one author, dealing with one specific topic only, goes by the term *monograph*. Most dissertations and scientific publications in a university context can be attributed to this latter group.

Each philology (i.e., the study of the literature and linguistics of a particular language) has bibliographical reference books or databases that can be used to search for further literature. For the study of all modern languages, such as German and Romance languages, and, in particular, for literatures in English, the *MLA International Bibliography*, compiled by the Modern Language Association (MLA), is the standard reference work. This bibliography has been on the market since 1921 and indexes several thousand new pieces of secondary literature published every year.

Most large university and departmental libraries have the *MLA International Bibliography* in its printed edition and additionally provide access to the accompanying online database. In order to find out what has been published on the novel *The Handmaid's Tale* (1985) by the Canadian author Margaret Atwood, for example, all you have to do is enter the name of the author together with the title of the literary text or a subject keyword, and the result page will list all entries of secondary literature on the required item. Overleaf is a sample entry for the above online search on Margaret Atwood. The abbreviations on the left margin stand for: TI = title, AU = author(s), SO = source,

IS = International Standard Serial Number, LA = language, PT = publication type, PY = publication year, DE = descriptors.

```
TI:    Margaret Atwood's The Handmaid's Tale: A
       Contextual Dystopia
AU:    Ketterer,-David
SO:    Science-Fiction-Studies (SFS), Greencastle, IN.
       1989 July; 16(2 (48)): 209-217.
       IS: 0091-7729
LA:    English
PT:    journal-article
PY:    1989
DE:    Canadian-literature; 1900-1999; Atwood,-
       Margaret;
       The-Handmaid's-Tale; novel-; dystopian-novel;
       treatment of historicity
```

The individual references of the *MLA Bibliography* contain rudimentary information about the contents and topic of the secondary text; most importantly, however, they provide the dates and references you will need for the successful retrieval of secondary literature (which can either be essays or book-length studies). In the example above, the title (TI) of the essay ("Margaret Atwood's *The Handmaid's Tale*: A Contextual Dystopia") is mentioned first, then the name of the author (AU) of the essay (Ketterer, David), followed by the name of the journal or anthology (SO) where the essay was published (*Science Fiction Studies*) together with the year, volume, and page numbers of the journal (1989 July; 16 (2 [48]): 209–217). For book publications, the place of publication and the publisher are also listed. In addition, the field descriptor (DE) provides brief information about the content and topic of the secondary text. These keywords offer a first quick insight into the relevance of a secondary text to your own research.

If your library does not subscribe to the online version of the *MLA Bibliography*, you will have to consult the printed edition. This can be very time-consuming, since you have to check every annual volume of the bibliography individually. The *Subject Index* of the printed bibliography permits you to search for secondary literature on a variety of topics, including subjects such as "feminist literary criticism," "detective fiction," or "utopias." The *Author Index* is divided into national literatures and periods, listing the secondary literature that has been published on individual literary texts in the course of a certain year. For example, in order to search for articles and books published on the novel *Mrs Dalloway* (1925) by the English author Virginia Woolf, you have to look up the section "English literature" and the further subdivision "contemporary" in the individual annual volumes. Under the author's name, you will find a list of secondary sources published in that year on Woolf's respective literary works. Here is a sample search result from the 1956 volume:

```
Baldanza, Frank. "Clarissa Dalloway's 'Party
Consciousness.' " MFS, 11, 24-30.
```

If you need a complete list of secondary literature about an author or text, it is necessary to consult all annual volumes by repeating the process described above. The *MLA International Bibliography* goes back to the year 1921 – in our example, you would have to check the volumes from 1925 onward, since Woolf's *Mrs Dalloway* was published in that year.

Although the *MLA International Bibliography* is the most comprehensive reference work for modern languages and literatures and is usually sufficient for the needs of the beginner, it does not, of course, list *all* published items of secondary literature. Therefore, many university libraries offer facilities that grant the researcher additional access to extensive international, computerized databases and bibliographies. This complex search method is of little interest to the beginner and probably only worthwhile in the context of a larger research project, such as a thesis or dissertation.

An easy and fast way to find book-length studies on a specific topic that are not included in the online version of the *MLA International Bibliography* is to use the online catalogues of large research libraries such as the Library of Congress or the British Library. Most universities also provide links to catalogues such as *Online Public Access Catalogue (OPAC)* or *Online Computer Library Center (OCLC)*, which is also referred to as *OCLC WorldCat*. These networks allow you to screen a large number of international library catalogues simultaneously by simply filing one search. The program then systematically checks the different library holdings for the requested keywords.

For larger research projects that require complete – or nearly so – lists of secondary literature, it is indispensable to consult other printed or computerized general bibliographical sources or reference works that specialize in certain areas. The best guidebook to these sources is James L. Harner's *Literary Research Guide: An Annotated Listing of Reference Sources in English Literary Studies*, 5th ed. (New York: The Modern Language Association, 2008).

Once you have found references to secondary literature in the *MLA Bibliography* (or any other standard reference work), you can begin to search for this material in the departmental or university library. If it is necessary to use books or journals that are not available at your home institution, there is the option of ordering them at the main university library through the interlibrary loan system. Moreover, certain articles that you come across during your research may be available online. In such cases, you should definitely make use of these sources and cite them in your paper as electronic documents. How these and other types of secondary material are documented correctly in a scholarly paper will be the focus of the next chapter.

6

HOW TO WRITE A RESEARCH PAPER

To write a successful seminar paper or scholarly essay in the field of literature, you should observe a few conventions. Apart from the requirements of an accurate critical apparatus, which will be discussed later in this chapter, these basic rules mainly concern the **structural organization** of your research paper. Most importantly, it has to be logically organized and contain an introductory paragraph, a main part, and a conclusion.

The first or **introductory paragraph** fulfills several functions: the initial sentence or sentences should lead the reader to the topic by moving from more general statements on the overall subject matter to the actual focus of the paper. A feasible strategy is to depart from what is commonly known to the reader and then highlight the new and particular aspects that the paper will contribute to the state of research in the field. These original contributions are pointed out in the **thesis statement**, which should be part of the introductory paragraph and serve the reader as a first orientation concerning the content, methodology, and structure of your paper.

One part of the thesis statement has to briefly define the specific focus of the paper, and here it is crucial to narrow down the **topic** in a sensible and practicable way. Good scholarly papers are characterized by a clearly and convincingly focused topic. For example, there is little use in choosing a topic as undifferentiated as "Christine de Pizan's

The Book of the City of Ladies" for a seminar paper. Taking into consideration the numerous publications on this particular piece of literature, it is essential to concentrate on one specific aspect for analyzing the text, for example "Christine de Pizan's *The Book of the City of Ladies* as a Predecessor of Modern Feminist Literary Theory." Of course, you should not select the focus of the paper indiscriminately. On the contrary, ideally, the paper tackles a new as well as central aspect of the text.

An additional part of the thesis statement explains how you approach your topic (i.e., which **method** you use in your analysis). After reading this part, the reader should be able to associate the paper with a theoretical and methodological school or approach, similar to the ones discussed in Chapter 4. In the concrete case of the example mentioned above, the approach combines biographical facts and selected passages of Pizan's book with central aspects of feminist literary criticism.

Furthermore, the introductory paragraph gives an idea of what aspects of the topic are presented in what order. This **road map** makes the structure of the paper transparent and comprehensible from the very beginning and thereby provides the reader with a basic sense of orientation. In the given example, you could argue, for instance, that you will first document Pizan's personal position on literature about women, then summarize some of the central aspects of twentieth-century feminist approaches, and finally show how Pizan's positions coincide with these recent feminist debates.

Naturally, these individual parts of the thesis statement cannot always be presented separately, since they are often intricately interwoven with each other. For example, the topic may suggest the methodology, or the road map and the theoretical approach might be interconnected. Therefore, it will be advisable at times to combine topic and approach, or methodology and road map. In what manner you will actually render these three aspects of the thesis statement in the introductory paragraph depends largely on the individual paper. However, it is essential that all three aspects are clearly stated and comprehensible for the reader.

To sum up, the introductory paragraph briefly outlines the topic, methodology, and structure of your paper. In order to check whether you have written an informative introductory paragraph, you should ask yourself the following questions:

1   *What* is the paper about?
2   *How* (i.e., with what method) do I approach the topic?
3   *When* in the course of the paper am I dealing with which issues?

If you are able to answer the questions *what?*, *how?*, and *when?* in your introduction, you will most likely provide a thesis statement that informs the reader about the choice of your subject matter, your methodological approach, and the sequence of your arguments. Here is a possible introductory paragraph:

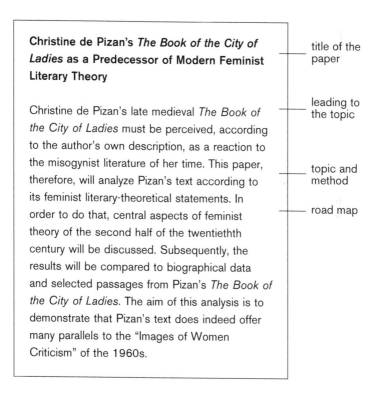

Christine de Pizan's *The Book of the City of Ladies* as a Predecessor of Modern Feminist Literary Theory ——— title of the paper

Christine de Pizan's late medieval *The Book of the City of Ladies* must be perceived, according to the author's own description, as a reaction to the misogynist literature of her time. This paper, therefore, will analyze Pizan's text according to its feminist literary-theoretical statements. In order to do that, central aspects of feminist theory of the second half of the twentiethth century will be discussed. Subsequently, the results will be compared to biographical data and selected passages from Pizan's *The Book of the City of Ladies*. The aim of this analysis is to demonstrate that Pizan's text does indeed offer many parallels to the "Images of Women Criticism" of the 1960s.

——— leading to the topic

——— topic and method

——— road map

Every subsequent **paragraph** or section of the main part of your paper should be a self-contained argument that develops one particular aspect of the overall topic. Here, it is crucial that every paragraph has a **topic sentence** that highlights the main idea of the paragraph and establishes a connection to the overall topic of the paper (i.e., the thesis statement). Equally important is the proper placement of a paragraph within the structure of the entire paper. The sequence of the individual paragraphs should be logical and comply with the sequence of argumentation that you established in your road map.

Transitions from one paragraph to the next enhance the inner coherence of the paper and guide the reader when advancing through your arguments. Ideally, one paragraph should connect with the next paragraph. The easiest way to achieve this is to incorporate a transitional phrase in the topic sentence at the beginning of each new paragraph. This way, the topic sentence not only introduces a new idea, but also links the idea of the new paragraph to the previous one. By smoothly leading the reader through your arguments, this technique increases the logic of your paper and thereby becomes one of the cornerstones of lucid writing in general. Here is a sample paragraph from the main part of a paper:

Using modern feminist literary theory for the analysis of this medieval book is not an arbitrary methodological decision. Many literary documents, as well as Pizan's own biography, prove that the author was engaged in a heated scholarly discussion about the literary portrayal of women at the end of the fourteenth century.	topic sentence, connecting to previous paragraph
Additionally, Pizan's criticism of a patriarchal image of women in the works of male authors shows strong similarities to the "Images of Women Criticism" of the 1960s.	further discussion of one aspect of the topic sentence

The first and most obvious visual signs of badly organized writing are single-sentence paragraphs. If almost every sentence of your paper forms a paragraph of its own, you have to improve the organization and logical structure of your text. This can be achieved by connecting single sentences in units of thought with identifiable topic sentences so that they make up coherent paragraphs. As a kind of checklist for a successful paragraph, you can ask yourself the following questions:

1 Does the paragraph develop a single, coherent aspect of the overall topic or argument?
2 Does the paragraph begin and end with smooth and logical transitions?
3 Is the paragraph positioned correctly within the overall paper?

Moreover, also turn a critical eye toward possible subchapters. Quite frequently, papers contain so many headings that almost every paragraph becomes a separate chapter, which definitely means taking things too far for a seminar paper of less than ten pages. The central problem in this respect is that many people think they can circumnavigate transitions between individual units of thought by simply inserting subchapter headings. However, a subheading can only fulfill the function of introducing a new aspect. It cannot link or connect two paragraphs or units of thought and will therefore leave the reader puzzled by the breaks in the overall flow of your argumentation. To prevent this from happening, it is helpful if you read through your text while leaving out all (sub)chapter headings. This will reveal whether you have organized the text in a coherent and comprehensible way, whether the sequence of individual sections flows naturally, and, most importantly, whether you have supported your paragraphs with appropriate transitional links.

At the end of the paper, a **concluding paragraph** should briefly and concisely summarize the most important results of your discussion. This is your final opportunity to remind the reader once more of your overall line of argumentation by repeating the thesis statement and by giving a short summary of your results. Furthermore, good concluding paragraphs contain a kind of outlook that transcends the actual findings of your research and places them in a wider context. For example, you could point out the exemplary nature of your paper and how your approach would lead to valuable results when applied to other works. Basically, the outlook should expand the focus and context of your paper, thus demonstrating that your approach could possibly have wider implications that go beyond the limitations of the paper at hand. Here is a possible concluding paragraph:

Naturally, it is not possible to regard all of the book's complex aspects from only one modern feminist point of view. Nevertheless, Pizan's biography, as well as the structure and content of her work, seems to call for such an approach.	repetition of the thesis statement
Through an overview of the most important realizations of modern feminism, as well as the discussion of crucial examples of the text, it has been confirmed that Pizan's main concern can indeed be seen as a predecessor of the "Images of Women Criticism" of the 1960s.	summary of the results
Based on these results, one may conclude that any feminist literary discussion must be sparked by criticism of prevalent patriarchal images of women – be it in the late Middle Ages or in the second half of the twentieth century.	outlook

The best way to check if your introduction and conclusion are efficient is to read only the first and last paragraphs of your paper. If these two passages mention all of the central questions and methodological steps as well as provide a summary of the major results, then they fulfill their functions. In other words, these two sections of your paper should put in a nutshell the basic information about content, methodology, and results.

You might rightly add that not all published scholarly articles observe this rather rigid structure. However, most college courses in England and America require these composition guidelines. For the beginner, this technique has the advantage that it provides clear-cut rules for enhancing the effectiveness and readability of texts by stressing unity and logic. Although these rules may appear simple in theory, they are difficult to put into practice. It is therefore essential not to give up and to persist in trying to organize your paper according to these guidelines.

Every academic discipline follows further conventions that are concerned with the documentation of sources, a feature of scholarly writing that is often subsumed under the term **critical apparatus**.

In the field of English and American literature, there are particularly strict rules for documentation, which have been published in a handbook by the aforementioned Modern Language Association, the largest and most influential association of literary scholars worldwide. This MLA style sheet allows consistent citation and documentation of sources (e.g., bibliographies). Therefore, it serves as the guideline for all major presses and journals publishing on English literature and is standard in most literature departments around the world. The following guidelines are simplified versions of the most important rules that are explained in great detail in the *MLA Handbook for Writers of Research Papers* (7th ed., 2009) (not to be confused with the *MLA International Bibliography*).

Scholarly writing in literary studies is characterized by a consistent and accurate critical apparatus that must contain all primary and secondary texts used. This should enable the reader to retrace the sources of quotations and paraphrases at any time. Therefore, it is vital to collect all necessary information concerning a text, including the author or editor's name, the title of the text, the journal or anthology containing the essay, the year of publication, the volume, and the page numbers. For books, the place of publication and the name of the publisher must be mentioned, too. This information usually appears on the first pages of a book or in the masthead of a journal.

The literature used in a paper can be incorporated either in the form of direct **quotations** or as **paraphrases**: short passages from primary texts are usually integrated as direct quotations, larger units of meaning as paraphrases. Secondary literature is generally paraphrased, except for important, fundamental statements that are sometimes quoted word for word. Short, direct quotations of less than four lines are integrated into the running text, marked by quotation marks at the beginning and end. Longer citations form a separate paragraph, indented on the left, without quotation marks. If a passage is not quoted in its entirety, the left-out parts are replaced by three periods in square brackets [. . .].

If a scholarly paper refers to a certain piece of primary or secondary literature, a **parenthetical citation** gives the bibliographical reference. After the quote or the paraphrase, the corresponding page number is listed together with either the title and page reference (*Anatomy of Criticism* 22), or the author's name and page number (Frye 22). If several works by one author are used, in addition to the author's name and page number the title must be listed; for example, (Greenblatt, *New World Encounters* 75). Full documentation of sources is provided only in the bibliography.

Another aspect of many scientific papers is footnotes, which serve a dual function: first, they permit you to expand on a thought that is not directly relevant to the general argument in the text; second, they allow you to refer to further sources for additional background reading. This is an example of such a bibliographical footnote:

[1] For a different approach, see Frye 56.

All of the pieces of parenthetical information in the text, or in footnotes, refer to the **bibliography** at the end of a paper, which lists all primary and secondary literature used in alphabetical order. The reader can thus easily identify the sources of the works cited. Therefore, when documenting sources in footnotes or bibliographies, it is necessary to provide all of the bibliographical information in the correct sequence of "who," "what," "where," "when" (author, title, place of publication, name of publisher, and year of publication). Below, you will find some basic examples for the citation of different kinds of sources.

Book publication by one author

Last Name, First Name. *Title of the Text.* Place of Publication: Name of Publisher, Year of Publication. Print.

Frye, Northrop. *Anatomy of Criticism: Four Essays.* Princeton, NJ: Princeton University Press, 1957. Print.

Because of the alphabetical order of the entries in the bibliography, the last name of the author comes before the first name. In order to visually distinguish a book from an essay or article, the title is written in italics. Information on the place of publication, as well as the date of publication can be found on the first few pages of a book. In order to make it easier for the user to identify the type of source, the newest edition of the *MLA Handbook* suggests that, at the end of each entry, the media format of the source should be mentioned; for example, "Print" or "Web."

Book publication by two authors

Gilbert, Sandra M., and Susan Gubar. *The Madwoman in the Attic: The Woman Writer and the Nineteenth-Century Imagination*. New Haven, CT: Yale University Press, 1979. Print.

If the titles of scholarly works consist of two parts, the subtitle is usually separated from the title by a colon (:), as in the preceding example.

Essay in a journal

Last Name, First Name. "Title of Essay." *Name of Journal* Volume and Issue Number (Year of Publication): Page Numbers. Print.

Booth, Wayne C. "Kenneth Burke's Way of Knowing." *Critical Inquiry* 1 (1974): 1–22. Print.

Bibliographical entries have to contain the exact page numbers (from beginning to end) of the quoted essay. In contrast to book publications and anthologies, the name of the publisher and place of publication are never provided for journal articles.

Anthology by one author

Greenblatt, Stephen, Ed. *New World Encounters*. Berkeley, CA: University of California Press, 1993. Print.

In recent years an increasing number of primary and secondary sources have become available in electronic form, either on CD-ROM, DVD, or online. The rules for citing these new media are similar to those for printed publications, and it is essential to follow them in an equally consistent manner. You generally have to include author, editor, title – or, if it is a film or DVD, the director and the leading actors. When referring to CD-ROMs, you have to include "CD-ROM" before mentioning the place of publication. If it is a DVD, this has to be mentioned at the end of the entry:

CD-ROM as an entry in a bibliography

Shakespeare, William. *Macbeth*. Ed. A. R. Braunmuller. New York: Voyager, 1994. CD-ROM.

DVD as an entry in a bibliography

It's a Wonderful Life. Dir. Frank Capra. Perf. James Stewart, Donna Reed, Lionel Barrymore, and Thomas Mitchell. 1946. Republic, 2001. DVD.

Online articles and books are cited like their printed counterparts. However, it is necessary to include the date when you accessed the source. Since online sources can be easily modified, this exact date will document which version of the page you refer to in your paper. In front of this date, "Web" is added to specify the format. The uniform resource locator (URL) (i.e., the Internet address) should only be added if the website is difficult to find.

Online article as an entry in a bibliography

Tolson, Nancy. "Making Books Available: The Role of Early Libraries, Librarians, and Booksellers in the Promotion of African American Children's Literature." *African American Review* 32 (1998): 9–16. *JSTOR.* Web. 1 Oct. 2012.

The examples above cover the most common types of entries in bibliographies. Detailed instructions for documenting book reviews, translations, new editions, films, online publications, or CDs can be found in the *MLA Handbook*. In order to find out how to cite these special cases, it is necessary to consult the detailed alphabetical index at the end of the handbook.

It used to require some experience to be able to transform the reference information contained in articles and books into accurate bibliographical entries and a consistent list of works cited. However, today most major online catalogues or databases, such as *WorldCat* or the *MLA International Bibliography*, let you directly **export entries** in the citation format of your choice. For example, when you look up a book or an article in the *MLA Bibliography*, you get a list of all the relevant bibliographical information in a catalogue-like entry, separating out author, title, journal name, issue number, pages, and so on. Instead of copying and pasting this information, or typing it in manually from the printed source, you can simply export the entire entry in the specific citation format you need. Most databases let you choose among the most common style sheets, including MLA, Harvard, Chicago, and

APA. In your case, you will most likely need MLA style and therefore export your entry in that format. This way, you automatically receive a relatively accurate MLA-conforming citation of a given book or article. Most people, when they have to create a bibliographical entry – even if they have the actual copy of the source in hand – search it in a database and export the reference in the desired citation format. Compared with doing it the old-fashioned manual way, importing minimizes the risk of typing errors or inconsistent citations.

If you want to do all of your citing and referencing – not just your bibliography – in an automated way, then you should use **citation management software**. Professional programs, such as *EndNote* or the free open-source software *Zotero*, let you create your private database into which you can download bibliographical entries in the citation format of your choice from web pages, databanks, and online library catalogues. While composing your essay in your word-processing program, the citation manager allows you to integrate bibliographic information in the format of your choice. For example, you start by specifying that you need your paper to conform to MLA style. Whenever you want to cite a specific source in your paper, you just click on this particular reference in the program's database and it will automatically insert that reference as a parenthetical citation, and, at the same time, add this entry to your list of works cited (i.e., your final bibliography). If you later decide that you need your paper to follow a different style sheet, one mouse click will change the entire critical apparatus of your essay from MLA style, which uses parenthetical documentation, to, for example, Chicago style, which relies on footnotes instead. Despite the high degree of automation, or maybe because of it, these programs might, in a small number of instances, produce minor errors. It is therefore absolutely essential to check the results of the bibliography for possible inconsistencies or little flaws before you finalize the document and submit your essay.

These programs not only help you to manage your citations, but also let you link the digital copies of the primary and secondary sources you use with your private bibliographical database. This way, you can cite a source and also quickly pull up the text as a PDF file without having to search for it on your computer. As helpful as these programs are in storing data and creating consistent citations, they have no impact on the creative process of your writing or the originality of your argument, which is, of course, the main goal of a research paper. In other words, citation software can be very handy but is no more than a helpful tool to speed up your writing and data management.

Example of a title page

Jones 1   pages
                                           numbered

Chris Jones
Professor Lement
English 410 Contemporary Utopian Fiction
October 14, 2013

                                           book title in
                                           italics

Gender in Ursula Le Guin's *The Dispossessed*

    Until recently much scholarship on Le Guin's fiction   first line of
has tended to take one of two forms. On the one hand,   every
there are studies which analyze the structural features   paragraph
of Le Guin's fiction without linking her narrative   indented
innovations to contemporary feminist debates. On the
other hand, there are gender-specific approaches,
which have taken their bearings from a critique of the
perceived limitations of her female characters and her
inclination toward an overall "maleness" in her portrayal
of androgynes. The following reading of Ursula Le
Guin's *The Dispossessed* tries to combine these two
trends in scholarship: first, to analyze the gender-
specific aspects of her novel and then, in a second
step, to connect them to the overall structural features
of the text.

    Although Le Guin took feminist accusations   double quotes
seriously – and in her essay "Is Gender Necessary?   for essays
Redux," apologized for not having explored "androgyny   and short
from a woman's point of view as well as a man's"   stories
(Le Guin, "Gender" 7)[1] – she also hinted at the
intricate gender pattern in her novel. She stated that
the androgynes

                                                           longer quotes
    have no myth of process at all. Their calendar calls   as separate
    the current year always the Year One, and they   paragraphs
    count backward and forward from that. In this, it
    seems that what I was after again was a balance: three periods
    the […] linearity of the 'male', the pushing forward   to mark
    to the limit, […] and the circularity of the 'female'. elisions
    (Le Guin, *The Dispossessed* 12)   parenthetical
                                                           reference

    1 Le Guin, having to justify her male perspective,
clearly shows that the feminism of the 1970s and   bibliographical
1980s had little interest in concepts of maleness; also   footnote
see Moi 177–179.

Example of a page from a bibliography

List of works cited

Aristotle. *The Complete Works of Aristotle: The Revised Oxford Translation.* Ed. Jonathan Barnes. 2 vols. Princeton, NJ: Princeton University Press, 1984. Clayton, GA: InteLex, 1994. CD-ROM. — book on CD-ROM

Derrida, Jacques. *Of Grammatology.* Trans. Gayatri Chakravorty Spivak. Baltimore, MD: Johns Hopkins University Press, 1974. Print. — book translation

Child, L. Maria, Ed. *The Freedman's Book.* Boston, MA: Ticknor and Fields, 1866. Google Book Search, Web. 15 May 2008. — book online

It's a Wonderful Life. Dir. Frank Capra. Perf. James Stewart, Donna Reed, Lionel Barrymore, and Thomas Mitchell. 1946. Republic, 2001. DVD. — film, DVD

Le Guin, Ursula K. *The Dispossessed.* 1974. London: Grafton, 1986. Print. — book reprint

---. *The Left Hand of Darkness.* London: Macdonald, 1969. Print. — book by the same author

---. "Is Gender Necessary? Redux." *Dancing at the Edge of the World: Thoughts on Words, Women, Places.* New York: Grove, 1989. 7–16. Print. — essay in a book

Moi, Toril. *Sexual/Textual Politics.* 2nd ed. London, New York: Routledge, 2002. Print. — book reprint (2nd edition)

Showalter, Elaine. "Feminist Criticism in the Wilderness." *The New Feminist Criticism.* Ed. Elaine Showalter. London: Virago, 1985. 243–270. Print. — essay in anthology

Tolson, Nancy. "Making Books Available: The Role of Early Libraries, Librarians, and Booksellers in the Promotion of African American Children's Literature." *African American Review* 32 (1998): 9–16. JSTOR. Web. 1 Oct. 2013. — essay online

The above examples of a title page and a page from a bibliography illustrate some of the most important formatting and documentation guidelines for research or seminar papers. Since papers are designed to be corrected or reviewed by readers, double-spaced lines and generous margins on both sides of the text leave room for notes and comments. It is also important to include your name, the title of the paper, the instructor's name, and the name of the course on the first page or on a separate cover page.

Although the MLA style is the most popular one in the field of literary studies, it should be mentioned that it is not the only way to cite sources and format a paper. There are other style guides, such as the style sheet of the APA (American Psychological Association) or *The Chicago Manual of Style*. Your own university and professors will let you know which one they prefer, and whether there are any other rules to consider. Nevertheless, most scholarly papers follow MLA guidelines, and most publishers in literary studies require the MLA style sheet. Ultimately, though, publishing houses will often adjust the manuscripts to fit their own preferred format in the final publication.

SUGGESTIONS FOR FURTHER READING

The works mentioned below are basic study aids and reference books in the field of English-language literatures and can be found in most university and departmental libraries. The list is, of course, not intended to be comprehensive. Of the large number of available texts, only user-friendly works have been selected. Although general in scope, they nevertheless provide more focused information on particular topics than the chapters of this introduction.

Works marked with an asterisk (*) are recommended as a first choice of further reading for the beginner because of their conciseness and clarity. General reference works precede more focused texts in the list.

GENERAL LITERARY TERMINOLOGY

*M. H. Abrams and Geoffrey Galt Harpham, *A Glossary of Literary Terms*, 10th ed. (Boston, MA: Wadsworth Cengage Learning, 2012); 432 pp.

> This comprehensive reference book explains basic literary terminology, introduces the most important theoretical movements in literary criticism, and lists titles for further reading; it can be used as a concise study aid for the beginner and as a terminological reference work throughout one's studies of literature.

J. A. Cuddon, *Dictionary of Literary Terms and Literary Theory*, 4th ed. (New York: Penguin, 2011); 991 pp.

> This very comprehensive and inexpensive terminological dictionary provides additional information that goes beyond Abrams and Harpham's survey.

Encyclopedia of Literature and Criticism, Ed. Martin Coyle et al. (London: Routledge, 1993); 1328 pp.

> A collection of essays on important issues of literary studies with references for further reading. Besides traditional areas – periods, genres, and theories – approximately 100 pages are devoted to Anglophone literatures outside England and the United States.

AUTHORS AND WORKS

The Oxford Companion to English Literature, Ed. Margaret Drabble, 7th ed. (Oxford and New York: Oxford University Press, 2009); 1184 pp.

The Oxford Companion to American Literature, Ed. James D. Hart, 6th ed. (Oxford and New York: Oxford University Press, 1995); 800 pp.

> These comprehensive, alphabetically arranged reference works provide basic factual information about major English and American authors and literary texts.

International Literature in English: Essays on the Major Writers, Ed. Robert L. Ross (New York: Garland, 1991); 784 pp.

> Collection of survey essays on the most important writers of "Commonwealth literature" or "new literatures in English"; includes suggestions for further reading.

Encyclopedia of Post-Colonial Literatures in English, Ed. Eugene Benson and L. W. Conolly, 2 vols. (London: Routledge, 1994); each volume approx. 900 pp.

> An alphabetically arranged reference work on the major regions, authors, themes, and genres of literatures in English outside England and the United States with references to secondary sources.

LITERARY THEORY

The Norton Anthology of Theory and Criticism, Ed. Vincent B. Leitch, 2nd ed. (New York: Norton, 2010); 2624 pp.

Critical Theory Since Plato, Ed. Hazard Adams and Leroy Searle, 3rd ed. (Boston, MA: Thomson/Wadsworth, 2005); 1545 pp.

> Anthologies of representative primary texts of literary theory from classical antiquity to the present.

*Jeremy Hawthorn, *A Glossary of Contemporary Literary Theory*, 4th ed. (London and New York: Edward Arnold, 2000); 274 pp.

> Concise, alphabetically organized survey of the most important terms of postmodernist literary theory.

The Johns Hopkins Guide to Literary Theory and Criticism, Ed. Michael Groden, Martin Kreiswirth, and Imre Szeman, 2nd ed. (Baltimore, MD, and London: Johns Hopkins University Press, 2005); 985 pp.

Encyclopedia of Contemporary Literary Theory: Approaches, Scholars, and Terms, Ed. Irena R. Makaryk (Toronto, Buffalo, New York, and London: University of Toronto Press, 1993); 656 pp.

> Comprehensive, alphabetically arranged reference books with short essay-like entries on the most important movements, proponents, and terms in literary theory, as well as references to further literature.

*Peter Barry, *Beginning Theory: An Introduction to Literary and Cultural Theory*, 3rd ed. (Manchester and New York: Manchester University Press, 2009); 290 pp.

> Introduction to the most important theoretical developments in the twentieth century; suitable for beginners.

*Raman Selden, Peter Widdowson, and Peter Brooker, *A Reader's Guide to Contemporary Literary Theory*, 5th ed. (Harlow, NY: Pearson Longman, 2005); 302 pp.

Lois Tyson, *Critical Theory Today: A User-Friendly Guide*, 2nd ed. (New York: Routledge, 2006); 464 pp.

Lucid introductions to recent literary theory for the beginner. These books may be supplemented by:

Raman Selden, *Practicing Theory and Reading Literature: An Introduction* (Lexington, KY: University Press of Kentucky, 1989); 206 pp.

Lois Tyson, *Using Critical Theory: How to Read and Write about Literature*, 2nd ed. (New York: Routledge, 2011); 368 pp.

These introductory texts apply different critical approaches to major texts in order to illustrate the possibilities of various methodologies in sample interpretations.

Terry Eagleton, *Literary Theory: An Introduction*, 3rd ed. (Minneapolis, MN: University of Minnesota Press, 2008); 240 pp.

Widely used introduction to literary theory, which provides a thorough and accessible survey of the field.

Jonathan Culler, *Literary Theory: A Brief Insight* (New York: Sterling Publishing, 2009); 196 pp.

Very concise introductory outline of essential movements in literary theory.

Works on specific areas of literary theory

The following texts are introductions to specific areas of literary theory and are slightly more demanding than the surveys mentioned above.

Structuralist theory: Terence Hawkes, *Structuralism and Semiotics*, 2nd ed. (London and New York: Routledge, 2003); 176 pp.

Psychoanalytic literary theory: Elisabeth Wright, *Psychoanalytic Criticism: Theory in Practice* (London and New York: Methuen, 1987); 212 pp.

Marxist literary theory: Terry Eagleton, *Marxism and Literary Criticism*, 2nd ed. (London and New York: Routledge, 2002); 96 pp.

Deconstruction: Christopher Norris, *Deconstruction: Theory and Practice*, 3rd ed. (London and New York: Routledge, 2002); 234 pp.

Feminist literary theory: Toril Moi, *Sexual/Textual Politics*, 2nd ed. (London and New York: Routledge, 2002); 221 pp.

Reception theory: Robert C. Holub, *Reception Theory: A Critical Introduction* (London and New York: Routledge, 2003); 189 pp.

New historicism: Catherine Gallagher and Stephen Greenblatt, *Practicing New Historicism* (Chicago, IL: University of Chicago Press, 2001); 249 pp.

> Especially, the "Introduction" (1–19) offers an excellent overview of the methods and fields of New Historicism.

Postcolonial theory: Peter Childs and Patrick Williams, *An Introduction to Post-Colonial Theory* (London and New York: Prentice Hall, 2007); 240 pp.

Postcolonial studies: *Post-Colonial Studies: The Key Concepts*, Ed. Bill Ashcroft, Gareth Griffiths, and Helen Tiffin, 2nd ed. (London and New York: Routledge, 2007); 288 pp.

GENRES

Collections of primary literary texts

Literature Online (http://lion.chadwyck.co.uk)

> One of the most comprehensive full-text databases of English and American literature with numerous links to similar databases. Access is limited to subscribers.

The Norton Introduction to Literature, Ed. Alison Booth et al., 10th ed. (London and New York: Norton, 2005); 2360 pp.

> A collection of primary texts in English, of different genres and periods, with some additional terminological information, as well as guidelines for the interpretation of texts.

The Norton Anthology of English Literature, Ed. M. H. Abrams et al., 9th ed., 2 vols. (London and New York: Norton, 2012); each volume approx. 3000 pp.

The Norton Anthology of American Literature, Ed. Nina Baym et al., 8th ed., 2 vols. (London and New York: Norton, 2011); each volume approx. 2600 pp.

The Norton Anthology of Literature by Women: The Traditions in English, Ed. Sandra M. Gilbert and Susan Gubar, 3rd ed. (London and New York: Norton, 2007); 2452 pp.

> These three collections of primary texts in English provide a representative selection of works from different periods and genres. They are also a good means by which the beginner may judge which literary works are traditionally considered canonical (i.e., important texts in the field).

New Worlds of Literature: Writings from America's Many Cultures, Ed. Jerome Beaty and J. Paul Hunter, 2nd ed. (London and New York: Norton, 1994); 980 pp.

> An anthology of literary texts in English from the United States, Canada, and the Caribbean that deliberately shifts the emphasis from the "Anglo-Saxon" tradition to authors of different ethnic and cultural backgrounds.

Fiction

Paul Innes, *Epic* (London: Routledge, 2013); 160 pp.

> Traces the classical genre of the epic from its ancient roots to postmodernist adaptations.

*Jeremy Hawthorn, *Studying the Novel: An Introduction*, 6th ed. (New York: Bloomsbury, 2010); 240 pp.

> A very basic introduction to the history and the elements of the novel with references for further reading.

Shlomith Rimmon-Kenan, *Narrative Fiction: Contemporary Poetics*, 2nd ed. (London and New York: Routledge, 2002); 192 pp.

> Comprehensible introduction to the foundations of narrative theory for the beginner.

The Columbia History of the British Novel, Ed. John J. Richetti et al. (New York: Columbia University Press, 1994); 1064 pp.

The Columbia History of the American Novel, Ed. Emory Elliott (New York: Columbia University Press, 1991); 800 pp.

> Collections of essays on important novelists by literary historians.

Ian Watt, *The Rise of the Novel: Studies in Defoe, Richardson and Fielding* (first published in 1957; Whitefish, MT: Kessinger Publishing, 2010); 320 pp.

Classic study on the origins of the English novel and its socio-cultural background in the eighteenth century.

Michael McKeon, *The Origins of the English Novel, 1600-1740*, 2nd ed. (Baltimore, MD: The Johns Hopkins University Press, 2002); 560 pp.

Recent standard study of the early English novel. In contrast to Watt's book, it argues that the genre evolved before the eighteenth century.

Poetry

The New Princeton Encyclopedia of Poetry and Poetics, Ed. Alex Preminger et al., rev. ed. (Princeton, NJ: Princeton University Press, 1993); 1382 pp.

Standard encyclopedic reference work on the major areas of poetry and literary theory.

The Norton Introduction to Poetry, Ed. J. Paul Hunter et al., 8th ed. (New York: Norton, 2002); 670 pp.

Accessible primary text anthology with important poems of the Anglophone traditions combined with helpful discussions of all major aspects of poetry in general.

*Laurence Perrine et al., *Perrine's Sound and Sense: An Introduction to Poetry*, 13th ed. (Boston, MA: Thomson/Wadsworth, 2010); 480 pp.

Donald Hall, *To Read a Poem*, 2nd ed. (Fort Worth, TX: Harcourt Brace Jovanovich, 1992); 432 pp.

Both are introductions to the elements and terminology of poetry with numerous examples suitable for beginners.

Modern Poems: An Introduction to Poetry, Ed. Richard Ellmann and Robert O'Clair, 2nd ed. (New York: Norton, 1989); 526 pp.

This anthology of essential English and American poetry of the nineteenth and twentieth centuries provides biographical information, explanations of texts, and a brief 50-page overview of basic poetic elements.

Cleanth Brooks and Robert Penn Warren, *Understanding Poetry*, 4th ed. (New York: Harcourt Brace Jovanovich, 1988); 602 pp.

> Classic text on the structuralist analysis of poetry, which, despite its rigid approach, offers a good survey of the terminological and formal aspects of poetry as well as illustrative readings of poems.

The Columbia History of American Poetry, Ed. Jay Parini (New York: Columbia University Press, 1993); 894 pp.

> A collection of essays on major American poets by leading literary historians.

Drama

The Cambridge Guide to Theatre, Ed. Martin Banham, 2nd ed. (Cambridge: Cambridge University Press, 1995); 1247 pp.

> Illustrated, alphabetically arranged reference work with brief entries on the major playwrights, plays, and dramatic terms.

*Robert Cohen, *Theatre: Brief Version*, 9th ed. (New York: McGraw-Hill, 2010); 327 pp.

Robert W. Corrigan, *The World of Theatre*, 2nd ed. (Madison, WI: Brown & Benchmark, 1992); 408 pp.

> Richly illustrated, comprehensive introductions to drama that go beyond the narrow English and American contexts and include aspects of directing and performance.

Martin Esslin, *An Anatomy of Drama* (New York: Hill & Wang, 1977); 125 pp.

> Very concise and accessible first survey of the most important aspects of drama.

Phyllis Hartnoll, *Theatre: A Concise History*, 3rd ed. (London: Thames & Hudson, 1998); 304 pp.

> Richly illustrated general overview of the historical development of drama covering the whole range of text, directing, and performance.

Simon Trussler, *The Cambridge Illustrated History of British Theatre* (Cambridge: Cambridge University Press, 2000); 404 pp.

Comprehensive, richly illustrated history of theater in England from its beginnings in the Middle Ages to the 1990s.

Film

IMDb – Internet Movie Database (www.imdb.com)

Largest global database on almost every publicly released movie, including information on actors, directors, reviews, or plots.

Film encyclopedias

International Dictionary of Films and Filmmakers, Ed. Nicolet V. Elert et al., 4th ed., 4 vols. (Detroit and New York: St. James Press, 2000); each volume approx. 1250 pp.

Very comprehensive reference work on different aspects of international film with individual volumes on films, directors, actors and actresses, and scriptwriters and producers.

Ephraim Katz, *The Film Encyclopedia*, 6th ed. (New York: Harper Colins, 2008); 1584 pp.

Affordable, alphabetically organized reference book on the most important terms, figures, and works in the film industry and film criticism.

Susan Hayward, *Cinema Studies: The Key Concepts*, 3rd ed. (London and New York: Routledge, 2006); 586 pp.

Alphabetical reference work on basic terms, names, and concepts in film studies and film theory.

Leonard Maltin, *Movie and Video Guide* (New York: Signet, n.d.); 1580 pp.

Very inexpensive, annually published (and therefore up-to-date) reference work on the most important movies.

The Oxford Guide to Film Studies, Ed. John Hill and Pamela Church Gibson (Oxford and New York: Oxford University Press, 1998); 624 pp.

Standard reference work with articles on central aspects of film studies.

Introductions to film

*David Bordwell and Kristin Thompson, *Film Art: An Introduction*, 9th ed. (New York: McGraw-Hill, 2010); 544 pp.

Louis Giannetti, *Understanding Movies*, 12th ed. (Boston, MA: Allyn Bacon, 2010); 576 pp.

Bruce F. Kawin, *How Movies Work* (Berkeley, CA: University of California Press, 1992); 574 pp.

These three books provide lucid introductions to the history, genres, and elements of film with many examples and illustrations.

James Monaco, *How to Read a Film: Movies, Media, and Beyond*, 4th ed. (New York and Oxford: Oxford University Press, 2009); 736 pp.

A classic introduction to film.

Film history

*David Parkinson, *History of Film* (New York: Thames & Hudson, 2002); 264 pp.

Very concise and richly illustrated survey of the history of international film.

Gerald Mast and Bruce F. Kawin, *A Short History of the Movies*, 11th ed. (New York: Pearson Longman, 2010); 784 pp.

David Bordwell and Kristin Thompson, *Film History: An Introduction*, 3rd ed. (New York: McGraw-Hill, 2009); 800 pp.

David A. Cook, *A History of Narrative Film*, 3rd ed. (London and New York: W. W. Norton, 1996); 1,087 pp.

All three books are comprehensive and accessible surveys of the history of international film.

Film adaptations

**Film and Literature: An Introduction and Reader*, Ed. Timothy Corrigan, 2nd ed. (New York: Routledge, 2011); 488 pp.

An anthology of major theoretical texts on the interrelation of film and literature, together with some introductory explanations.

Thomas Leitch, *Film Adaptation and Its Discontents: From* Gone With the Wind *to* The Passion of the Christ (Baltimore, MD: Johns Hopkins University Press, 2007); 372 pp.

Offers a good, general overview of the interaction between the different media of literature and film.

Seymour Chatman, *Coming to Terms: The Rhetoric of Narrative in Fiction and Film* (Ithaca, NY: Cornell University Press, 1990); 240 pp.

Overview of the interaction between film and literature from a narratological perspective.

Adaptations: From Text to Screen, Screen to Text, Ed. Deborah Cartmell and Imelda Whelehan (London: Routledge, 1999); 247 pp.

Exemplary analyses of filmed literature.

The Encyclopedia of Novels into Film, Ed. John C. Tibbetts and James M. Welsh, 2nd ed. (New York: Facts on File, 2005); 586 pp.

Useful, alphabetically organized reference work of important novels and their filmed versions.

Film theory
Robert Stam, *Film Theory: An Introduction* (Oxford: Blackwell, 2000); 392 pp.

Survey of basic film theory in the twentieth century. May be combined with the following text.

Film and Theory: An Anthology, Ed. Robert Stam and Toby Miller (Oxford: Blackwell, 2000); 880 pp.

Thematically arranged selection of "primary texts" in film theory of the past decade.

Critical Dictionary of Film and Television Theory, Ed. Roberta E. Pearson and Philip Simpson (London: Routledge, 2001); 498 pp.

Alphabetically organized reference book including fundamental terms, names, and concepts of film theory.

Film Theory and Criticism: Introductory Readings, Ed. Gerald Mast et al., 7th ed. (New York and Oxford: Oxford University Press, 2009); 912 pp.

A collection of illustrative "primary texts" in film theory and film criticism from the birth of the medium to the present.

LITERARY HISTORY

*G. C. Thornley and Gwyneth Roberts, *An Outline of English Literature*, rev. ed. (London and New York: Longman, 1994); 216 pp.

*Peter B. High, *An Outline of American Literature* (London and New York: Longman, 1986); 256 pp.

Both books offer concise, illustrated surveys of the most important periods, authors, and works in British and American literature from their origins to the present. They are characterized by illustrative readings of texts that shed light on larger mechanisms while avoiding long lists of dates and facts.

Hans-Peter Wagner, *A History of British, Irish and American Literature* (Trier: Wissenschaftlicher Verlag Trier, 2003); 550 pp.

Illustrated one-volume survey of the periods of British, Irish, and American literary history, their main representatives and texts.

Andrew Sanders, *Short Oxford History of English Literature*, 3rd ed. (Oxford: Oxford University Press, 2004); 766 pp.

The Oxford Illustrated History of English Literature, Ed. Pat Rogers (Oxford and New York: Oxford University Press, 2001); 528 pp.

Peter Conn, *Literature in America: An Illustrated History* (Cambridge: Cambridge University Press, 1989); 587 pp.

Three accessible, illustrated literary histories that cover the major periods of English and American literature.

A Literary History of England, Ed. Albert C. Baugh, 2nd ed. (London: Routledge, 1967); 1876 pp.

Classic literary history that is still very helpful for reference and as an initial overview of the older periods of British literature.

Columbia Literary History of the United States, Ed. Emory Elliott (New York: Columbia University Press, 1988); 1263 pp.

Single-volume, quite demanding standard work with essays on American literature from its beginnings to the present.

The Cambridge History of American Literature, Ed. Sacvan Bercovitch, 18 vols. (Cambridge: Cambridge University Press, 1994–2006); each volume approx. 900 pp.

Standard work on American literary history with essays by leading scholars in the field. These complex volumes are not suitable for the beginner but rather are useful for students or scholars who need a specialized survey of a particular period.

HOW TO WRITE A RESEARCH PAPER

*Joseph Gibaldi, *MLA Handbook for Writers of Research Papers*, 7th ed. (New York: Modern Language Association, 2009); 292 pp.

Detailed standard style sheet with formal rules on how to document sources in a literary research paper, including current information on computer-assisted research. This handbook is frequently revised, therefore it is important to use the most recent edition.

James L. Harner, *Literary Research Guide: An Annotated Listing of Reference Sources in English Literary Studies*, 5th ed. (New York: Modern Language Association, 2008); 826 pp.

Very detailed compilation of possible sources for bibliographical searches. It provides lists of general bibliographical works that are similar to the *MLA International Bibliography*, but also mentions a number of other reference works on various disciplines and areas of literary study.

Jeannette A. Woodward, *Writing Research Papers: Investigating Resources in Cyberspace*, 2nd ed. (Lincolnwood, IL: NTC/Contemporary Publishing Group, 1999); 317 pp.

Useful guide to writing seminar papers with the help of Internet resources. Offers addresses of important websites and criteria for evaluating which sites are relevant and reliable.

Alice Oshima and Ann Hogue, *Writing Academic English*, 4th ed. (White Plains, NY: Pearson Longman, 2006); 337 pp.

> Very accessible introduction to writing academic papers with numerous practical examples and exercises. It focuses on all important aspects of text production, ranging from sentence structure to paragraph organization.

WorldCat (www.worldcat.org)

> Worldwide, free-of-charge network of several thousand major library catalogues, allowing easy large-scale searches of book publications by author, title, or key words. Retrieved bibliographical entries or whole lists of entries can be exported in different citation formats, including MLA, Chicago, or APA styles.

MLA International Bibliography

> Largest continually updated online database, listing secondary sources (mostly articles and books) in the field of modern languages and literatures since 1926. Its online access is restricted to subscribers only, but available through most university libraries. Retrieved bibliographical entries can be exported in different formats, including MLA, Chicago, or APA styles.

Zotero (www.zotero.org)

> Free open source citation management software that lets you import bibliographical data from online sources, databases, and catalogues. By docking onto your word processor, *Zotero* allows you to integrate these bibliographical data when writing your research papers and enables you to format or reformat your papers according to the style sheet of your choice, including MLA, Chicago, or APA.

GLOSSARY OF LITERARY AND CINEMATOGRAPHIC TERMS

This survey of the most important terms in literary criticism and film studies can be used either as a concise reference section or as a way of testing your knowledge. The numbers refer to the pages in the text where the respective terms are dealt with in more detail.

acoustic dimension of film, 82: most recently acquired feature of *film*. Not developed until the 1920s, it radically changed the medium because information no longer had to be conveyed merely by means of visual effect, such as facial expression, gestures, or subtitles, but could also rely on language (dialogue and *monologue*), recorded music, or sound effects.

act, 63: major structuring principle of *drama*; it is traditionally subdivided into *scenes*. *Elizabethan theater* adopted this formal structure from classical antiquity, dividing the *plot* into five acts; in the nineteenth century, the number of acts was reduced to four, in the twentieth century, generally to three. Sometimes acts are abandoned altogether in favor of a loose sequence of *scenes*.

actio, 105: conceptual step in *rhetoric* concerning the techniques of delivering a perfect speech.

actor, 70: agent that stands at the intersection of *text*, *transformation*, and *performance* in *drama* and thereby distinguishes the *performing arts* from literary texts in the narrow sense of the term. The actor is the mediator of the combined concerns of the author and the director in the performance, the last phase of drama. Traditional actor training distinguishes between the *internal method* (with a focus on emotional immersion) and the *external method* (stressing technique).

affective fallacy, 109: "wrong belief in subjective effects"; important term of *new criticism*, attacking any kind of *interpretation* that considers the reader's emotional reactions to a *text* as relevant to the scholarly analysis of the text; see also *intentional fallacy*.

alienation effect, 107: according to the German playwright and theoretician Bertolt Brecht, the alienation effect should guarantee that in dramatic performances, actors – and, above all, the audience – maintain a critical distance from the play in order to be aware of the artificial and illusory nature of a theatrical performance; see also *defamiliarization*.

alliteration, 54: type of *rhyme* in which the first consonant is repeated within the same line; see also *assonance*.

amphitheater, 67: see *Greek theater*.

anapest, 53: *foot* in which two unstressed syllables are followed by a stressed syllable (˘˘´), as for example, in "Ănd thĕ sheén | ŏf thĕir spéars | wăs lĭke stárs | ŏn thĕ seá."

Anglophone literatures, 97: see *postcolonial literature*.

archetypal criticism, 108: based on the depth psychology of C. G. Jung, this text-oriented approach analyzes texts according to collective motifs or archetypes of the human unconscious which are shared by various periods, cultures, or languages and appear in myth and literature (e.g., mother figure, shadow, and so on); see also *myth criticism*.

article, 5: one of the shorter forms of *secondary sources* on a specific topic, *text*, or author published in a *journal* or *collection of essays*. The term "article" is used synonymously with *essay*, which, however, also refers to a semiliterary *genre* in the seventeenth and eighteenth centuries.

aside, 63: form of *monologue* in *drama*. It is not meant to be heard by the other figures of the play, providing information only for the audience.

assonance, 54: a type of *rhyme* in which the first vowel of a word is repeated later in the same line; see also *alliteration*.

Augustan age, 91: see *eighteenth century*.

auteur theory, 130: movement in *film theory*, created and advocated by Andrew Sarris and François Truffaut, which, similar to *author-oriented approaches* in literature, views a *film* director's œuvre as an expression of his or her particular style.

author-oriented approaches, 114–116: movements in *literary criticism* that try to establish a direct connection between a literary *text* and the biography of the author; see also *biographical criticism*.

ballad, 41: subgenre of *narrative poetry*. It is situated between the longer *epic* poetry and the shorter *lyric poetry*. It is characterized by well-rounded *plots* and complex narrative techniques, but it is not sufficient in range and size to match the proportions of the epic or the *romance*. It traditionally uses a *quatrain* form.

bibliography or **list of works cited**, 6, 146–149: alphabetical list of *primary* and *secondary sources* used in a scholarly paper to document sources; see also *footnotes* and *critical apparatus*.

Bildungsroman, 13: German for "novel of education"; the term is also applied in English for a subgenre of the *novel* that generally shows the development of a *protagonist* from childhood to maturity.

biographical criticism, 114: *author-oriented approach* in *literary criticism* that tries to establish a relation between the biography of an author and his or her works.

book review, 127: critical evaluation or discussion of book-length *primary* or *secondary sources* in a *journal* or newspaper.

breeches role, 72: an aspect of *performance* in *drama* where a woman appears onstage in male clothing. *Elizabethan theater* gave an additional spin to this tradition since, according to convention, only men were allowed onstage – resulting in men playing women who dress up as men.

camera angle, 78: position of the camera or *framing* in relation to an object that is represented; it is possible to distinguish between high angle, straight-on angle, or low angle depending on the position of the camera.

camera movement, 78: early feature of *film* that coincides with the development of lighter camera equipment, thus enabling the medium to abandon the static perspective of the *proscenium stage*.

canon, 122: term originally used for holy *texts*. It now refers to the entirety of those literary texts that are considered to be the most important in *literary history*.

catharsis, 59: Greek: "cleansing"; term from Aristotle's theory of *drama*. It argues that *tragedy* has a cleansing and purging effect on the viewer.

character, 21–25: figure presented in a literary *text*, including main character or *protagonist* and *minor character*. Recurring character types in drama are called *stock characters*.

characterization, 23–25: the figures in a literary text can either be characterized as types or individuals – see *typification* and *individualization*. Types that show only one dominant feature are called *flat characters*. If a figure is more complex, the term *round character* is applied. In both cases, a figure has to be presented either through *showing* (dramatic method) or *telling* (narration); see also *modes of presentation*.

chiasmus, 50: arrangement of letters, words, and phrases in the form of a cross (from the Greek letter *chi*, χ); it is most commonly used in two adjacent lines of a poem.

chorus, 71: in classical *Greek theater* the chorus, a group of reciters or chanters, was positioned in the *orchestra* between the audience and the *actors*. Early Greek drama did not depend on dialogue between the figures of a play as much as on dialogue between figures and the chorus. The chorus generally recited lyrical poems, either commenting on the action of the play or addressing the actors in a didactic manner.

climax, 18: also called crisis or turning point; crucial element of traditional *plot* when the action undergoes decisive changes. In linear plots, the climax is preceded by *exposition* and *complication* and followed by the resolution.

close reading, 110: central term in *new criticism*. It is often used as a synonym for intrinsic or text-immanent interpretation; see also *affective fallacy* and *intentional fallacy*.

closet drama, 61: stylized subgenre of *drama* that is not intended to be performed but to be read in private.

collection of essays or **anthology**, 5: collection of *secondary sources* (*articles*) on specific topics compiled by one or several editors. If the anthology is published in honor of a well-known scholar, it is also referred to as a *Festschrift*.

comedy, 59: subgenre of *drama* with witty, humorous themes intended to entertain the audience. It is often regarded as the stylized continuation of primitive regeneration cults, such as the symbolic expulsion of winter by spring. This fertility symbolism culminates in the form of weddings as standard happy endings of traditional comedies.

comedy of manners or **Restoration comedy**, 60: popular form of English *drama* in the second half of the seventeenth century, mainly portraying citizens from the upper ranks of society in witty dialogues.

Commonwealth literature, 97: see *postcolonial literature*.

comparative literature, 124–127: *context-oriented approach* that compares and contrasts literary texts of different origins, languages, and periods – the main areas of research being interliterary comparison (comparing literatures of different languages and cultures) and transliterary comparison (comparing literary texts with other media).

complication or **conflict**, 18: element of traditional *plot*. During the complication, the initial *exposition* is changed in order to develop into a *climax*; in linear plots, it is preceded by the exposition and followed by the climax and *denouement*.

concluding paragraph, 143: final paragraph of a scholarly paper that rephrases the *thesis statement*, summarizes the most important points or results, and puts them in a larger context.

concrete poetry, 47: movement in *poetry* that focuses especially on the visual form of a poem, including the shape and layout of letters, lines, and *stanzas*.

context-oriented approaches, 119–127: various movements and schools that approach a literary *text* not merely as an intrinsic, independent work of art, but as part of a wider context. The context can be historical (e.g., *new historicism*), national (e.g., *literary history*), socio-political (e.g., *Marxist literary theory*), generic (e.g., poetics), or gender-related (e.g., *feminist literary theory*).

couplet, 56: *stanza* form that consists of two lines.

critical apparatus, 6, 144: formal element of *secondary sources* that encompasses *footnotes* or endnotes (or *parenthetical documentation*), a *bibliography* (or list of works cited), and possibly an index of key words, names, or titles.

cultural studies, 121: movement which gained momentum in the 1990s that is interested in culture as a comprehensive discourse-based phenomenon and thus shows striking structural analogies to trends in *deconstruction* and *new historicism*.

dactyl, 53: *foot* in which a stressed syllable is followed by two unstressed syllables ('˘˘), as, for example, in "Júst fŏr ă | hándfŭl ŏf | sílvĕr hĕ | léft ŭs."

deconstruction, 112: one of the recent and complex movements of *text-oriented approaches*, based on the works of the French philosopher Jacques Derrida; like *semiotics*, it regards *texts* as systems of *signs*, but differs from traditional schools of *structuralism* by concentrating on the interaction of the *signifiers*, almost abandoning the concept of a *signified*; see also *poststructuralism*.

defamiliarization, 106: stylistic device used to make the reader aware of literary conventions; related to the Brechtian *alienation effect*; see also *metafiction* and *Russian formalism*.

denouement, 18: French term for resolution, the last element of a linear *plot* in which the *complication* of the action is resolved after the *climax*.

detective novel, 14: subgenre of the *novel* that centers on uncovering a crime.

directing, 65: level of *transformation* between the *text* and the *performance* of *drama* and *film*. It includes conceptual steps that are not directly accessible to the audience but determine the performance; involves the choice of script, casting, and accentuation of the play, props, *lighting*, scenery, and rehearsals.

discontinuous narrative, 81: refers to narratives in literature and film that do not follow a linear plot line. Especially, recent film increasingly works with discontinuous narrative structures that force the viewer to reconstruct the plotline out of temporarily fragmented scenes; see also *plot*.

discourse, 4: term referring to oral or written expression within a certain thematic framework, as, for example, historical, economic, political, or feminist discourse; see also *genre* and *text type*.

dispositio, 105: conceptual step in *rhetoric* concerning the organization of material for a speech.

drama, 58–72: one of the three classical literary *genres*, involving the levels of *text*, *transformation*, and *performance*. Besides the written word, drama also relies on aspects of the *performing arts*, including a number of nonverbal means of expression mainly of a visual kind, such as stage design, scenery, facial expressions, gestures, makeup, props, and *lighting*.

editing, 79: one of the final processes in the production of a *film* when the various shots are cut and rearranged in a particular sequence; see also *montage*.

eighteenth century, 91: period also known as the *neoclassical*, *golden*, or *Augustan age*. It brought about major innovations and changes in English literature due to the introduction of newspapers and literary magazines as well as the evolution of the *novel* and the *essay* as new *genres*.

elegy, 40: classical form of *lyric poetry*. Its main theme is a lament for a deceased person.

Elizabethan age, 89: period in English *Renaissance* history, culture, and *literature* during the reign of Queen Elizabeth I (1558–1603).

Elizabethan theater, 67: renewed form of drama in the English *Renaissance* under the reign of Queen Elizabeth I (1558–1603); William Shakespeare and Christopher Marlowe are among its most important representatives.

elocutio, 105: conceptual step in *rhetoric* concerning the verbalization of a speech with the help of rhetorical figures.

end rhyme, 55: *rhyme* scheme based on identical syllables at the end of certain lines of a poem.

English or **Shakespearean sonnet**, 56: the traditional *sonnet* form in English literature, which consists of three *quatrains* and one *couplet*, and uses iambic pentameter as its *meter*; its fourteen lines follow the *rhyme* pattern abab cdcd efef gg.

epic, 9: long and complex form of *narrative poetry*. It differs drastically from *lyric poetry* in length, narrative technique, portrayal of *characters*, and *plot*. At the center of its complex plot stands a national hero who has to prove himself in numerous adventures and endure trials of cosmic dimensions. In the modern age, the epic has been overshadowed by the *novel*; see also *romance*.

epistolary novel, 13: subgenre of the *novel* that relates the *plot* in *first-person narration* using letters of correspondence as its medium.

essay, 5: semiliterary *genre*; popular in the seventeenth and eighteenth centuries, dealing with a particular topic in a scholarly manner while, at the same time, using a literary style. The literary essay shares features of both *primary* and *secondary literature*. Today, the term "essay" is also used synonymously with *article*.

exposition, 18: first element of a linear *plot* when the initial situation of the enfolding action is revealed; in a linear plot, the exposition is followed by the *complication*, the *climax*, and the *denouement*.

expressionism, 69: movement in various fields of art and *literature* in the early twentieth century. It is characterized by the exaggeration of certain aspects of the "object" portrayed (e.g., strong lines in painting or the emphasis on *types* in the *characterization* of figures in literature); it is often seen as a countermovement or reaction to *realism*.

external method, 70: one of the two major methods in actor training in which the actor imitates the moods required by a role through the use of certain techniques, rather than through actually feeling these moods, as is the case with the *internal method*.

eye rhyme, 55: type of *rhyme* that is based on syllables with identical spelling but different pronunciation.

feminist film studies, 131: branch of *film theory* that discusses issues such as the "male gaze" – a concept famously researched by scholar Laura Mulvey. According to this theory, traditional Hollywood cinema recreates the logic of male visual perception, consequently objectifying and eroticizing the "fragmented" female body in filmic representation.

feminist literary theory, 122: encompasses recent *context-oriented approaches* whose different methodologies focus on the female gender as a starting point for literary analysis; see also *gender theory*.

Festschrift, 5: *collection of essays* in honor of a distinguished scholar; see also *secondary source*.

fiction, 9–36: term to differentiate the literary prose genres of *short story*, *novella*, and *novel* from *drama* and *poetry*; in older *secondary sources* it is often used synonymously with *epic*.

figural narrative situation, 28: *point of view* in which the narrator moves into the background, suggesting that the *plot* is revealed solely through the actions of the *characters* in the text. This technique is a relatively recent phenomenon that developed with the rise of the modern *novel*, mostly as a means of encouraging the reader to judge the action without an intervening commentator. Also see *narrative situation*.

film, 72–84: in spite of different means of expression, *drama* and film are often summarized under the heading *performing arts* because of their use of *actors*. From a formalist–structuralist perspective, however, film seems closer to the *novel* than to drama because of its "fixed" (i.e., recorded) character; see also *spatial*, *temporal*, and *acoustic dimension of film*.

film narratology, 130: branch of *film theory* that adapts and questions literary concepts like *point of view* or the role of the narrator for the study of *film*.

film semiotics, 130: movement in *film theory* that tries to explain *film* as a language-like semiotic system, restricted by a number of media-specific codes that create filmic narration.

film stock, 76: the raw material onto which individual *frames* are photographed. The deliberate use of color or black-and-white, high or low contrast film stock produces structural effects that indirectly influence levels of content; see also *spatial dimension of film*.

film studies, 129: scholarly discipline devoted to the study and interpretation of film; see also *film theory*.

film theory, 129–131: theoretical and methodological foundation of film studies, partly paralleling developments in *literary theory*, but in general pursuing its own media-specific goals; also see *film*.

first-person narration, 27: *point of view* in which one of the *characters* who is part of the *plot* tells the story, referring to herself or himself in the first person singular.

flashback, 19: device in the structuring of a *plot* that introduces events from the past in an otherwise linear narrative; see also *foreshadowing*.

flat character, 21: in contrast to a *round character*, this kind of figure displays only one dominant character trait; see also *characterization*.

focalization, 32: one of the two main aspects of the *narrative situation* (the other one is the *narrative voice*). It denotes through whose eyes the reader experiences the plot and, thus, what amount of information is provided by the narrator. The character through whose eyes the reader sees the action is called the focalizer or reflector. A narrative with internal focalization assumes a character's point of view and knowledge. In externally focalized narratives the narrator is less knowledgeable than the characters. Zero focalization corresponds to an omniscient *point of view*, in other words, the narrator knows more than the characters.

foot, 53: according to the sequence of stressed and unstressed syllables, it is possible to distinguish five important metrical feet: (1) *iambus*:

an unstressed syllable followed by a stressed syllable (˘´); (2) *trochee*: a stressed syllable followed by an unstressed syllable (´˘); (3) *spondee*: two stressed syllables (´´); (4) anapest: two unstressed syllables followed by a stressed syllable (˘˘´); (5) *dactyl*: a stressed syllable followed by two unstressed syllables (´˘˘).

footnote or **endnote**, 146: references to *primary* or *secondary sources*, or additional commentary, either as a footnote at the bottom of the page or as an endnote at the end of a research paper.

foreshadowing, 19: device in the structuring of *plot* that brings information from the future into the current action; see also *flashback*.

formalism, 105–109: term that is mostly used synonymously with *structuralism* to characterize *text-oriented approaches* in the first half of the twentieth century which focused on the formal aspects of a literary work; see also *Russian formalism*.

framing, 77: segment of a scene, person, or object represented on *film*. It is closely connected to terms such as close-up, medium, and long shot that refer to the distance between the camera and the filmed object or person, as well as to the choice of which segment of a *setting* is to be represented. Similar effects can be achieved with wide-angle or telephoto lenses; see also *mise en scène*.

French feminism or *écriture féminine*, 122: movement in feminism that views the female physical anatomy as responsible for a specifically feminine kind of writing that manifests itself in plot, content, narrative structure, and textual logic.

gender theory, 122–124: recent context-oriented movement which, unlike *feminist literary theory*, no longer focuses exclusively on women, but includes issues concerning both genders in the *interpretation* of literary *texts*.

genre, 3: term to classify the traditional literary forms of *epic* (i.e., *fiction*), *drama*, and *poetry*. These categories or genres are still commonly used, although the epic has been replaced by the *novel* and *short story*; see also *discourse* and *text type*.

golden age, 91: see *eighteenth century*.

gothic novel, 14: subgenre of the *novel* with an eerie, supernatural setting. It was particularly popular in the late eighteenth century.

Greek theater, 67: open-air amphitheater consisting of an *orchestra* and a *skene* (stage building). The audience was seated in semicircles around the orchestra. The *actors* moved between the skene and the orchestra, and the *chorus* was positioned in the orchestra between the audience and the actors. In the *comedies* and *tragedies* of classical Greek *drama*, all actors wore masks.

hermeneutics, 101: traditional term for the scholarly *interpretation* of a *text*.

heterodiegetic narrator, 31: important term in *narratology* to describe a narrator who is not part of the story world and, therefore, has unlimited knowledge and authority. The opposite is true for a *homodiegetic narrator*; see also *narrative situation*.

historical novel, 13: subgenre of the *novel* with *characters* and *plot* in a realistic-historical context. New journalism, which recounts real events in the form of a novel, is a related movement in the second half of the twentieth century.

history play, 60: subgenre of *drama*. In the English tradition, it dates back to the *Renaissance* and dramatizes historical events or personalities.

homodiegetic narrator, 31: important term in *narratology* to describe a narrator who is part of the story world and, consequently, has only a limited view of the action and particularly of the other characters' thoughts. The opposite is true for a *heterodiegetic narrator*; see also *narrative situation*.

iambus, 53: *foot* in which an unstressed syllable is followed by a stressed syllable (˘´), as, for example, in "Thĕ cúr | fĕw tólls | thĕ knéll | ŏf pár | tĭng dáy."

imagery, 40: term that derives from the Latin "imago" ("picture") and refers mainly to the use of concrete language to lend a visual quality to abstract themes in a poem; see also *imagism*.

images of women criticism, 122: early phase of *feminist literary theory* that focuses on the representation of women in *texts* by male authors.

imagism, 46: literary movement in the early twentieth century closely associated with Ezra Pound. It attempts to reduce and condense *poetry* to essential "images." Concrete language without decorative elements is employed to achieve a strong visual effect or *imagery*.

individualization, 23: *characterization* that emphasizes a multiplicity of character traits in a literary figure, rather than one dominant feature; see also *typification*.

intentional fallacy, 109: a wrong belief in the author's intention; important term of *new criticism*, aimed against *interpretations* that try to reconstruct the author's original intentions when writing a *text* and thereby neglect intrinsic aspects of the text; see also *affective fallacy*.

interior monologue, 30: narrative technique in which a figure is exclusively characterized by his or her thoughts without any other comments; it is influenced by psychoanalysis and related to the *stream-of-consciousness technique*.

internal method, 70: one of the two main methods in actor training. It builds on individual identification of the actor with his or her part. In contrast to the external method, which tries to simulate personal feelings, this method works with the internalization of emotions and situations that are required in the part. This approach, which goes back to Konstantin Stanislavsky and his pupil Lee Strasberg, is also referred to as "The Method."

internal rhyme, 54: type of *rhyme* that is not based on *end rhyme* but rather on *alliteration* or *assonance*; most *Old English* and some *Middle English* poetry uses internal rhyme.

interpretation, 101: modern term for *hermeneutics* and exegesis (i.e., the search for the meaning of a *text*); sometimes seen in opposition to evaluative *literary criticism*.

introductory paragraph, 139: the first paragraph of a scholarly paper, which informs the reader about the focus, methodology, and structure of the entire paper; see also *thesis statement*.

inventio, 105: conceptual step in *rhetoric* concerning the selection of themes for a speech.

journal, 5: regularly issued scholarly publication that contains *essays* and sometimes *notes*, *book reviews*, or *review essays*; see also *secondary source*.

lighting, 77: visual element used in *film* and *drama* to enhance levels of content.

literary criticism, 127: systematic, scholarly approach to literary *texts*, often used synonymously with *interpretation*; see also *literary theory*.

literary history, 119: *context-oriented approach* that mainly deals with the chronological and period-specific classification of literary *texts*. This movement is informed by historical methodology; it dates and categorizes literary works and examines the influence of earlier works on later works.

literary theory, 101: also referred to as *critical theory*; philosophical and methodological basis of *literary criticism*, including varying approaches to texts; the respective schools can be grouped according to *text-*, *author-*, *reader-*, and *context-oriented approaches*.

literature, 1–7: vague umbrella term for written expression; it conventionally refers to *primary* and *secondary sources*; see also *text*.

lyric poetry, 37: term for a variety of short poetic forms such as the *sonnet*, the *ode*, and the *elegy*. In contrast to the more complex and longer *narrative poetry*, it usually revolves around a single event, impression, or idea.

Marxist literary theory, 119: *context-oriented approach* based on the writings of Karl Marx (1818–1883) and other Marxist theorists. It analyzes literary *texts* as expressions of economic, sociological, and political backgrounds. Conditions of production in particular periods are examined with respect to their influence on literary writings of the time.

memoria, 105: conceptual step in *rhetoric* concerning the technique of remembering a speech.

metafiction, 107: "fiction about fiction"; term for self-reflexive literary *texts* that focus on their own literary elements, such as language, narrative, and *plot* structure; it is a main feature of *postmodernism*.

metaphor, 44: *rhetorical figure* that "equates" one thing with another without actually "comparing" the two (e.g., "My love is a red, red rose"); see also *simile*.

meter, 52: element of the *rhythmic–acoustic dimension* of *poetry*; stressed and unstressed syllables of a line can be organized in *feet*. In order to describe the meter of a verse, one indicates the name of the foot and the number of the feet used (e.g., iambic pentameter = 5 iambuses in each line).

Middle English period, 87: period of linguistic and literary history. It is considered to begin with the invasion of England by the French-speaking Normans in the eleventh century and ends with the advent of the *Renaissance* at the end of the fifteenth century; dominant literary genres are the *romance* and the tale.

minor character, 28: figure in a literary *text* who – in contrast to the *protagonist* – does not occupy the center of attention.

minority literatures, 96: problematic umbrella term for movements in *literature* toward the end of the twentieth century that are represented by marginalized gender groups (women, gays, and lesbians) and ethnic groups (e.g., African Americans, Chicanos, and Chicanas).

mise en scène, 77: French for "to place on stage"; the term refers to the arrangement of all visual elements in a theater production. In film, it is used as an umbrella term for the various elements that constitute the framing, including camera distance, camera angles, lenses, and lighting, as well as the positioning of persons and objects in relation to each other.

modernism, 94: period of literary and cultural history in the first decades of the twentieth century. It can be seen as a reaction to the realist tendencies of the late nineteenth century. New narrative structures, *points of view* (e.g., *stream-of-consciousness technique*), and other literary forms of expression are introduced under the influence of the visual arts and psychoanalysis.

modes of presentation, 25: similar to the presentation of *characters* and events in a literary work, it is possible to distinguish between explanatory characterization based on narration (*telling*) and dramatic characterization based on dialogues and *monologues* (*showing*).

monograph, 5: scholarly or book-length publication on a specific topic, *text*, or author; see also *secondary source*.

monologue or **soliloquy**, 62: long speech onstage that is not aimed at a direct dialogue partner. In the *aside*, a special form of monologue, a character onstage passes on information to the audience that is not accessible to the other figures in the play.

montage, 79: *editing* technique in *film*. Its effects resemble those of *rhetorical figures* in *literature* (e.g., metaphorical meaning): by combining two different images, the meaning of one object can be associated with the other, as occurs in the relationship between tenor and vehicle in *metaphor*. Montage is closely associated with the innovations of the Russian filmmaker Sergei Eisenstein.

mystery and **miracle play**, 59: medieval dramatic forms which adapt religious-allegorical or biblical themes to be performed outside of the church; together with classical Latin drama, they influenced the revival of *drama* in the *Renaissance*.

myth criticism, 108: approach that investigates the mythological deep structures of literary *texts* and uses them as a basis for *interpretation*; see also *archetypal criticism*.

narrative poetry, 37: in contrast to the shorter and more focused *lyric poetry*, it includes *genres* such as the *epic*, the *romance*, and the *ballad*, all of which tell a story with a clearly defined *plot*.

narrative situation, 26–33: term in *narratology* that focuses mainly on two aspects: the *narrative voice* (who speaks?) and the *focalization* (who sees?). Generally speaking, a narrative can be presented from either an authorial, figural, or first-person point of view. Another way of specifying the *narrative situation* is to define whether the text has a *heterodiegetic* or a *homodiegetic narrator*.

narrative voice, 26: one of the two main aspects of the *narrative situation* (the other one is *focalization*), denoting who speaks, that is, who is the narrator of the story.

narratology, 130: area of literary and *film theory* that focuses on the study of the narrative structure of a *text* in the widest sense of the term; see also *narrative situation*, *heterodiegetic narrator*, *homodiegetic narrator*, and *focalization*.

narrator, 26: term in *narratology*, denoting the authority who tells a story; see also *narrative situation*, *heterodiegetic narrator*, *homodiegetic narrator*.

naturalism, 93: term denoting *texts* from the end of the nineteenth century that aim at a realistic depiction of the influence of social and environmental circumstances on *characters* in literary texts; see also *realism*.

neoclassical age, 91: see *eighteenth century*.

new criticism, 109–111: one of the most important Anglo-American *text-oriented approaches* in the decades after World War II; it differentiates *interpretation* from source studies, socio-historical background studies, and history of motifs, as well as *author-oriented* biographical or *psychoanalytic literary criticism* and *reception history* in order to free *literary criticism* from extrinsic elements (i.e., those outside of the text) and bring the focus back to the literary text as such; see also *structuralism*, *affective fallacy*, *intentional fallacy*, and *close reading*.

new historicism, 120–121: recent *context-oriented approach* that builds on *poststructuralism* and *deconstruction* but also includes historical dimensions in the discussion of literary *texts*, presupposing a structural similarity between literary and other *discourses* within a given historical period.

note, 5: short *secondary source* in a scholarly *journal*, which treats a very specific aspect of a topic in only a few paragraphs.

novel, 12: important *genre* of prose *fiction* that developed in England in the eighteenth century; the *epic* and the *romance* are indirect precursors. Structurally, the novel differs from the epic through more complex *character* presentation and *point of view* techniques, its emphasis on *realism*, and a more subtle structuring of the *plot*.

novella or **novelette**, 17: subgenre of prose *fiction*. Due to its short length and idiosyncratic narrative elements, it assumes a position between the *short story* and the *novel*.

ode, 40: traditional form of *lyric poetry* on a serious, mostly classical theme and consisting of several *stanzas*.

Old English or **Anglo-Saxon period**, 87: earliest period of English literature and language between the invasion of Britain by Germanic tribes (Angles, Saxons, Jutes) in the fifth century AD and the conquest of England by William the Conqueror in 1066; the most important *genres* are the *epic* and *poetry* (including charms and riddles).

omniscient point of view, 26: *point of view* that describes the action from an omniscient, God-like perspective by referring to the *protagonist* in the third person. It is therefore often imprecisely termed third-person narration.

onomatopoeia, 38: linguistic term for a word that resembles the sound produced by the object it denotes (e.g., "cuckoo"); in *poetry*, it attempts to emphasize the meaning of a word through its acoustic dimension.

orchestra, 67: space in the center of the stage in a classical Greek amphitheater. The seating was arranged in semicircles around the *orchestra*; see also *Greek theater*, *chorus*, and *skene*.

paraphrase, 145: summary in one's own words of a passage from a *secondary* or *primary source*; see also *quotation*.

parenthetical citation, 145: part of the *critical apparatus* of a scholarly paper. It allows the reader to retrace the original sources of *paraphrases* and *quotations* by giving author (or title of the source) and page number(s) in parentheses; alternative documentation systems are *footnotes* or *endnotes*.

performance, 70–72: last phase in the *transformation* of a dramatic *text* into a staged play; see also *drama* and *actor*.

performing arts, 73: umbrella term for artistic expressions that center on the *performance* of an *actor* in a stage-like setting; see also *drama* and *film*.

philology, 103–104: summarizes an approach in traditional *literary criticism*. It deals especially with "material" aspects of *texts*, such as the editing of manuscripts, and the preservation or reconstruction of texts. The term *philology* can also refer to one of the different languages in literary studies or linguistics, including English, German, or French.

picaresque novel, 13: subgenre of the *novel*. It recounts the episodic adventures of a vagrant rogue (Spanish: "pícaro") who usually gets into trouble by breaking social norms; it attempts to expose social injustice in a satirical way.

plot, 18–21: logical combination of different elements of the action in a literary *text*. In an ideal linear plot, the initial situation or *exposition* is followed by a *complication* or conflict that creates suspense and then leads to a *climax*, crisis, or turning point. The climax is then followed by the resolution or *denouement*, which usually marks the end of a text; see also *discontinuous narrative*.

poetry or **poem**, 36–58: literary *genre* that differs from prose genres in the use of verse, *rhyme*, and *meter*. In modern prose poems or experimental poetry, these classical elements are no longer valid; however, the wording and the deliberate use of certain structural elements of syntax and *rhetorical figures* mark these works as poetic forms; see also *narrative poetry* and *lyric poetry*.

point of view, 26–33: see *narrative situation*.

postcolonial literature, 97: umbrella term that refers to *texts* from former colonial territories in the Caribbean, Africa, India, and Australia that have attracted the attention of contemporary literary critics; in the English context sometimes also referred to as "new literatures in English," *Commonwealth literature*, or *Anglophone literatures*.

postmodernism, 96: movement in literary and cultural history in the second half of the twentieth century which takes up issues that were treated by *modernism* – for example, innovative narrative techniques and *plot* patterns – by dealing with them in an academic, often self-reflexive way; see also *metafiction*.

poststructuralism, 110: umbrella term for the *text-oriented* schools in *literary theory* in the second half of the twentieth century, such as *semiotics* and *deconstruction*, that go beyond the traditional schools of *structuralism* and *formalism*.

primary source, 5: term for a literary *text*, usually belonging to one of the three traditional *genres*; see also *secondary source*.

proscenium stage, 68: dominant *stage* form since the Baroque. Because of its box-like shape, which creates the impression of a self-contained and independent world of the play, it was the preferred stage for realist *drama*.

protagonist, 27: technical term for the main *character* in a literary *text*; see also *minor character*.

psychoanalytic literary criticism, 115: movement in *literary criticism* that applies the methods of Sigmund Freud's psychoanalysis; psychological traits of the author are examined in the *text*, and literary *characters* are analyzed as if they were real people; see also *archetypal criticism*.

psychological film theory, 129: branch of *film theory* with special focus on studying the mental effects and processes when watching a *film*, and applying a psychological framework to the interpretation of films.

Puritan age, 90: religiously motivated movement that dominated English culture from 1649 to 1660; the term is also used for the colonial period in the seventeenth and eighteenth centuries as the first literary movement on the North American continent.

quatrain, 56: *stanza* that consists of four lines.

quotation, 145: passage that has been taken word for word from a *primary* or *secondary source*; see also *paraphrase*.

reader-oriented approach, 116–118: school in *literary criticism* in the second half of the twentieth century. It concentrates on the relation between *text* and reader. The most important movements are *reception theory*, reader-response theory, reception-aesthetic, and *reception history*.

realism, 93: term for the period in *literary history* toward the end of the nineteenth century that was preoccupied with translating "reality" into *literature*; it is also used as a general term for any kind of realistic portrayal in literature; see also *naturalism*.

realism movement, 130: approach in *film theory* after World War II. It regards elements of composition, such as *mise en scène* and *framing*, as the basis of filmic reality.

reception history, 118: *reader-oriented approach* that deals with the reception of a *text* by the reader; sales figures, critical statements, and reviews from magazines and scholarly *journals* provide data for a synchronic analysis (i.e., one that takes place within a certain period) of readers' reactions, as well as a diachronic analysis (i.e., one that compares historical periods) of the reception of texts.

reception theory, 116: also reception aesthetic or reader-response theory; movement in the interpretation of texts that focuses primarily on the reader. It stands in contrast to intrinsic or *text-oriented approaches*; see also *reception history*.

Renaissance, 88: period in literary and cultural history that traditionally encompasses the sixteenth and parts of the seventeenth century; in England, the *Renaissance* is often subdivided into periods named after the rulers of the time, such as the *Elizabethan age* (for Queen Elizabeth I) or *Jacobean age* (for King James). The classical *genre* of *drama* experiences its first revival in English literature; linguistics often applies the term *early modern period*.

Restoration comedy, 60: see *comedy of manners*.

review article, 127: longer form of the *book review*. It discusses a number of pieces of *secondary literature* on a particular topic.

rhetoric, 104–105: precursor of modern *text-oriented approaches* which dates back to the practice of oratory in classical antiquity. As a source of rules for good public speech, it contains detailed instructions for every phase of oratory: *inventio* (finding themes), *dispositio* (structuring material), *elocutio* (wording with the aid of *rhetorical figures*), *memoria* (techniques for remembering a speech), and *actio* (delivery of a speech).

rhetorical figures or **figures of speech**, 43: a number of stylistic forms that mostly use language in its "nonliteral" meaning; see *metaphor, simile, symbol*.

rhyme, 54: element of the *rhythmic-acoustic dimension* of a poem. In English, it generally includes *internal rhymes* (based on *alliteration* and *assonance*), *end rhymes* (the most frequent kind of rhyme in modern poems, based on identical syllables at the end of certain lines), and *eye rhymes* (which play with identical spelling but different pronunciation of words and syllables).

rhythmic–acoustic dimension, 51–58: umbrella term for elements of *poetry* such as sound, *rhyme*, *meter*, and *onomatopoeia*.

romance, 10: most classical romances were written in prose, most medieval ones in verse. Because of its advanced use of *narrative situation* and the structuring of *plot*, the romance is, despite its verse form, regarded as the first direct precursor of the *novel*. In contrast to the *epic*, the romance is more focused in terms of plot, and with its emphasis on realism, less concerned with cosmic or national issues.

romanticism, 92: movement in *literary history* in the first half of the nineteenth century. It appears more or less simultaneously in American and English literature. Nature *poetry* and individual, emotional experiences play important roles. Romanticism may be seen as a reaction to the Enlightenment with its political changes throughout Europe and America at the end of the eighteenth century. In America, romanticism partly overlaps with *transcendentalism*.

round character, 21: figure that is rendered through a number of different character traits; see also *flat character* and *characterization*.

running time, 80: length of a film or of an episode of a television series. In most cases the running time is not identical with the plot time portrayed; see also *foreshadowing* and *flashback*.

Russian formalism, 106: *text-oriented approach* that developed in Russia during and after World War I. It was interested in the nature of literary language and is famous for the concept of *defamiliarization*; see also *structuralism*.

scene, 63: subdivision of *acts* in traditional *drama,* and therefore the smallest unit in the overall structure of a play.

secondary source, 5: scholarly *text type*, including *notes, essays, book reviews*, and *monographs* that usually deal with *primary sources*.

semiotics, 111–114: *text-oriented approach* in the second half of the twentieth century that defines the *text* as an interdependent network of *signs*. It expands the notion of text to include nonverbal systems of signs, such as *film*, painting, fashion, or geography. The basis for this complex theory is the concept of language of the Swiss linguist Ferdinand de Saussure, which is based on the terms *signifier* and *signified*; see also *deconstruction* and *poststructuralism*.

setting, 33–36: dimension of literary *texts* including the time and place of the action. The setting is usually carefully chosen by the author in order to indirectly support *plot, characters*, and *narrative situation*.

short story, 15: short *genre* of prose *fiction* that is related to fairy tales and myths. Medieval and early modern cycles of narratives are indirect models. Generally, the short story differs from the *novel* in length, in its less complex *plot* and *setting*, its less differentiated *characterization* of figures, and its less elaborate use of *point of view*.

showing, 24: *mode of presentation* that, in contrast to narration or *telling*, relies on dramatic presentation (e.g., direct speech).

sign, 111: meaningful element within a closed system (e.g., *text*); see also *semiotics*.

signified, 111: the linguist Ferdinand de Saussure divided language into two basic dimensions: the mental concept (e.g., the idea of a tree), termed the *signified*; and that concept's manifestation in language (the sequence of sounds or letters in the word "T-R-E-E"), termed the *signifier*; see also *semiotics* and *deconstruction*.

signifier, 111: see *signified*.

simile, 43: *rhetorical figure* that "compares" two different things by connecting them with "like," "than," "as," or "compare" (e.g., "Oh, my love is like a red, red rose"); see also *metaphor*.

skene, 67: stage building behind the orchestra in a classical Greek amphitheater; also see *Greek theater* and *chorus*.

soliloquy, 63: see *monologue*.

sonnet, 40: poem with a strict *rhyme* scheme; it is often used for the treatment of "worldly love" in *poetry*. According to the rhyme scheme and the kind of *stanza*, it is possible to distinguish between *English* or *Shakespearean*, Spenserian, Italian, and Petrarchan sonnets.

spatial dimension of film, 76–79: umbrella term for a number of heterogeneous aspects in *film*, such as *film stock*, *lighting*, *camera angle*, *camera movement*, *point of view*, *editing*, and *montage*; see also *mise en scène*.

spondee, 53: *foot* with two stressed syllables ($''$), as, for example, in "Góod stróng | thíck stú | pé fý | íng ín | cénse smóke."

stage, 67: the various designs of theater stages can be reduced to the two basic types of the *amphitheater* and the *proscenium stage*; most other common forms combine elements of these two.

stanza, 56: element of the visual dimension of a poem that can be classified according to the number of its lines, *meter*, and *rhyme*; most poems are the *couplet* (2 lines), *tercet* (3 lines), and *quatrain* (4 lines); see also *sonnet*.

stock character, 71: recurring *flat character* in *drama*; examples include the boastful soldier, the cranky old man, and the crafty servant.

stream-of-consciousness technique, 30: narratological technique (related to *interior monologue*) that is used to represent the subconscious associations of a literary character. It reflects a groundbreaking shift in cultural paradigms during the first decades of the twentieth century; the most famous example is the final section of James Joyce's novel *Ulysses* (1922).

structuralism, 105–109: umbrella term for *text-oriented approaches* that use formal-structural aspects (intrinsic approach) in the *interpretation* of *texts* and neglect historical, sociological, biographical, and psychological dimensions; the most important schools are *Russian formalism* and the Prague school of structuralism in the first half of the twentieth century. In the Anglo-American context, *new criticism* developed as a related movement; see also *semiotics* and *deconstruction*.

stylistics, 104–105: *text-oriented approach* focusing on the description of stylistic characteristics of authors, *texts*, or periods; it deals with grammatical structures (vocabulary, syntax), elements of sound (phonology), and overarching forms (*rhetorical figures*) of texts.

symbol, 42: term for "objects" in a literary text that transcend their material meaning; it is possible to distinguish between *conventional symbols* (which are commonly known) and *private symbols* (which are created by an author for a particular text).

telling, 23: one of the two basic *modes of presentation* in literary *texts*. In contrast to *showing*, it relies mostly on narration.

temporal dimension of film, 79–81: includes aspects such as slow motion, fast motion, *plot* time, length of film, *flashback*, and *foreshadowing*.

tercet, 56: *stanza* that consists of three lines.

text, 1–7: term often used synonymously with *literature*; in recent usage, it is also applied to denote nonverbal *sign* systems such as fashion, *film*, geography, and painting; see also *semiotics* and *deconstruction*.

text-oriented approaches, 103–114: movements or schools in *literary theory* that concentrate on the "textual" or intrinsic levels of literature. They deliberately exclude extrinsic aspects (i.e., those external to the text) concerning the author (biography, complete works), audience (class, gender, age, ethnic origin, education), or context (historical, social, or political conditions). The text-oriented approaches include *philology*, *rhetoric*, and *stylistics*, as well as the formalist-structuralist schools of *Russian formalism*, Prague school of structuralism, *new criticism*, *semiotics*, and *deconstruction*.

text type, 4: linguistic term used for the classification of forms of expression that are mostly written, but are not necessarily of a literary kind. It includes *primary* and *secondary sources*, *texts* of everyday use, advertisements, or instruction manuals; see also *genre* and *discourse*.

textual criticism, 103: important branch of *philology* that is concerned with the reconstruction of the physical basis of a literary text as, for example, editions of texts or manuscripts.

theater of the absurd, 61: movement in twentieth-century *drama* that abandons traditional *plot* structures and conventional *character* presentation in favor of new modes of portraying the disillusioned human condition after World War II.

thesis statement, 139: part of the *introductory paragraph* of a scholarly paper; in a clear and concise way, it informs the reader about the thematic focus, methodology, and structure ("road map") of the paper.

three unities, 63: rules concerning the unity of place, time, and action in *drama*, deriving from (mis)interpretations of Aristotle's *Poetics* in the *Renaissance* which argue that, in a "good" play, the place of the action should not change, the time of the *plot* presented should correspond more or less to the length of the *performance*, and the action should follow a linear plot.

topic sentence, 141: opening sentence of a paragraph in the main part of a scholarly paper. It emphasizes the specific aspect discussed in the respective paragraph and links it to the overall topic of the paper.

tragedy, 58: subgenre of *drama* with serious themes, usually depicting the downfall of an important figure, intended to have a purging effect on the audience; see also *catharsis*.

transcendentalism, 93: period in the first half of the nineteenth century in the United States. It became the first important uniquely American literary movement; it was partly influenced by romantic enthusiasm for nature and German idealism.

transformation, 65–70: steps involved in staging a dramatic text or a performance; see also *directing*.

trochee, 53: *foot* in which a stressed syllable is followed by an unstressed syllable (´˘), as, for example, in "Thére thĕy | áre, mў | fíftў | mén ănd | wómĕn."

typification, 22: typified *characters* display one dominant feature which often represents an abstract idea or the general traits of a group of persons. Medieval allegorical depictions of figures preferred typification in order to personify vices, virtues, or philosophical and religious positions; see also *individualization*.

utopian novel, 14: subgenre of the *novel* describing alternative worlds with the aim of revealing and criticizing existing socio-political conditions.

REFERENCES

"Against Wens." *Anglo-Saxon Poetry*. Trans. R. K. Gordon. London: Dent, 1970. 87. Print.

Andrew, S. O. *Sir Gawain and the Green Knight: A Modern Version of the XIV Century Alliterative Poem in the Original Metre*. London: Dent, 1929. Print.

Aristotle. *Aristotle's Poetics: The Argument*. Trans. Gerald F. Else. Leiden: Brill, 1957. Print.

Atwood, Margaret. *The Edible Woman*. New York: Bantam Books, 1991. Print.

Auden, W. H. "Twelve Songs." *Collected Poems*. Ed. Edward Mendelson. London: Faber and Faber, 1976. 116–122. Print.

Bashō, Matsuo. "The Ancient Pond." Trans. Donald Keene. *Japanese Literature: An Introduction for Western Readers*. Rutland, VT: Tuttle, 1977. Print.

Beowulf. Trans. Seamus Heaney. New York: Norton, 2000. Print.

Browning, Robert. "The Bishop Orders His Tomb at Saint Praxed's Church." *The Poetical Works of Robert Browning*. Vol. 1. Leipzig: Tauchnitz, 1872. 235–239. Print.

———. "The Lost Leader." *The Poems of Browning*. Ed. John Woolford and Daniel Karlin. Vol. 2. London: Longman, 1991. 176–179. Print.

———. "One Word More." *The Poetical Works of Robert Browning*. Vol. 1. Leipzig: Tauchnitz, 1872. 285–292. Print.

Burns, Robert. "A Red, Red Rose." *Poems and Songs*. Ed. James Kinsley. Oxford: Oxford UP, 1979. 582. Print.

Byron, George Gordon, Lord. "The Destruction of Sennacherib." *The Poetical Works of Lord Byron*. London: Oxford UP, 1911. 82. Print.

Coleridge, Samuel Taylor. *The Poems of Samuel Taylor Coleridge*. Ed. Ernest Hartley Coleridge. Oxford: Oxford UP, 1935. Print.

Cortázar, Julio. *Hopscotch*. Trans. Gregory Rabassa. New York: Pantheon–Random House, 1966. Print.

"Cuccu." *Mittelenglische Lyrik*. Ed. Werner Arens and Rainer Schönwerling. Stuttgart: Reclam, 1980. Print.

cummings, e. e. "l(a." *Complete Poems 1904–1962*. Ed. George J. Firmage. New York: Liveright, 1994. 673. Print.

Dostoyevsky, Fyodor. *Crime and Punishment*. Ed. George Gibian. Trans. Jessie Coulson. New York: Norton, 1964. Print.

Eco, Umberto. "Regretfully, We Are Returning . . . Reader's Reports." 1972. *Misreadings*. Trans. William Weaver. San Diego, CA: Harcourt Brace, 1993. 33–46. Print.

Erlich, Victor. *Russian Formalism*. 4th ed. The Hague: Mouton Publishers, 1980. Print.

Faulkner, William. *The Sound and the Fury*. Harmondsworth: Penguin, 1978. Print.

Frost, Robert. "Stopping by Woods on a Snowy Evening." *The Poems of Robert Frost*. New York: Random House, 1946. 238. Print.

Gray, Thomas. "Elegy Written in a Country Church-Yard." *Gray's Poems*. Ed. John Bradshaw. London: Macmillan, 1895. 34–38. Print.

Hemingway, Ernest. "Homage to Switzerland." *The Short Stories of Ernest Hemingway*. New York: Scribner's, 1953. 422–435. Print.

Herbert, George. "Easter Wings." *The Poems of George Herbert.* Ed. Arthur Waugh. London: Oxford UP, 1913. 43–44. Print.

Homer. *The Iliad of Homer: Rendered into English Blank Verse.* Trans. Edward Earl of Derby. 2 vols. London: Murray, 1856. Print.

Hugo, Victor. *The Hunchback of Notre Dame.* Trans. Catherine Liu. New York: The Modern Library, 2002. Print.

Joyce, James. *Ulysses.* Ed. Declan Kibert. London: Penguin, 2000. Print.

Kafka, Franz. *The Trial.* Trans. Richard Stokes. London: Modern Voices, 2005. Print.

Keats, John. "Ode on a Grecian Urn." *The Poetical Works of John Keats.* Ed. H. W. Garrod. London: Oxford UP, 1956. 209–210. Print.

Langland, William. *Piers Plowman: The Prologue and Passus I–VII of the B Text as Found in Bodleian MS. Laud Misc. 581.* Ed. J. A. W. Bennett. Oxford: Clarendon Press, 1972. Print.

Melville, Herman. *Moby Dick.* London: Penguin, 1994. Print.

Poe, Edgar Allan. "The Fall of the House of Usher." *Poe's Tales of Mystery and Imagination.* Ed. Pádraic Colum. London: Dent, 1959. 128–144. Print.

Pope, Alexander. "An Essay on Criticism." *Pastoral Poetry and An Essay on Criticism.* Ed. E. Audra and Aubrey Williams. New Haven, CT: Yale UP, 1961. 195–326. Print.

Pound, Ezra. "In a Station of the Metro." *Selected Poems.* Ed. T. S. Eliot. London: Faber and Faber, 1967. 113. Print.

Proust, Marcel. *In Search of Lost Time: Swann's Way.* Trans. C. K. Scott Moncrieff and Terence Kilmartin. Rev. D. J. Enright. Vol. 1. New York: The Modern Library, 2003. Print.

Puig, Manuel. *Kiss of the Spider Woman.* Trans. Thomas Colechie. New York: Vintage–Random House, 1991. Print.

Quarles, Francis. *Emblems and Hieroglyphics of the Life of Man, Modernized.* 4 vols. London: Cooke, n.d. Print.

Rhys, Jean. *Wide Sargasso Sea.* New York: Popular Library, 1966. Print.

"Riddle 44." *The Exeter Book*. Ed. George Philip Krapp and Elliott van Kirk Dobbie. London: Routledge, 1936. 204–205. Print.

Salinger, J. D. *The Catcher in the Rye*. Boston, MA: Little, Brown, 1951. Print.

Sartre, Jean Paul. *Nausea*. Trans. Lloyd Alexander. New York: New Directions, 2007. Print.

Shakespeare, William. *The Complete Works of Shakespeare*. Ed. David Bevington. 3rd ed. Glenview, TL: Scott, Foresman and Company, 1980. Print.

Stevens, Wallace. "Anecdote of the Jar." *Selected Poems*. London: Faber and Faber, 1976. 36. Print.

Tolstoy, Leo. *War and Peace*. Trans. and rev. Alexandra Kropotkin. New York: Literary Guild of America, 1949. Print.

Twain, Mark. "A True Story." *Sketches: New and Old*. New York: Harper, 1906. 265–272. Print.

Vonnegut, Kurt. *Slaughterhouse-Five: Or the Children's Crusade*. London: Triad–Grafton, 1989. Print.

Walther von der Vogelweide. "Under the Lime Tree." Trans. Raymond Oliver. *Poems without Names: The English Lyric, 1200–1500*. Ed. Raymond Oliver. Berkeley, CA: University of California Press, 1970. 125–127. Print.

Williams, Carlos William. "This Is Just to Say." *The Collection of Earlier Poems of William Carlos Williams*. New York: New Directions, 1966. 354. Print.

Woolf, Virginia. *Mrs Dalloway*. Harmondsworth: Penguin, 1972. Print.

AUTHOR AND TITLE INDEX

Abbess of Castro, The (1832) 17

Abish, Walter (1931–) 113–114

Achebe, Chinua (1930–2013) 97

Adding Machine, The (1923) 69

Addison, Joseph (1672–1719) 16, 91

Adorno, Theodor (1900–1969) 119

Adventures of Huckleberry Finn, The (1884) 93

Adventures of Sherlock Holmes (1905) 75

Aeneid (c.31–19 BC) 10, 34, 86

Aeschylus (c.525–456 BC) 58, 129

After Magritte (1971) 70

"Against Wens" (c. tenth century AD) 37

Albee, Edward (1928–) 69, 96

Alciatus, Andreas (1492–1559) 90

All for Love (1677) 61

Alphabetical Africa (1974) 114

"Altar, The" (1633) 47

American Graffiti (1973) 82

Anakreon (c.580–495 BC) 86

"Ancient Pond, An" (1686) 47

Andreae, Johann Valentin (1586–1654) 14

"Anecdote of the Jar" (1919) 45

Angel at My Table, An (1984) 97

Apocalypse Now (1979) 17

Apuleius (second century AD) 10

Aquis Submersus (1876) 17

Arcadia (c.1580) 89

Aristophanes (c.448–380 BC) 58, 86, 129

Ariosto, Lodovico (1474–1533) 10

Aristotle (384–322 BC) 18, 58, 61, 63, 106, 110

Arnheim, Rudolf (1904–2007) 130

Artist, The (2011) 82

As You Like It (c.1599) 44, 72

Atwood, Margaret (1939–) 14, 33, 97

Auden, W. H. (1907–1973) 42, 51

Aue, Hartmann von (c.1165–1215) 88

Autobiography [of Benjamin Franklin] (1771–1788) 28

Bachtin, Michail (1895–1975) 125
Bacon, Francis (1561–1626) 7, 89
Baraka, Amiri (1934–) 69
Baron in the Trees, The (1957) 13, 34
Barry Lyndon (1975) 77
Barth, John (1930–) 96
Barthes, Roland (1915–1980) 112
Bashō, Matsuo (1644–1694) 47
Battle of Maldon, The (c.1000) 87
Bazin, André (1918–1958) 130
Beckett, Samuel (1906–1989)
    62–64, 66, 69, 96
Beda Venerabilis (673–735) 87
Bell Jar, The (1963) 97
Beloved (1987) 97
Beowulf (c. eighth century AD) 54,
    87
Bhabha, Homi (1949–) 121
Bible 15, 88, 100–101, 128
Bierce, Ambrose (1842–1914) 94,
    114
Birth of a Nation, The (1915) 75
"Bishop Orders His Tomb at Saint
    Praxed's Church, The" (1845) 53
Blackton, Stuart J. (1874–1941)
    75
Blake, William (1757–1827) 92
Boccaccio, Giovanni (1313–1375) 6,
    15–16, 87–88
Böll, Heinrich (1917–1985) 16
Bordwell, David (1947–) 130
Borges, Jorge Luis (1899–1986) 17,
    96
Bradstreet, Anne (c.1612–1672) 91
Brando, Marlon (1924–2004) 71
Brecht, Bertolt (1898–1956) 107
Broch, Hermann (1886–1951) 95
Brothers Karamazov, The (1879–1880)
    94
Brown, Dan (1964–) 15
Browning Robert (1812–1889) 53
Burckhardt, Jacob (1818–1897) 121

Burns, Robert (1759–1796) 43
Butler, Judith (1956–) 123, 131
Byron, George Gordon [Lord Byron]
    (1788–1824) 50–51, 53

Cabinet of Dr Caligari, The (1919) 75
Calderón, Pedro (1600–1681) 90
Calvino, Italo (1923–1985) 13, 34
Camões, Luíz Vaz de (1524–1580)
    89
Campanella, Tommaso (1568–1639)
    14
Canterbury Tales, The (c.1387) 16, 87
Cantos, The (1915–1962) 95
Canzoniere (1379) 88
"Cask of Amontillado, The" (1846)
    108
Castle, The (1926) 115
Castle of Otranto, The (1764) 14
Catastrophe (1982) 66
Catcher in the Rye, The (1951) 27, 32,
    115
Catullus (84–54 BC) 86
Cervantes, Miguel de (1547–1616)
    12, 90
Chatman, Seymor (1928–) 130
Chaucer, Geoffrey (c.1343–1400)
    15–16, 87
Chrétien de Troyes (c.1140–1190)
    88
Christianopolis (1619) 14
Christie, Agatha (1890–1976) 14
Cinderella (1899) 74
Citizen Kane (1941) 77
City of the Sun (1602) 14
*Civilization of the Renaissance in Italy,
    The* (1860) 121
Cixous, Hélène (1937–) 122
Clarissa (1748–1749) 12, 91
Coleridge, Samuel Taylor
    (1772–1834) 41, 43, 53, 55–56,
    92

Color Purple, The (1980) 97
Confessions (c. AD 397–398) 28, 86
Congreve, William (1670–1729) 61
Conrad, Joseph (1857–1924) 17
Coppola, Francis Ford (1939–) 17
Cornwell, Patricia (1956–) 15
Corrections, The (2001) 97
Cortázar, Julio (1914–1984) 19, 96
Count of Monte Christo, The
    (1844–1846) 13
Country Wife, The (1675) 61
Crime and Punishment (1866) 28
Criminal of Lost Honour, The (1792)
    14
Cromwell, Oliver (1599–1658) 60,
    89
Crooklyn (1994) 78
Crucible, The (1953) 62
Crying of Lot 49, The (1966) 96
"Cuckoo Song" (c.1250) 38
Culture and Society (1958) 121
cummings, e. e. (1894–1962) 50–51
Curtius, Ernst Robert (1886–1956)
    124

Daldry, Stephen (1961–) 81
Dangerous Liaisons, The (1782) 13
Dante Alighieri (1265–1321) 10,
    34, 88
David Copperfield (1849–1850) 93
Da Vinci Code, The (2003) 15
Dean, James (1931–1955) 71
Decameron (c.1349–1351) 15–16,
    88
Declaration of Independence (1776)
    60
Defoe, Daniel (c.1660–1731) 12, 91
Derrida, Jacques (1930–2004) 113
Descartes, René (1596–1650) 92
De Sica, Vittorio (1901–1974) 75
"Destruction of Sennacherib, The"
    (1815) 53

Devil's Dictionary, The (1906) 114
Devil's Elixirs, The (1816) 14
Dexter (2006–) 83
Dickens, Charles (1812–1870) 13,
    16, 27, 93
Dickinson, Emily (1830–1886) 93
Dictionary of the Khazars, The (1984)
    19, 113
Dimension (1991–1997) 94
Divine Comedy, The (c.1307–1321)
    10, 34, 88
Doll's House, A (1879) 94
Do the Right Thing (1989) 76
"Don Juan" (1819) 50
Don Quixote (1605–1615) 12, 90
Dostoyevsky, Fyodor (1821–1881)
    28, 94, 115
Double Indemnity (1944) 75
Double or Nothing (1971) 96
Dracula (1897) 14
Dryden, John (1631–1700) 61, 91
Dumas, Alexander (1802–1870) 13
Dutchman (1964) 69
Dylan, Bob (1941–) 40

"Easter Wings" (1633) 47–48, 90
Ecclesiastical History of the English
    People (731) 87
Eco, Umberto (1932–) 14, 112,
    127–128
Edible Woman, The (1969) 33
Eisenstein, Sergei (1898–1948) 75,
    79, 129
Élégies (1556) 40
"Elegy Written in a Country
    Church-Yard" (1751) 40, 42, 51,
    53–54
Eliot, George [Mary Ann Evans]
    (1819–1880) 93
Eliot, T. S. (1888–1965) 7, 95
Emblemata (1531) 90
Emblems (1635) 49–50

Emerson, Ralph Waldo
    (1803–1882) 93–94
Emilia Galotti (1772) 61, 92
Émile, or On Education (1762) 13
Emperor Jones, The (1920) 95
Epic of Gilgamesh (third to first
    millennium BC) 19, 86, 103
Erec (late twelfth century) 88
Essay on Criticism, An (1711) 51
Euphues (1578) 89
Euripides (c.480–406 BC) 58, 129
*European Literature and the Latin
    Middle Ages* (1948) 124
Exeter Book (tenth century AD) 38

Faerie Queene, The (1590; 1596) 10,
    89
"Fall of the House of Usher, The"
    (1840) 34
Fassbinder, Rainer Werner
    (1946–1982) 76
Faulkner, William (1897–1962) 31,
    95
Fear of Flying (1973) 97
Federman, Raymond (1928–2009)
    96
Fielding, Henry (1707–1754)
    12–13, 91
Film Language (1963) 130
Finnegans Wake (1939) 95
Fitzgerald, F. Scott (1896–1940)
    28
Flaubert, Gustave (1821–1880) 94
Fleming, Victor (1883–1949) 77
Forster, E. M. (1879–1970) 21
Forster, Marc (1969–) 80
Forrest Gump (1994) 78
Fowles, John (1926–2005) 96
Frame, Janet (1924–2004) 97
Frankenstein, or the Modern Prometheus
    (1818) 92
Franklin, Benjamin (1706–1790) 28

Franzen, Jonathan (1959–) 97
Frazer, J. G. (1854–1941) 108
French Lieutenant's Woman, The (1969)
    96
Freud, Sigmund (1856–1939) 30,
    115–116
Frisch, Max (1911–1991) 96
Frogs, The (c.405 BC) 86, 129
Frost, Robert (1874–1963) 52, 55
Frye, Northrop (1912–1991) 108
Fuentes, Carlos (1928–2012) 96

Gambler, The (1867) 115
Genette, Gérard (1930–) 31–32
Gerusalemme Liberata (1581) 89
Godard, Jean-Luc (1930–) 76
Goethe, Johann Wolfgang
    (1749–1832) 13, 40, 91–92,
    124
Golden Ass, The (second century AD)
    10
Golden Bough, The (1890–1915) 108
Gramsci, Antonio (1891–1937)
    119
Grass is Singing, The (1950) 97
Gray, Thomas (1716–1791) 40, 42,
    53–54
Great Gatsby, The (1925) 28
Great Train Robbery, The (1903) 79
Greenblatt, Stephen (1943–) 120
Griffith, D. W. (1875–1948) 75
Grimmelshausen, Hans Jacob
    Christoph von (c.1621–1626)
    12–13, 90

Habermas, Jürgen (1929–) 119
Hamlet (c.1601) 33, 60, 116
Handmaid's Tale, The (1985) 14, 97
Handke, Peter (1942–) 96
Haneke, Michael (1942–) 83
Harriot, Thomas (c.1560–1621) 120
Harris, Julie (1925–) 71

Hauptmann, Gerhart (1862–1946) 94

Hawthorne, Nathaniel (1804–1894) 93

Haynes, Todd (1961–) 81

Hazanavicius, Michel (1967–) 82

Heart of Darkness (1902) 17

Hemingway, Ernest (1899–1961) 16, 24, 32, 95

Henry V, King (c.1600) 71

Heptameron (1558) 15

Herbert, George (1593–1633) 47–48, 50, 90

Herder, Johann Gottfried (1744–1803) 92

Herodotus (c.480–425 BC) 100

Herzog, Werner (1942–) 76

High Noon (1952) 80

Hillerman, Tony (1925–2008) 15

Histories (fifth century BC) 100

Hoffmann, E.T.A. (1772–1822) 16, 116

"Homage to Switzerland" (1933) 24

Homer (c. seventh century BC) 9, 19, 43

Hopscotch (1963) 19

Horace (65–8 BC) 86

Horla, Le (1887) 17

Hours, The (2002) 81

Howells, William Dean (1837–1920) 93

Hugo, Victor (1802–1885) 23

Hunchback of Notre Dame, The (1831) 23

Ibsen, Henrik (1828–1906) 94

Iliad (c. seventh century BC) 9, 43, 86

I'm not there (2007) 81

Importance of Being Earnest, The (1895) 69

"In a Station of the Metro" (1916) 46

Inferno (c.1307–1321) 34

Infinite Jest (1996) 98

In Search of Lost Time (1913–1927) 28

In the Penal Colony (1919) 115

Intrigue and Love (1784) 61

Irigaray, Luce (1932–) 122

Irving, Washington (1783–1859) 16

Iser, Wolfgang (1926–2007) 117

Jakobson, Roman (1896–1982) 106

James, Henry (1843–1916) 94

Jarmusch, Jim (1953–) 80–81

Jaws (1975) 83

"Job" (c. fifth–fourth century BC) 15

Jong, Erica (1942–) 97

Joseph Andrews (1742) 12

Joyce, James (1882–1941) 30, 33, 95, 104, 115

Joy Luck Club, The (1993) 76

Jung, C. G. (1875–1961) 108

Kafka, Franz (1883–1924) 29, 32, 115

Kant, Immanuel (1742–1804) 92

Keats, John (1795–1821) 40, 44–46, 92, 110

Killers, The (1946) 75

Kiss of the Spider Woman (1976) 24

Kingston, Maxine Hong (1940–) 97

Koyaanisqatsi (1983) 79

Kracauer, Siegfried (1889–1966) 130

Kristeva, Julia (1941–) 122

"Kubla Khan" (1816) 55

Kubrick, Stanley (1928–1999) 77, 80

Lacan, Jacques (1901–1981) 116, 131

Laclos, Pierre Choderlos de (1741–1803) 13

Lady in the Lake (1946) 79

Lang, Fritz (1890–1976) 75

Langland, William (*c.*1332–1387) 22, 54–55, 87

laudibus sanctae crucis, De (*c.*810) 47

Lay of Hildebrand (*c.*840) 88

Lazarillo de Tormes (1554) 13

Lee, Spike (1957–) 76–78

Lessing, Doris (1919–) 97

Lessing, Gotthold Ephraim (1729–1781) 21, 61, 92

Leucippe and Clitphon (late second century AD) 86

Lévi-Strauss, Claude (1908–2009) 108

Library of Babel, The (1941) 17

Life of Gargantua and of Pantagruel, The (1532–1564) 90

Literary Research Guide (2008) 138

Locke, John (1632–1704) 92

Long Day's Journey into Night (*c.*1941; published 1956) 69, 115

Lorca, Federico García (1898–1936) 96

Lord of the Rings, The (2001–2003) 78

Lost in the Funhouse (1968) 96

"Lost Leader, The" (1845) 53

Lucas, George (1944–) 82

Lukács, Georg (1885–1971) 119

Lusiads, The (1572) 89

Lyly, John (*c.*1554–1606) 89

Lyrical Ballads (1798) 92

Madame Bovary (1857) 94

Mad Men (2007–) 83

Magritte, René (1898–1967) 70

Malory, Thomas (*c.*1408–1471) 87

Man, Paul de (1919–1983) 113

Man Without Qualities, The (1930–1942) 95

Mariachi, El (1992) 76

Marlowe, Christopher (1564–1593) 60, 89

Márques, Gabriel García (1927–) 96

Marx, Karl (1818–1883) 62, 119–120, 127, 131

Mather, Cotton (1663–1728) 91

Maupassant, Guy de (1850–1893) 17

Maurus, Rabanus (AD 780–856) 47

Méliès, Georges (1861–1938) 74

Melville, Herman (1819–1891) 23, 28, 93

Memento (2000) 81

Merchant of Venice, The (*c.*1596–1598) 66

Metamorphoses (1 BC–AD 10) 86

"Metrical Feet: Lesson for a Boy" (1806) 53

Metropolis (1926) 75

Metz, Christian (1931–1993) 130

Middlemarch (1871–1872) 93

Midsummer Night's Dream, A (1595) 68

Miller, Arthur (1915–2005) 62

Milton, John (1608–1674) 10, 89, 115

MLA Handbook for Writers of Research Papers (2009) 145–146, 148

MLA International Bibliography (since 1921) 135–137, 145, 148

Moby Dick (1851) 23, 28, 93

Molière (1622–1673) 90

Montaigne, Michel de (1533–1592) 7, 89

Montgomery, Robert (1904–1981) 79

More, Thomas (1477–1535) 14, 88

Morrison, Toni (1931–) 97

Morte d'Arthur, Le (1470) 87

Mrs Dalloway (1925) 31, 35, 80–81, 95

Mulvey, Laura (1941–) 131
Münsterberg, Hugo (1863–1916) 129
Murder on the Orient Express (1934) 14
"Murders in the Rue Morgue, The" (1841) 118
Musil, Robert (1880–1942) 95
Mystery Train (1989) 81

Nabokov, Vladimir (1899–1977) 7, 97
Name of the Rose, The (1980) 13, 15, 112
Narration in Film (1985) 130
Nathan the Wise (1779) 92
Native Son (1940) 97
"Nature" (1836) 93
Nausea (1938) 30
Navarre, Marguerite de (1494–1549) 15
New York Review of Books, The (since 1963) 127
New York Times Book Review, The (since 1896) 127
New Yorker, The (since 1925) 16
Newman, Paul (1925–2008) 71
Nolan, Christopher (1970–) 81

O'Neill, Eugene (1888–1953) 69, 95, 114–115
"Occurrence at Owl Creek Bridge, An" (1891) 94
"Ode on a Grecian Urn" (1820) 40, 44, 46, 110
Odets, Clifford (1906–1963) 62
Odyssey (c. seventh century BC) 10, 19, 80, 86
Oedipus the King (c.425 BC) 64, 86
Omeros (1990) 97
"One Word More" (1855) 53
Opitz, Martin (1597–1639) 61
Orientalism (1978) 121

Orlando Furioso (1532) 10, 89
Ovid (43 BC–AD 17/18) 86

Pale Fire (1962) 7
Pamela (1740–1741) 12–13, 91
Paradise Lost (1667) 10, 89
Paradise Regained (1671) 89
Pavić, Milorad (1929–2009) 19, 114
Pessoa, Fernando (1888–1935) 96
Petrarca, Francesco (1304–1374) 56, 88
Photoplay, The (1916) 129
Pickwick Papers, The (1836–1837) 16
Piers Plowman (c.1360–1386) 22, 54, 87
Plath, Sylvia (1932–1963) 97
Plautus (c.254–184 BC) 60, 86
Poe, Edgar Allan (1809–1849) 16–17, 34–35, 93, 108–109, 116, 118
Poems on Various Subjects (1773) 91
Poetics, The (fourth century BC) 58, 63, 106, 110
Pope, Alexander (1688–1744) 51–52, 91
Porter, Edwin S. (1870–1941) 74, 79
Pound, Ezra (1885–1972) 46, 95
"Prodigal Son, The" (Luke 15,11; first century AD) 15
Prometheus Unbound (1820) 61
Propp, Vladimir (1896–1970) 107–108
Proust, Marcel (1871–1922) 28
Puig, Manuel (1932–1990) 24–25
Pulp Fiction (1994) 81
Pynchon, Thomas (1937–) 96–97, 115

Quarles, Francis (1592–1644) 49–50

Qur'an (c. seventh century AD)
    100

Rabb, Ellis (1930–1998) 66
Rabbit (1960–2001) 98
Rabelais, François (c.1494–1553) 90
Racine, Jean (1639–1699) 90
Ransom, J. C. (1888–1974) 109
Red and the Black, The (1830) 94
"Red, Red Rose, A" (1796) 43
Reggio, Godfrey (1940–) 79
"Regretfully, We are Returning . . .
    Reader's Reports" (1972) 128
Reinhardt, Max (1873–1943) 65
Rhys, Jean (1890–1979) 32–33
Rice, Elmer (1892–1967) 69
Richard II, King (1597) 60, 67
Richardson, Samuel (1689–1761)
    12–13, 91
"Riddle 44" (tenth century AD) 38
Rilke, Rainer Maria (1875–1926) 95
"Rime of the Ancient Mariner, The"
    (1798) 41, 43
Rise of Silas Lapham, The (1885) 93
Rise of the Novel, The (1957) 119
Robinson Crusoe (1719) 12, 91
Rodriguez, Robert (1968–) 76
Roman Elegies (1795) 40
Romeo and Juliet (1595) 18, 67
Ronsard, Pierre de (1524–1585) 40
Rosencrantz and Guildenstern Are Dead
    (1966) 62
Rosseau, Jean-Jacques (1712–1778)
    13, 92
Rossellini, Roberto (1906–1977) 75
Rotterdam, Erasmus of
    (c.1466–1536) 88
Rushdie, Salman (1947–) 97

Said, Edward (1935–2003) 121
Salinger, J. D. (1919–2010) 13, 27,
    32, 115

"Sandman, The" (1817) 116
Sappho (c.600 BC) 86
Sarris, Andrew (1928–2012) 130
Sartre, Jean-Paul (1905–1980) 30
Satanic Verses (1988) 97
Saussure, Ferdinand de (1857–1913)
    111, 113
Saving Private Ryan (1998) 76
Scarlet Letter, The (1850) 93
Schiller, Friedrich (1759–1805) 14,
    61, 92
Schindler's List (1993) 77
Scott, Sir Walter (1771–1832) 13
"Seafarer, The" (c. ninth century AD)
    87
Second Shepherds' Play (c.1425) 59
Seneca (c.4 BC–AD 65) 60
Shakespeare, William (1564–1616)
    18, 33, 44, 56–57, 60, 63,
    66–68, 71–72, 89, 103,
    115–116, 120
Shaw, George Bernard (1856–1950)
    61, 68, 94
Shelley, Mary (1797–1851) 92
Shelley, Percy Bysshe (1792–1822)
    61, 92
She's Gotta Have It (1986) 77
Shklovsky, Victor (1893–1984) 106
Shyamalan, M. Night (1970–) 117
Sidney, Philip (1554–1586) 89
Simplicissimus (1669) 12–13, 90
Simpsons, The (1989–) 115
Siodmak, Robert (1900–1973) 75
Sir Gawain and the Green Knight
    (fourteenth century) 10–11, 23,
    87
Sixth Sense, The (1999) 64, 81, 117
Slaughterhouse-Five (1969) 20
Sleepwalkers, The (1931–1932) 95
Soderbergh, Steven (1963–) 81
"Sonnet 73" (1609) 56
Sophocles (497–406 BC) 58, 64, 86

Sopranos, The (1999–2007) 83

Sorrows of Young Werther, The (1774) 13, 91

Sound and the Fury, The (1929) 31, 95

Spectator, The (1711–1712; 1714) 16, 91

Spenser, Edmund (c.1552–1599) 10, 56, 89

Spielberg, Steven (1946–) 76–77, 83

Stanislavsky, Konstantin (1863–1938) 65, 71

Stanzel, Franz Karl (1923–) 26

St. Augustin of Hippo (AD 354–430) 28, 86

Stay (2005) 80

Steele, Sir Richard (1672–1729) 16

Stein, Gertrude (1874–1946) 95

Stendhal [Marie-Henri Beyle] (1783–1842) 17, 94

Sterne, Laurence (1713–1768) 12, 27, 91, 106–107

Stevens, Wallace (1879–1955) 45–46

Stoker, Bram (1847–1912) 14

"Stop all the Clocks, Cut Off the Telephone" (1936) 42

Stoppard, Tom (1937–) 62, 70, 95

"Stopping by Woods on a Snowy Evening" (1923) 52, 55

Storm, Theodor (1817–1888) 17

Strasberg, Lee (1901–1982) 65, 71

Strike (1924) 79

Structural Anthropology (1958) 108

Sunset Boulevard (1950) 19, 82

Swift, Jonathan (1667–1745) 91

Taming of the Shrew, The (c.1592) 66

Tarantino, Quentin (1963–) 81

Tasso, Torquato (1544–1595) 89

Tate, Allen (1899–1979) 109

Tatius, Achilles (second century AD) 86

Tatler, The (1709–1711) 16, 91

Tempest, The (c.1611) 120

Teseida (c.1339) 6

Terence (c.185–159 BC) 86

"That time of year thou may'st in me behold" (1609) 56

Thesaurus Linguae Graecae 104

Things Fall Apart (1958) 97

"This Is Just to Say" (1934) 57

Thoreau, Henry David (1817–1862) 93

Thousand and One Nights (fourteenth and subsequent centuries) 15

Three Lives (1909) 95

Times Literary Supplement, The (since 1902) 127

To the Lighthouse (1927) 95

Tolstoy, Leo (1828–1910) 26, 32

Tom Jones (1749) 12–13, 91

Traffic (2000) 81

Travesties (1974) 62, 96

Trial, The (1925) 29, 115

Trier, Lars von (1956–) 80, 83

Tristram Shandy (1759–1767) 12, 27, 91, 106

"True Story, A" (1874) 22

Truffaut, François (1932–1984) 76, 130

Tschechow, Anton P. (1860–1904) 16

Twain, Mark [Samuel Langhorne Clemens] (1835–1910) 22–23, 93–55

24 (2001–2010) 80

Twin Peaks (1990–1991) 83

2001: A Space Odyssey (1968) 80

Ulysses (1922) 30, 33, 95, 104

Unamuno, Miguel de (1864–1936) 96

Uncle Tom's Cabin (1903) 75
"Under the Lime Tree" (*c.*1200) 39
Updike, John (1932–2009) 98
Utopia (1516) 14, 88

Vega, Lope de (1562–1635) 90
Virgil (70–19 BC) 10, 34, 86
"Visual Pleasure and Narrative
    Cinema" (1975) 131
Vogelweide, Walther von der
    (*c.*1170–1230) 39
Voltaire (1694–1778) 92
Vonnegut, Kurt (1922–2007) 20–21
Vondel, Jost van den (1587–1679)
    90

Waiting for Godot (1952) 62–64, 69,
    96
Waiting for Lefty (1935) 62
Walcott, Derek (1930–) 97
Walden, or Life in the Woods (1854)
    93
Walker, Alice (1944–) 97
Wallace, David Foster (1962–2008)
    98
Walpole, Horace (1717–1797) 14
"Wanderer, The" (*c.* ninth-tenth
    century AD) 87
Wang, Wayne (1949–) 76
War and Peace (1869) 26
Waste Land, The (1922) 7, 95
Watt, Ian (1917–1999) 119
Waverly (1814) 13
Way of the World, The (1700) 61
We (1924) 14
Weavers, The (1893) 94
Wellek, René (1903–1995) 124
Welles, Orson (1915–1985) 77, 130

Wenders, Wim (1945–) 76
Wheatley, Phillis (*c.*1753–1784) 91
"When Lilacs Last in the Dooryard
    Bloom'd" (1865–1866) 40
White Ribbon, The (2009) 83
Whitman, Walt (1819–1892) 40,
    93
Wide Sargasso Sea (1966) 32
Wiene, Robert (1881–1938) 75
Wilde, Oscar (1854–1900) 61, 69
Wilder, Billy (1906–2002) 19, 75,
    92
Wilhelm Meister's Apprenticeship
    (1795–1796) 13, 91
William the Conqueror
    (*c.*1028–1087) 87
Williams, Raymond (1921–1988)
    121
Williams, William Carlos
    (1883–1963) 57
Wilson, Robert (1941–) 66
Wimsatt, William K. (1907–1975)
    109
Winthrop, John (1588–1649) 91
Wizard of Oz, The (1939) 77
Woman Warrior, The (1976) 97
Woolf, Virginia (1882–1941) 31,
    35–36, 80–81, 95
Wordsworth, William (1770–1850)
    92
Wright, Richard (1908–1960) 97
Wycherley, William (1641–1715)
    61

Zamyatin, Yevgeny (1881–1937) 14
Zemeckis, Robert (1952–) 78
Zinnemann, Fred (1907–1997) 80
Zoo Story, The (1958) 69, 96

SUBJECT INDEX

acoustic dimension of film 82–84
act 63, 68
actio 105
actor 58–59, 62, 65–73, 78, 107
actor training 70
advertising 4, 22, 112
aesthetics of reception 116
affective fallacy 109, 116
African American 22–23, 69–70,
    76, 91, 97, 120
agent 108
alienation effect 107
allegory 12
alliteration 54–55
alphabet 1–2, 47, 55, 104
amphitheater 67
anapest 53
Ancient Greek literature 2, 36, 86,
    88, 98
Anglo-Saxon 38, 54–55, 87
Anglo-Saxon period 87
Anglophone literature 97
anthology 128, 136, 145, 147, 151
anthropology 112
APA style 149, 151

archetypal criticism 108–109
architecture 66, 112, 121
Aristotle's unities 61, 63, 69
art history 105, 112
Arthurian romance 10, 88
article 5, 6, 127, 133–138, 144,
    146–149
aside 63, 107
assonance 54
audience 19, 58–59, 62–73, 83, 88,
    102–103, 107
audio-literature 2
Augustan age 91
"auteur" theory 130–131
authorial narrative situation 26
author-oriented approaches
    114–116
autobiography 29, 96, 107

ballad 37, 41
bard 2
Baroque 10, 47–48, 61, 67, 89–91
bibliography 6, 135–138, 145–151
Bildungsroman 13
biographical criticism 102, 114

biography 102–103, 107, 114
blank 107, 117–118
blank verse 54
Blu-ray 74
book review 5, 6, 127, 129, 135, 148
bourgeois tragedy 61, 92
breeches role 72

caesura 55
camera angle 73, 77–79
camera movement 75–76, 78
canon 4, 45, 100, 115, 122–123, 128
canon revision 122
carmen figuratum 47
carnivalesque 125
catharsis 59
CD-ROM 104, 147, 151
censorship 60
change of narrative perspective 32–33
character 10–12, 16, 18, 21–34, 44, 46, 62, 67, 69–72, 77–82, 84, 107–108, 110, 112, 115
characterization 22–25, 35–36, 64
character presentation 4, 11, 21–25, 31, 41, 80–81
character typology 21–25, 107–108
charm 37–38, 87–88
chiasmus 50–51
Chicago style 148–149, 152
Chicano, Chicana 97
Chinese 46–47, 97
choir 71
chorus 67, 71
chronotopos 125
cinema 3, 15, 25, 73–76, 79–83, 131
citation management software 149
class 12, 16, 23, 103, 120

classical antiquity 36, 40, 47, 59, 63, 86, 106, 128
climax 11, 17–19, 59, 63–64, 89
close reading 110
close-up shot 77
closet drama 61
collage 94
collection (of essays) 5, 19, 135
colonial age 90–91
colonial literature 91, 120
color movie 76
comedy 59–60, 68, 71, 108
comedy of manners 60
Commonwealth 60, 89, 97
Commonwealth literature 97
comparative literature 124–126
complication 18, 63–64
computer 3, 78, 104, 131, 137–138, 149
concluding paragraph 143
concordance 104
concrete poetry 47, 51, 90
conflict 18
context-oriented approaches 101, 119–127
conventional symbol 42
couplet 56–57
covert narrator 32
crisis 18
critical apparatus 6–7, 139, 144–145, 149
cubism 36, 94
cultural studies 102, 121
cut 79, 81, 129

dactyl 53
database 133–135, 137, 148–149
date of publication 146
deconstruction 103, 111–114, 118, 120–121, 123, 126, 131
deep structure 108–109
defamiliarization 79, 82, 106–107

denouement 18, 63–64
depth psychology 108
detective novel 14–15
dialogism 125
dialogue 24–25, 61–62, 66–67, 69, 71, 75–76, 82, 107, 130–131
diegetic score 92
dimeter 54
directing 65
director 65–67, 70–71, 74–82, 129–130
discontinuous narrative 81
discourse 2–5, 9, 18, 21, 24–25, 37, 54, 58–75, 84, 86, 88–90, 92, 94–95, 98, 104, 106–107, 115, 128–129
dispositio 105
dissertation 5, 135, 137
documentation of sources 5, 144–146
drama 1–4, 9, 14–16, 19, 27, 38, 41–55, 62, 65, 68, 77, 86, 96, 103–104
dramatic characterization 24–25
dramatis personae 71
drawing-room comedy 68
dream 20, 75, 80, 83, 99–100
dress 72
DVD 74, 147–148

early modern English 14, 89
écriture feminine 123
editing 73, 75, 79
edition 7, 88, 102–104, 127, 135–136, 148
editor 5, 7, 88, 128, 134–135, 145, 147
Egypt 86
eighteenth century 87, 90–92, 98, 119
elegy 40, 42, 51
Elizabethan age 90, 119

Elizabethan theater 63, 67, 71–72
elocutio 105
emblem 48–50, 90
encyclopedia 1, 113–114
endnote 6
EndNote 149
end rhyme 55
English sonnet 56–57
Enlightenment 61, 91–92
epic 2–4, 9–14, 22–23, 27–28, 41, 86–89
epic poetry 3, 9, 11, 43, 86, 99
episode 10, 35, 59, 78, 80–81, 84
epistolary novel 13, 91
essay 5–7, 16, 89–93, 131, 135–136, 139, 145–150
etymology 36
evaluation 24–25, 101, 127–129
exegesis 100–101
experimental poetry 37, 51, 58
exposition 18, 63–64, 107
expressionism 69, 96
expressionist theater 61, 66, 69
external focalization 32
external method 70
extradiegetic score 82–83
eye rhyme 54–56

fairy tale 15
fast motion 73, 79
feminist film studies 73, 131
feminist literary theory 23, 122–124
Festschrift 5–6, 135
fiction 4–5, 9–36, 58, 71–75, 86, 90
figural narrative situation 11, 26, 28–29, 32–33, 41
figure 17, 19, 22–32, 35–37, 60, 71, 75
figure of speech 43
film 3, 9, 14, 17–21, 72–84, 112, 121, 129–131, 147–148
film music 3, 82

film narratology 130
film semiotics 130
film stock 73, 76–77
film studies 73, 81, 129–131
film theory 73, 116, 129–131
first-person narration 13, 19, 27–28, 32–33
first-person narrative situation 26–28, 32, 41
first-person narrator 19
flashback 19, 74, 76, 79
flat character 10, 21, 71
focalization 26, 32
focalizer 32
foot 53
footnote 6–7, 98, 146, 149
foreshadowing 19, 74, 79
formalism 103, 105–109
frame narrative 15, 41
framing 77
free indirect discourse 30
French feminism 122

gender 23, 71–72, 97, 103, 117, 119–124, 127, 131
gender difference 122–124
gender theory 122–124
genre 3–4, 9
Globe Theatre 67
Golden Age 90
Gothic novel 14, 34
grammar 104
Greek theater 67, 71

haiku 46–47
Harvard style 148
hermeneutics 101
heroic drama 61
heterodiegetic narrator 31–32
historical novel 13
history 2, 10, 38, 60, 85, 119–120
history of motifs 109

history of reception 109, 118
history play 60
Hollywood 75, 131
homodiegetic narrator 31–32
humanities 101, 121
Humanism 88

iambus 53
iconoclasm 2
illustration 2
image 24, 40–47, 49–51, 79–80, 108
imagery 40, 44, 47, 51
images of women criticism 122
imagism 46
imago 40
implied reader 117–118
index 6–7, 135–136, 148
individualism 12
individualization 11, 23, 25
individualized character 23, 25
initial situation 18, 64
in medias res 17
intentional fallacy 109
interior monologue 30–31, 82
interlibrary loan 138
interliterary comparison 125
internal focalization 32
internal method 70–71
internal rhyme 54
interpretation 5–7, 24–25, 36, 66, 99–101, 104, 110, 113, 116–118, 127–128
intrinsic approach 106
introductory paragraph 139–141
inventio 105
irony 108, 110
Italian neorealist film 75
Italian sonnet 56

Jacobean age 89
Jesuit drama 90

journal 5, 127, 133–136, 145, 147–148

Latin 1, 40, 47, 86–87, 90
legal text 100–101, 104
length of film 80, 84
letter 1, 50–51, 55, 90, 111–112
lexis 105
lighting 50, 67, 77
linear plot 11, 19, 21, 63
lingua franca 87
linguistics 4, 89, 104, 135
list of works cited 6, 148–149
literariness 103, 106
literary award 127–128
literary criticism 3, 5–6, 9, 72–73, 96, 99–131
literary history 3, 9, 36, 85, 89, 91–93, 96, 118–119, 122, 128
literary theory 9, 14, 23, 44, 58, 61, 73, 84, 91, 101, 105, 111, 116, 119–120, 122–124
literature 1–7
long shot 77–78
lyra 36
lyric poetry 37, 39, 87

magazine 16, 22, 91, 118
magic 37–38, 99–100
main character 10–11, 23, 25, 27–29
makeup 58, 65, 69, 72, 80, 130
manifesto 46
manuscript 2, 102, 127
Marxist literary theory 119–120
mask 67, 69, 71
media studies 84
memoria 105
Mesopotamia 19, 86, 103
metafiction 107
metaphor 43–44, 46, 57, 79
meter 37, 52–58, 100, 104–106, 110

Middle Ages 2, 6, 10, 12, 15, 22, 36, 39, 47, 59, 86–88, 101
Middle English 10, 16, 38, 54, 87–88
Middle English period 87–88
mind-tricking narrative/film 64, 81
minor character 27–28
"minority" literatures 96
miracle play 59, 88
mise-en-scène 77, 130
MLA Handbook 145–146, 148
MLA style sheet 145, 148–149, 152
Modern Language Association (MLA) 135–138, 145–152
modernism 31, 94–98
modes of presentation 23, 25, 61, 69, 73
monograph 6, 133, 135
monologue 30–31, 62, 66, 82
monometer 54
montage 73, 79, 81, 129–130
morphology 106
music 2–3, 36, 38–40, 75, 82–84, 121, 125, 130
mystery play 59, 88
myth 10, 15, 64, 86, 108–109, 112
myth criticism 108

narration 26–33
narrative film 74–75
narrative perspective 4, 17, 26–33, 35, 41
narrative poetry 37
narrative situation 10–11, 17–18, 26–34, 44
narrative structure 10, 19, 21, 104, 107, 122–123
narrative voice 26
narratology 82, 130
narrator 17, 19, 23–34, 41, 79, 81, 93, 130
national literature 38, 87–88, 91, 124

natural sciences 5, 125
Naturalism 61, 93–94
neoclassical age 91
Neo-Latin tragedy 90
new criticism 103, 105, 109–111,
    116, 118, 120
new German cinema 76
new historicism 120–121, 127
newspaper 1, 16, 80, 91, 118, 127
note 5
novel 9–18
novella, novelette 17

ode 40, 46
off-Broadway 70
Old English 2, 37–38, 40, 54–55,
    87
Old English period 38, 40, 87
Old High German 88
omniscient point of view 29, 32
online 84, 133–138, 147–149
onomatopoeia 38–39
oracle 64, 99–100
oral poetry 2
orchestra 67
overt narrator 32

painting 1, 3, 46, 66, 70, 73, 95, 124
paradox 110
paragraph 139–145
paraphrase 5, 86, 110, 145
parenthetical citation 145, 149
parody 12, 61, 68, 107, 128
pentameter 54, 56
performance 24, 58–74, 107
performing arts 58, 72–73
periods 85–98
Petrarchan sonnet 56, 88
phenomenological approach 115
philology 103–104, 135
philosophy 101, 122
picaresque novel 13, 15

pictographic writing 2
picture poem 47, 50
place of publication 136, 145–147
play within the play 68
plot 18–21
plot time 80
poem 36–58
poetic language 37, 40–31, 51
poetics 3
poetry 2–5, 9–11, 36–58
point of view 11, 25–33, 36, 41,
    74, 79, 82, 94–95, 104, 106,
    114, 116, 130
popular culture 112, 121
postcolonial literature 97, 120
postcolonial theory 121
postcolonial studies 120
postmodernism 96–98, 114
poststructuralism 105, 110, 112,
    120–121
Prague school of structuralism 103,
    105
primary source 4–7, 101
printing 2, 12, 103, 119
private symbol 42–43
production 65–67, 70–72, 75, 77,
    83, 113
projection 36, 72, 74
properties, props 58, 65–70
proscenium stage 68, 70, 75, 79
prose 4, 9–18, 26, 30, 33–37, 59,
    69, 86, 89–90, 95, 99, 114
prose poem 37, 57
protagonist 26–33
psychoanalytic literary criticism
    115–116
psychological film theory 129
psychology 108
publisher 127–128, 136, 145–147,
    152
pun 110
Puritan age 60, 89

Puritan interregnum; Puritan
    Commonwealth 60, 89
Puritan Literature 90

quatrain 56
quotation 5, 145

race 23, 103, 120
radio 2, 81–82
reader 5, 19–20, 24–28, 32–33, 42,
    73, 95, 101, 107, 109, 116–118,
    122, 124, 126, 128, 131, 139
reader-oriented approaches 116–118
reader-response theory 116
realism 11–12, 16, 61, 65, 68, 73,
    93–94
realism movement 69, 130
reception 1, 17, 61, 73, 102–103,
    109, 116–119, 122, 124, 129
reception aesthetics 73, 116–117
reception history 109, 118
reception theory 116, 118, 129
reflector 32
religion 10, 15, 60, 90, 99–100,
    103, 109
Renaissance 40, 56, 60–61, 67–68,
    88–89, 98, 103–104, 121, 126
representation 22–23, 28, 58, 73,
    94, 111, 130
resolution 18, 63
Restoration comedy 60, 89
review article 6, 167
rhetoric 88, 103
rhetorical figures 37, 43–44, 79,
    104–105, 110, 114
rhyme 37, 52, 54–57, 99–100,
    105–106, 110
rhythm 51, 54, 57, 82, 105–106
rhythmic-acoustic dimension of
    poetry 51–58
riddle 37–38, 87–88
"road map" 140–142

romance 10–12, 15, 23, 37, 41,
    86–89, 91, 98, 108
Roman literature 86, 98
romanticism 40, 92–93, 98
round character 21, 23, 25, 71
running time 80
Russian formalism 103, 105–107
Russian montage theory 79,
    129–130

scansion 52
scene 63
scenery 58, 66–70, 74
science fiction 14, 75
screen 74, 80, 130
script 24–25, 63, 66, 72
secondary source 4–7, 127, 133,
    135, 137, 147, 149
semiotics 14, 103, 111–114, 118,
    121, 130–131
sensitivity of film material 77
setting 13, 16–18, 20–21, 23, 26,
    31, 33–36, 62–63, 67, 69, 74,
    77, 79, 94
Shakespearean sonnet 56
short story 4, 15–17, 23, 41
showing 232–235, 71
siglo de oro 90
sign 1–2, 57, 111–114
sign system 111–114
signified 111–114
signifier 111–114, 123
silent movie 75, 82, 130
simile 43–44, 79
singer 2, 40
skene 67
slow motion 79
soliloquy 63
song 2, 38–40, 86, 92
sonnet 40, 56–57, 88
sound 2–3, 38, 51–58, 72–73,
    75–76, 82–83, 106, 130

sound effect 82–83
source 4–7, 91, 101, 109, 127, 133–138, 144–152
Spanish golden age 90
spatial art 21
spatial dimension of film 76–79
speaker 41
Spenserian sonnet 56
spondee 53
stage 3, 58–75, 77, 79, 81
stanza 40, 44–46, 48, 51, 56–58
stock character 21, 71
stream-of-consciousness technique 30
structuralism 103, 105–109
structural organization 139
Sturm und Drang 92
style 7, 17–18, 24, 66, 90, 95, 98, 102, 104–105, 114, 122, 127, 130
style sheet 145, 148–149, 152
stylistics 103–105
subject index 135–136
suspense 17–19, 64, 83
syllable 47, 52–56
symbol 22, 42–45, 110
symbolism 12, 59
syntax 4, 104–105

talkies 130
telephoto lens 78
telling 23, 25
temporal art 21
temporal dimension of film 79–81, 83
tenor 44
tension 23, 29, 56, 92
tercet 56
tetrameter 54
text 1–7
text-oriented approaches 101–114, 116, 120–121, 123, 130

text type 3–7
textual criticism 3, 103–104
theater of the absurd 61, 63–64, 66, 69, 96
theology 100, 104
thesis 5, 137
thesis statement 139–144
third-person narration 26
three unities 61, 63, 69
topic sentence 141–142
tragedy 58, 60–61, 92, 108
transcendentalism 93–94, 98
transformation 62, 65–70, 72
transliterary comparison 125
trimeter 54
trochee 53
turning point 18
TV series 83
typification 22, 25
typified character 21–23, 25
typology 107–108

unity 17, 40, 52, 57–58, 63, 110
utopian novel 14

vehicle 44
verbal dimension of poetry 41–47, 57
verbal icon 44
visual dimension of poetry 47–51
voice 41
voice-over 19, 82
volume 82

Western 75, 78, 80
wide-angle lens 78
women's literature 96–97
WorldCat 137, 148
writing 1–4

zero focalization 32
Zotero 149